BETWEEN MEN ~ BETWEEN WOMEN
Lillian Faderman and Larry Gross, Editors

FAMILIES

WE

CHOOSE

KATH WESTON

FAMILIES WE CHOOSE

LESBIANS, GAYS, KINSHIP

COLUMBIA UNIVERSITY PRESS
NEW YORK

Columbia University Press
New York   Oxford

Library of Congress Cataloging-in-Publication Data

Weston, Kath, 1958–
    Families we choose : lesbians, gays, kinship / Kath
Weston.
    p.   cm.—(Between men~between women)
    Includes bibliographical references and index.
    ISBN 0-231-07288-0
    ISBN 978-0-231-11093-8 (pbk.)
    1. Gay couples—United States.   2. Gay parents—
United States.
3. Kinship—United States.   4. Gays—United States—
Family relationships.   I. Title.   II. Series.
HQ76.3.U5W48   1991
306.87—dc20   90-49349
                                                    CIP

Casebound editions of Columbia University Press books
are printed on permanent and durable acid-free paper.

Printed in the United States of America

c 10 9 8 7 6 5 4 3 2

BETWEEN MEN ~ BETWEEN WOMEN

LESBIAN, GAY, AND BISEXUAL STUDIES

Terry Castle and Larry Gross, Editors

Rebecca Alpert, *Like Bread on the Seder Plate: Jewish Lesbians and the Transformation of Tradition*

Emma Donoghue, editor, *Poems Between Women: Four Centuries of Love, Romantic Friendship, and Desire*

James T. Sears and Walter L. Williams, editors, *Overcoming Heterosexism and Homophobia: Strategies That Work*

Patricia Juliana Smith, *Lesbian Panic: Homoeroticism in Modern British Women's Fiction*

Dwayne C. Turner, *Risky Sex: Gay Men and HIV Prevention*

Timothy F. Murphy, *Gay Science: The Ethics of Sexual Orientation Research*

Cameron McFarlane, *The Sodomite in Fiction and Satire, 1660–1750*

Lynda Hart, *Between the Body and the Flesh: Performing Sadomasochism*

Byrne R. S. Fone, editor, *The Columbia Anthology of Gay Literature: Readings from Western Antiquity to the Present Day*

Ellen Lewin, *Recognizing Ourselves: Ceremonies of Lesbian and Gay Commitment*

Ruthann Robson, *Sappho Goes to Law School: Fragments in Lesbian Legal Theory*

Jacquelyn Zita, *Body Talk: Philosophical Reflections on Sex and Gender*

Evelyn Blackwood and Saskia Wieringa, *Female Desires: Same-Sex Relations and Transgender Practices Across Cultures*

William L. Leap, ed., *Public Sex/Gay Space*

Larry Gross and James D. Woods, eds., *The Columbia Reader on Lesbians and Gay Men in Media, Society, and Politics*

Marilee Lindemann, *Willa Cather: Queering America*

George E. Haggerty, *Men in Love: Masculinity and Sexuality in the Eighteenth Century*

Andrew Elfenbein, *Romantic Genius: The Prehistory of a Homosexual Role*

Gilbert Herdt and Bruce Koff, *Something to Tell You: The Road Families Travel When a Child Is Gay*

Richard Canning, *Gay Fiction Speaks: Conversations with Gay Novelists*

Laura Doan, *Fashioning Sapphism: The Origins of a Modern English Lesbian Culture*

Mary Bernstein and Renate Reimann, eds., *Queer Families, Queer Politics: Challenging Culture and the State*

Richard R. Bozorth, *Auden's Games of Knowledge: Poetry and the Meanings of Homosexuality*

Larry Gross, *Up from Invisibility: Lesbians, Gay Men, and the Media in America*

Linda Garber, *Identity Poetics: Race, Class, and the Lesbian-Feminist Roots of Queer Theory*

Richard Canning, *Hear Us Out: Conversations with Gay Novelists*

David Bergman, *The Violet Hour: The Violet Quill and the Making of Gay Culture*

In memory of Julie Cordell
1960–1983
who came looking for community

CONTENTS

PREFACE TO THE PAPERBACK EDITION

It was one of those quiet midwestern nights, the August sky so tranquil or restrained you felt compelled to shut the television off or plunge your hands into the steaming ground or maybe look over your shoulder and run. We were having a family talk, and I was there for the duration.

"What's the big deal? I just don't get it." My stepfather turned quizzically in my direction. "If you're gay, you're gay. So what? Why make such a fuss over nothing?"

The sincerity in his question tugged at me. I leaned back to give the wall a little support. Then I sat for a moment, still as the night around us, pulled ten years past into a comment made by someone I interviewed for *Families We Choose*. "I don't think straight people have any idea," she had insisted, "how painful family issues can be for lesbians and gay men."[1]

My stepfather had voiced a sort of liberal counterpoint to the classic myth that people who find themselves attracted to others of the same sex must learn to live without family. When I began the field research for this book in the mid-1980s, popular wisdom had it that lesbians, gay men, and bisexuals put kinship ties at risk whenever they decided to come out. Many worried that if they told relatives about their sexual identities, they would alienate the very people who had seen them through to adulthood. Otherwise sympathetic brothers and parents and cousins worried, in turn, that their loved ones would be doomed to a series of fleeting relationships that couldn't possibly last. As one woman's disapproving mother put it, "Even a dog shouldn't have to die alone."

In the end, sheer living usually dispelled such fears. Stories about coming out to relatives might have highlighted the threat of rejection, but the actual experience of being disowned turned out to be much more the exception than the rule. Many a family discovered ways to work out initial shock or misunderstanding or rage as the years passed. Some families even seemed to take the news in stride. The notion that same-sex couples lack staying power generally failed to convince after family members met gay people in long-term relationships. Yet these concerns about family betrayal and kinship lost are not to be taken lightly. People have to muster friendship, courage, and whatever flair they have for negotiation to dispatch this particular set of demons.

Of course there are still relatives who warn that their nephew's "tragic lifestyle" can only bring heartache. (Never mind that his sister's ten-year heterosexual marriage, which had not been preceded by any such dire predictions, ended unhappily.) But today the myth that queer sexuality spells the end of family ties coexists uneasily with my stepfather's mantra of tolerance for the twenty-first century: What's the big deal? His words allude to a contemporary tale of reversed expectations. For people who believe that the world has now become a safer place for queers, the shock occurs not when relatives offer acceptance, but when the act of bringing home a lover turns out to be a big deal after all.

One way to address my stepfather's question is to note the social and legal restrictions that lend continuing force to the myth of kinship lost. Put simply, it's still a "big deal" to live a life of same-sex attraction because very little in society is set up to acknowledge the family ties you propose to make. Certainly the gay, civil rights, and women's movements have had a combined impact on the way that institutions handle the issue of homosexuality. A few businesses now offer benefits to the unmarried partners of employees. Celebrities play gay characters on sitcoms with a regularity that would have been unimaginable ten years ago. Yet this is no straightforward narrative of progress. A lesbian who gets divorced on the cusp of the twenty-first century has every reason to live in terror of a court judgment that will declare her unfit to parent on the grounds of homosexuality alone. It's still very possible to lose your kid for having loved. Many insurance companies refuse to write joint policies for same-sex partners. Joint adoptions remain uncommon. Individuals have to struggle, on a case-by-case basis, to visit lovers in the hospital or in jail. New acquaintances still routinely assume that a gay man bears no financial responsibility for children, much less for a sibling or a lover's parents. When those same acquaintances learn that a bisexual woman does not have a partner, they may pity her isolation without ever suspecting that she has friends she considers family.

The very visibility sought by white middle-class leaders of the lesbian/gay movement, with their calls for everyone to abandon their closets, can be double-edged. Witness the speed with which the so-called Defense of Marriage Act passed through the U.S. Congress in 1996. Here is that relatively rare case of a law drafted in order to preempt a state of affairs which does not yet exist.[2] Just in case the State of Hawaii should legalize same-sex marriage, legislators at the federal level worked to ensure that no one would have to recognize these marriages across state lines. Come to find out, visibility makes for an excellent target.

There's another way to approach my stepfather's question. The matter of why gay people continue to "make a big deal" about sexual identity turns out to be inseparable from frequently voiced inquiries about why they can't just "keep it in the bedroom where it belongs."[3] And why not? Because sexuality is embedded in kinship in ways that everyone knows but many hesitate to speak. Where else would babies and fathers-in-law come from? How else would publishers find a market for the shelves of books that advise couples on how to put the masala back into their marriages? So the injunction for lesbians, bisexuals, and gay men to "keep it in the bedroom" puts us at a tremendous disadvantage. It's much easier to spare your co-workers the details of a flirtation or a weekend tryst than it is to scurry about inventing stories to explain why you have to leave a few minutes early to pick up a chosen family friend at the hospital or drop your lover off at the bus station or fetch the kid from soccer practice. It takes work—unconscionable, spirit-gutting work—to remember never to say any of their names. In the United States a person may be able to confine sex to the bedroom if he wants, but not so with kinship, or only at an unthinkable cost. Yet in some sense both are "about" sexuality.

When I undertook the research for *Families We Choose*, I did not set out to examine sexuality, or even family and kinship per se. My interests focused on identity, ideology, and social justice. Like many other young scholars, I could never quite grasp what people had seen in the arcane kinship terminology and genealogies painstakingly assembled by researchers of an earlier generation. By the time I arrived in graduate school, kinship studies occupied the paradoxical status of a canonical subject ("kinship, now that's real anthropology") and an area of study regarded as intellectually dead in the water ("been there, understood that").

After I began fieldwork in San Francisco in the mid-1980s, an event occurred that derailed, then rerailed, my plan of study. All around me, people had begun talking about something called "gay families," the "families we choose." Several months down the road, I concluded that I had stumbled across an entire discourse in the making. Enter my interest in ideology: I couldn't help but wonder about the unexpected popularity of a term such as "gay families" that had scarcely circulated before. Why were lesbians and gay men busy recasting close friends as kin? Why was everyone suddenly talking about making or taking in babies? Had people always sat around telling stories about the mother who learned to respect her gay son's lover when they had to work together to ease the son's dying? Could I explore such questions in a way that would convey the degree to which most queers share with their heterosexual neighbors some eminently "United Statesian" concerns about family loyalties and love? Could I begin to take account of race and class differences, while reminding readers just how revolutionary any claim to family is for people not so long ago condemned to the no-man's-land of kinship lost?

Over the past decade family issues have moved to the center of lesbian, gay, and bisexual lives in ways I could never have foreseen when *Families We Choose* went to press. "Are you planning to have kids?" has become a routine question directed at lesbian couples, even by heterosexual friends. Advocacy organizations have turned to the courts in an effort to gain legal recognition for "our families." Wedding ceremonies have become a staple of lesbian/bisexual/gay rights events, including the 1993 March on Washington and a 1996 group ceremony at San Francisco City Hall officiated by Mayor Willie Brown. PFLAG (Parents and Friends of Lesbians and Gays) chapters have flourished in localities across the country, with like groups organized by people of color to explore cultural differences in family relations.[4] Studies of lesbian/gay families have even helped rehabilitate kinship as a fit subject for anthropological inquiry.[5]

There's a history to these developments, a filament of organizing and social change that threads its way through the pages of *Families We Choose*. As the lesbian/gay movement gathered strength in the 1970s, it called upon "everyday queers" to disclose their sexual identities to society at large, or at least to parents and other close relatives. "To come out or not to come out" became the question of the day. To contemplate that question was to confront the possibility that biological connection might not be enough to make kinship, or to make it last. Although people seldom lost aunts or grandparents in the event, they knew too well that family ties could be severed by the shock of revelation. Everyone had heard stories about the parent who reacted by saying, "A son of mine would not do this. Get out of my sight! You were never really my son!" Kinship began to seem more like an effort and a choice than a permanent, unshakable bond or a birthright. The mute substance of genes, blood, and bone had to be transformed into something more. And if such efforts at transformation could fail—if blood could prove thinner than water—why dismiss out of hand the kinship potential of other sorts of social ties: the connecting tissue of friendship, say, or nonbiological parenthood, or a committed gay relationship?

Don't make the mistake, though, of thinking that because lesbians and gay men now claim chosen families, these are *freely* chosen families. There are constraints on any choice. Color, access to money, and social connections leave some people more constrained than others. Relatives and passersby subject people to constant judgments about the choices they have made, frequently ignoring the conditions of the choosing. Think about the conversations that circulate whenever someone, regardless of sexual identity, settles upon a mate. Does So-and-So's choice qualify as good or bad, socially acceptable or irresponsible, considerate of her parents' wishes or a slap in the face of the way she was raised? "I like how she treats your mother." "Did you see those ears?" "Forget the ears. He's driving a Mercedes!" "Isn't he kind of dark?" "You did good." "Is she cultural?" Race and racism, class and class pretensions, all go into the evaluative mix.

The not-so-free choices that configure a family incorporate material circumstances, culture, history, habit, and imagination. There are reasons why few sisters or brothers readily hand over a child to be raised by a lesbian or gay sibling. There are reasons why the phone circuits on Castro Street are not buzzing with parents who want to offer support by taking responsibility for arranging the same-sex marriages of their children. Arranged marriage, like the practice of adopting out a child to siblings, is standard operating procedure in some societies. Both practices introduce an element of choice into kinship. Yet these are not the most common aspects of the families gay men and lesbians have been fashioning in the United States.

Many other kinship practices fall within the realm of choice and possibility yet remain conspicuous by their absence. The 1980s could have witnessed a slew of court cases in which neighbors argued for visitation privileges on the basis of informal child care services rendered. They didn't. Where were the stories in the gay press about the adoption of an eldest child's lover by a parent who wanted to continue the family name and family business? How is it that even Oprah Winfrey has not produced a television show featuring lesbian lovers who are in the habit of handing over their paychecks to their partners? Why doesn't the national debate about same-sex marriage focus upon "spouse service" or dowries?[6] Will the next trend in gay family living popularize multigenerational joint families in which gay brothers (or sisters) bring their partners home to live with the sibs and Mom and Dad? Doubtful. Given the diasporas that have brought people from across the world to the United States, some of these kinship practices have undoubtedly gone on from family to family, community to community, and place to place. But not one of these practices has served as the focus of the visible public battles supposed to represent gay family concerns. If the choices that went into the making and the marketing of gay families were anywhere near as free or free-ranging as people like to think, we would be seeing more variety in the making.

Culture and economics are at work here, but also institutions. Think about the multiplicity of "choices" that greet you each time you take your shopping cart for a spin down the cereal aisle of a grocery superstore in the United States. Cereal companies work to limit the imagination at the very moment they seem to expand it by displaying a tantalizing array of multicolored boxes. Clearly there are many other ways to get that first meal of the day than by subscribing to the ones on offer. Likewise with the limited recognition accorded gay families to date. It is much easier for an institution such as a corporation to grant recognition to same-sex lovers by calling them "domestic partners" and treating them like honorary spouses than it is for corporate managers to creatively adapt policies to handle some of the culturally diverse scenarios described above. It is easier (though not easy) to go to court to fight for same-sex marriage than it is to battle for legal recognition of a family of friends in the absence of case-law precedent.

Or consider the "choice" of cover art for this new edition of *Families We Choose*. I examined a range of possibilities for the cover, all the while asking myself which image would bring what associations to whose mind. This 1989 photograph by Chantal Regnault, entitled "Revlon Boys," pictures three young men from one of the voguing houses in New York. Members of the House of Revlon created drag performances that pushed onlookers to think twice about what's guile and what's parody, what's staged and what's real, what's free and what's forced, when gender/race/class/sexuality meet. Voguing houses became home when members described themselves bonded by ties of kinship. But even decisions about how to depict a gay family are inevitably contentious and constrained.

I'm well aware that the selection of this particular photograph, in this particular placement, could be met by charges of misrepresentation. After all, the majority of people who appear in the pages of *Families We Choose* are not African-American men. Even though there are African-American men in the book, the choice of this image could also perpetuate the construction of race as an exclusively "black-white thing" in a way that Latinos, Asian Americans, Native Americans, and members of other groups have fought hard to dispel. For a book that engages a fairly diverse segment of San Francisco, no image drawn from a single race/class location can hope to represent a preponderance of the people in the study.[7] How can any one image hope to stand in for the whole of a complex and shifting queer population?

In choosing a photograph I also had to weigh issues of appropriation. Was this another white girl researcher using an African-American image to sell books? A legitimate question, and one not quite dispatched by the sobering thought that white (or Asian or Chicano or . . .) readers who cross the street when they see a black male coming are probably not going to be comfortable bringing home a book with an image of the same to "explain" things to Mom or Dad. Sales up or sales down? Time will tell.

What were the alternatives? Choose an image of queers of another color and face many of the same issues. Choose a white image and allow the popular misconstruction of "gay" as Anglo and inordinately wealthy to go unchallenged. (Turn to any book that promises general coverage of gay history, film, relationships, or even photography, and nineteen times out of twenty, you'll find a white image on the cover standing in for all lesbian/gay/bisexual lives.) Choose a rainbow photograph that depicts people of many colors and invite the dangerously utopian fantasies of harmony that *Families We Choose* attempts to undercut. Harmony is not easy to come by and people don't always learn about one another by getting along. Families, like "communities," are sites of conflict as well as support, violence as well as love. The family encounters I remember best from the time of my fieldwork were couched in acts of exquisite dailiness: macaroni wiped from a child's mouth, fingertips brushed shyly across shoulder, gun slammed nonchalantly on the table, voices lowered, voices raised, a carton of milk left out for me on the stoop.

In the end I decided to go with the image you see on the cover. These are not men I interviewed for the book, but men brought together in a family of their own making. I like this image because, unlike many other photographs that explicitly celebrate "our families," it signifies the potential of chosen kin to expand the notion of family well beyond couples and kids. Such a cover also serves as a reminder not to read the book through the author's body, either by whiting out the diversity of people interviewed or by perceiving it as a book about lesbians alone.[8]

Regnault's photograph deals a visual blow to the popular litigation strategy that portrays gay men and lesbians as deserving of rights because, except for this tiny little detail called sexuality, we're practically a white middle-class heterosexual you.[9] But are we? Child custody battles that invoke a white middle-class standard of parenthood do little for the unemployed black gay father or the underemployed Latina who works hard but lacks the money for the playpen, toys, diaper service, and extra bedroom a child "should" have. (Whose standards, whose "should"? Some groups would condemn the parent who "coldly" shunted her child off to a separate room to sleep alone.) Likewise, the right to pass on worldly goods to a partner without probate recedes in importance when there's nothing much to inherit. The value of domestic partnership lessens dramatically when nobody in the corporation receives a pension or health benefits. And if spending time with your family of friends is important to you but you have to work two jobs to make ends meet, all the family values in the world are not going to do you much good.

When the process of creating a book is over, what do you have? Once again, not free choice, but a necessarily uneasy selection hedged in by the legacies of mistrust, hope, violation, fantasy, and death sometimes known as "political considerations." As with race and class relations, so with the families we choose. As with the families we choose, so with the representation of what each of us has chosen.

Boston, Massachusetts *April 1997*

NOTES

1. It's not easy to undertake the task of reframing, with a new preface, a book that has already done more work in the world than an author dares hope. For assistance during this round of reflection, my thanks go to Helen Elaine Lee and Geeta Patel. They are in no way responsible for the positions I take here, nor in some instances would they agree. But their willingness to risk equanimity by visiting places of contention has been a lifesaver, and that's family to me.

2. See K. Anthony Appiah, "The Marrying Kind" (*The New York Review of Books* [June 20, 1996]:49–50): "The extreme unpopularity of gay marriage is, no doubt, why, in this election year, Bob Dole is cosponsoring a bill to deny federal recognition to gay marriages, even though no state has allowed any to take place, and even though marriage has always been largely a matter of state law, and Mr. Dole is from the party of state's rights."

3. Similarly, I have always been struck by the surprise many heterosexual readers of *Families We Choose* voice after they discover how very little information about sex appears in the 200-some pages of this book.

4. See Gali Kronenberg, "The Best Man: San Francisco Mayor Willie Brown Makes a Splash by Officiating at a Mass Same-Sex Wedding Ceremony," *The Advocate* (April 30, 1996):29–31. Lambda Legal Defense and Education Fund has led the shift in the focus of litigation, followed closely by organizations such as the West Coast-based National Center for Lesbian Rights (NCLR). In 1995 (ten years after the initial field research for *Families We Choose*), NCLR's Annual Report listed a caseload distribution weighted heavily toward family issues, with custody cases comprising 24.1 percent of the total, adoption 22.2 percent, partnership 13.3 percent, reproductive rights 9.2 percent, and domestic violence .5 percent. Lambda, an organization that serves gay male as well as lesbian clients, has pursued cases that involve second-parent and joint adoption, the rights of

nonbiological parents to custody or visitation, opposition to the deportation of immigrants who have been long-term partners of U.S. citizens, partners' rights to health benefits and bereavement leave, and the right of a surviving partner to remain in a rent-controlled apartment following a lover's death, as well as the high-profile same-sex marriage case of *Baehr v. Miike* (formerly *Baehr v. Lewin*) in the state of Hawaii. Of course the dockets of these organizations are not limited to family issues but extend, for example, to the filing of an amicus brief supporting a stay of execution in the case of *Burdine v. Scott*, in which a prosecutor urged a jury to sentence Calvin Burdine to death on the grounds that "sending a homosexual to the penitentiary certainly isn't bad punishment for a homosexual" (*The Lambda Update* 13 [3]:19).

5. See David Schneider's comments on turns and twists in the study of kinship in Richard Handler, ed., *Schneider on Schneider: The Conversion of the Jews and Other Anthropological Stories*, Durham: Duke University Press, 1995.

6. "Spouse service" is a play upon the ethnographic term "bride service," which refers to a marriage arrangement that requires a woman's spouse to labor for and otherwise serve his bride's parents and/or other relatives.

7. Given the history of identity politics in the United States, an image of a working-class white Jewish woman cannot stand, in any simple way, for an image of a middle-class WASP man, any more than an image of members of a voguing house can substitute for an image of members of an "old family" from the black middle class. Better not to try for that kind of representation.

8. Each of these "creative readings" happens far too frequently, if readers' reports are any guide.

9. Cf. Darren Rosenblum's argument that the legal strategies pursued in the course of the struggle for "gay rights" have skewed the fight for social justice in the direction of the white middle class, while ignoring the needs of queers who are poor, of color, gender bending, and/or "sexually subversive" ("Queer Intersectionality and the Failure of Recent Lesbian and Gay 'Victories,' " *Law and Sexuality* 4[1994]:83–122). Before the litigation started, well before the advocacy organizations ever arrived, a wide range of family forms had begun to emerge from the grass roots. (The establishment of voguing houses would be one.) Such families are not always amenable to legitimation under the rule of current law.

ACKNOWLEDGMENTS

The field research that forms the basis for this study was generously supported by grants from the American Association of University Women and the National Science Foundation. Many people provided encouragement that sustained me through the long process of translating my observations and insights into something more tangible. I especially would like to thank Steve Berlyn, Ed Cohen, Irene Heidenway, Nico Jones, Lisa Márquez, Kim Marshall, Celeste Morin, Kathy Phillips, Carla Schick, Cheri Thomas, and Darlene Weingand for reminding me why I had undertaken a project of this magnitude when I was feeling overworked and tempted to forget.

Ellen Lewin, Mary Pratt, Renato Rosaldo, Walter Williams, and Sylvia Yanagisako offered comments that helped me clarify my thinking and suggestions that significantly strengthened the manuscript. The women of the Lesbian Herstory Archives in New York and Lester Olmstead-Rose of Community United Against Violence in San Francisco directed me to background material that I otherwise might not have uncovered. In the face of an impending deadline, Lori Jervis rearranged her schedule to assemble bibliographic materials and proofread revised drafts of the manuscript. The final version of the text, for which I am solely responsible, owes much to Celeste Morin's critical eye, sense of balance, and willingness to argue a point.

My special thanks go to all the people in the Bay Area who contributed their stories, questions, time, wisdom, humor, patience, convictions, friendship, and resistance. You know who you are.

FAMILIES WE CHOOSE

LESBIANS, GAYS, KINSHIP

| # THE MONKEY CAGE AND
THE RED DESOTO

The rush and stampede for shelter from nature created the
wind.   —TONI CADE BAMBARA, *The Salt Eaters*

David Scondras, an openly gay man elected to the
Boston City Council, lists gaining recognition for an "extended concept of family" as one of his top priorities while in office. Domestic
partner legislation, which would allow an unmarried heterosexual or
gay partner to draw the same employment benefits as a married
spouse, is passed, vetoed, and finally written into law in San Francisco, only to be rescinded in citywide elections. In Minnesota, Karen
Thompson begins a protracted court battle for the right to visit her
lover of four years, Sharon Kowalski, who had been placed under the
legal guardianship of her father after being seriously injured in an
automobile accident.[1] Meanwhile, Jesse Jackson enters the presidential campaign with a pledge to support full legal rights for lesbian and
gay couples. The *New York Native* and *Village Voice* commemorate
gay pride week with feature articles on "the gay family." Geraldo
Rivera opens his nationally syndicated daytime television talk show
with a look of shock and the one-liner, "Is there a lesbian baby
boom?" Across the country, workshops on alternative (artificial) insemination and gay parenting spring up.

To note these developments of the 1980s was to witness the emergence of a discourse on gay families, a reconfiguration of the terrain
of kinship that continues to generate controversy among heterosexual
and gay people alike.[2] Gay families did not suddenly appear in isolation from conditions in society at large, but emerged as part of a wider
process which Rayna Rapp (1987:130) has described as the overt
politicization of kinship in the United States. Also debated during this
decade were new reproductive technologies; surrogate motherhood;

1

open adoptions; abortion rights; the increase in numbers of teenage mothers, working mothers, and single (mostly female and poor) parents; a rising divorce rate; and "blended families" that brought remarried spouses together with children from previous marriages. In urban areas skyrocketing rents added to the total of "unrelated" roommates sharing rental housing, while retired and disabled people experimented with a variety of cooperative living arrangements.[3]

This study begins by addressing a deceptively simple set of questions: What is all this talk about gay families? Where did those families come from, and why should they appear now? Associated with these questions are several broader areas of concern: What is the relation of a newly emergent discourse to social movements and social change? Are gay families inherently assimilationist, or do they represent a radical departure from more conventional understandings of kinship? Will gay families have any effect on kinship relations and social relations in the United States as a whole?

||||

The sign in the store window reads: "Closed so employees can be with their families for the holiday." I stand outside in a light drizzle, wondering whether the rainy season will come early this year and pondering the assumption conveyed in that handwritten note: surely all employees must have families. A hackneyed image of "the older homosexual" comes to mind, alienated from relatives and living out his or her last years alone in some garret. The stereotyped tragedy of "gay life" revolves around this presumed isolation, the absence of kin and stable relationships. Walking paradoxes in a land of marriage vows and blood ties, lesbians and gay men are popularly supposed to incarnate this most sexual and least social of beings. Where does the store owner think his lesbian and gay employees go for Thanksgiving?

||||

While many cultural anthropologists working abroad have busied themselves by classifying all sorts of relationships as "family" that might better be viewed through a different lens, within their own societies they have tended to overlook certain bonds regarded as kin by the "natives" themselves. Across the United States a person can find lesbians and gay men who echo Sylvia Yanagisako's and Jane Collier's (1987) assertion that families should not be confounded with genealogically defined relationships. Gay (or chosen) families dispute the old saying, "You can pick your friends, but you can't pick your relatives." Not only can these families embrace friends; they may also encompass lovers, coparents, adopted children, children from previous heterosexual relationships, and offspring conceived through alternative insemination. Although discourse on gay kinship features familiar symbols such as blood, choice, and love, it also redirects those symbols toward the task of demarcating different categories of family.

The longer I pursued my research, the more I became convinced that gay families could not be understood apart from the families in which lesbians and gay men had grown up. After looking at the entire universe of relations they considered kin, it became evident that discourse on gay kinship defines gay families vis-à-vis another type of family known as "straight," "biological," or "blood"—terms that many gay people applied to their families of origin. Previous studies of lesbians and gay men have tended to analyze each of these components in isolation. Many researchers have examined relations with "blood" and adoptive kin in the context of the literature on disclosure of sexual identity or the literary genre of coming-out stories. In contrast, discussion of lesbian and gay relationships often appears in the context of research on alternative forms of family. This study brings together these two areas of investigation in an effort to develop a more fruitful approach to understanding what "family" means and has meant to lesbians and gay men in the United States.

Nowhere in these pages will readers find an analysis of "the gay family." No such standardized creation exists, any more than there exists one uniform version of kinship called "the American family." The popular joke about growing up to marry and raise a family with 2.4 kids attests to the absurdity of such a claim. Here I am interested in family not so much as an institution, but as a contested concept, implicated in the relations of power that permeate societies.

Familial ties between persons of the same sex that may be erotic but are not grounded in biology or procreation do not fit any tidy division of kinship into relations of blood and marriage. David Schneider's (1968) classic study of "American kinship" outlines a symbolics grounded in precisely this division: the contrast between what he calls the order of nature, which invokes the "shared substance" of blood, and the order of law, based upon a customary "code for conduct." Lesbian and gay relationships seem to cut across these categories of law and nature. In approximately half of the states, statutes that outlaw sex between two women or two men remain on the books. For over a century some have labeled homosexuality a perversion of nature comprised of "unnatural acts." Little or no legal status exists for the relationships gay people create and may consider kin, relationships that include but are not limited to couples.

This cultural positioning of gay people outside both law and nature has generated one type of response which appropriates these terms to protest exclusion from the realm of kinship. Various gay organizations have worked for the abolition of sodomy laws and the establishment of some sort of legal recognition for lesbian and gay couples, as well as for nonbiological coparents. On a personal level, individuals sometimes take legally sanctioned ties as a point of reference in evaluating their own relationships. Al Collins characterized his connection to his partner this way:

> We bought rings after we had been together about six months and we said vows to each other and it was just like . . . to us it was a formal commitment and bond and marriage, although it wasn't sacramented by law of the church. But to the two of us, it's law.

Others, like Frank Maldonado, argued for the naturalness of gay relations.

> I have this childhood memory of being about six, and my father had this red DeSoto, and we used to take drives. It was a convertible. And we passed this church where there was a wedding, and my mother said, "Oh, it's a double wedding." And I said, "Oh, is that two men getting married and two women getting married?" I mean, it just seemed real natural to me.

Frank's romantic depiction of childhood innocence operated to make pejorative views of homosexuality themselves appear unnatural—merely social fictions. Charlyne Harris described her first visit to a lesbian bar to make a similar point: "It was a trip how . . . just things came real natural for me: approaching other women, dancing with other women. I didn't feel weird or nothing about it. It's like this was *natural*, and that was what I was supposed to be doing." Charlyne discussed what Schneider would call code for conduct ("what I was supposed to be doing"), not blood ties. Her usage of "nature" mixed Schneider's terms, linking nature to biology as well as custom by opposing "natural" desires to the "artificiality" of social expectations.

In contexts like this, where individuals appeal to nature in order to contest dominant cultural representations, nature does indeed appear to be "a category of challenge rather than an element in a stable binary contrast" (Bloch and Bloch 1980:31).

|||||

On a rare day without interviews, when I'm tired of hanging out in living rooms, storefront offices, and bars, I travel down the Peninsula to use the library at Stanford University. In the "HQ" section that organizes works on homosexuality, the older volumes are still imprinted with "locked stack" labels.

|||||

Because meanings are inseparable from practice, the level of resistance in the United States to granting gay families legitimacy should not be surprising. At stake is far more than a cultural nostalgia for more customary ways of symbolically constituting relationships. Applying for insurance coverage, filing taxes, and fighting child custody cases are just three instances that interpolate the symbolic oppositions which inform gay kinship into everyday experience. The material and emotional consequences that hinge upon which interpretation of kinship prevails are truly far-reaching. Who will be authorized to make life-and-death decisions when lovers and other members of gay families are hospitalized or otherwise incapacitated? Will court rulings continue to force some parents to choose between living with their children and living with a lesbian or gay partner? Should a biological grandfather who has never spoken to his grandchild because he disapproved of his daughter's lesbianism retain more legal rights vis-à-vis that child than a nonbiological coparent who has raised the child for ten years? Will the phrase "related by blood or marriage" be allowed to stand as a justification for refusing lovers public accommodations; denying them visiting rights at nursing homes, prisons, and hospitals; disqualifying gay families for family discounts; or withholding the right to pass on a rent-controlled apartment after death? How will conflicting conceptions of kinship play themselves out during disputes over death or inheritance, which are so often complicated by strained relationships with blood or adoptive family? A person need not be especially politically oriented or active to worry about the way such conflicts will translate into the most personal areas of their lives.

I know that if something were to happen to [my lover], her family would just fly her back home, and I would not be allowed to the funeral. I would die. I can't tell you. . . . And even now that we've accumulated . . . it's not a whole bunch of wealth, but to us, it's our little wealth! What should happen to our belongings?

Although people in the United States tend to imagine kinship as a discrete and private domain, many ostensibly nonfamilial arenas are infused with heterosexist presumptions and regulated by kinship.[4] As the law currently stands, lesbians and gay men cannot sue a third party for wrongful death of a partner, nor can they qualify for the exemption from probate that many states offer when all property is willed to a spouse. Immigration laws bar from the country gay men and lesbians who are not citizens, while the Immigration and Naturalization Service refuses to consider the hardship of separation as a ground for establishing residency or citizenship (as they will for married heterosexual couples and blood kin), even when gay people can document years of coresidence, shared ownership of property, and public ceremonies affirming their commitment to a relationship. Rather than stationing gay partners together in one place, the military threatens them with dishonorable discharge. When a new Chicago Housing Authority policy forbade "unrelated" guests from spending the night in public housing, "eight men who had been living with their girlfriends in one housing project married them in a mass ceremony" ("Shotgun Wedding" 1989). Leaving aside the civil rights implications for everyone involved in that situation, lesbian and gay residents had no such recourse. Zoning laws in many communities also restrict the number of "unrelated" persons who may live in housing classified as a "single family dwelling." Though a contradictory mix of outcomes has greeted lesbians and gay men in their efforts to argue the significance of gay family relationships, the battle itself has clearly begun.

Given these inequities, does it make sense to argue that gay families represent an alternative form of family, a distinctive variation within a more encompassing "American kinship"? Because any alternative must be an alternative *to* something, this formulation presumes a central paradigm of family shared by most people in a society. In the United States the nuclear family clearly represents a privileged construct, rather than one among a number of family forms accorded equivalent status. Although representations of nuclear families would not accurately describe the households where many people reside, they do supply one cultural framework for configuring kinship that people can draw upon to interpret the world around them. At the Portland Zoo on a midsummer afternoon, I joined a group of visitors surrounding a cage that contained one infant and four adult monkeys. The human bystanders—concerned only with constructing a standardized kinship triad from the group of five animals—quickly identified what they called "the father," "the mother," and "the baby." When one of the adult females disappeared inside the zoo building, a woman next to me took the hand of the child at her side and said, "Let's go. The mommy monkey left to make lunch."

But just as representations are contestable, so nuclear families do not constitute the timeless core of what it means to have kin in this society, relative to which all other forms of family must appear as derivative variations or marginal alternatives. A more useful approach to the analysis of gay families involves moving beyond the study of static variations and the celebration of diversity to examine historical transformations in kinship, ideology, and social relations—transformations that could not have come about without conflict, contradictions, difference, and struggle.

|||||

On the day of the annual Gay Pride Parade, hundreds of thousands are expected to march down Market Street in San Francisco, and the corners of major intersections have become impassable. As I watch, the young man next to me provides a running "camp" commentary for the benefit of his friends. Hi-Tech Gays, a Silicon Valley group, goes by ("Show us your hardware!"), followed by a lone drag queen in peacock feathers ("What's she with, faggots for attention?") and a group throwing condoms into the crowd ("Here's one for you Carter, and you Jack, and definitely one for you Richard"). "Dykes with Bikes" has grown to mammoth proportions, now an eight-block-long contingent of women, motorcycles, honking horns, and cheering onlookers. This year persons with AIDS (PWAs) and AIDS organizations lead the march.

|||||

The fieldwork that provides the basis for my analysis was conducted in the San Francisco Bay Area during 1985–1986, with a follow-up visit in 1987. San Francisco is a port city with a large and extremely diverse population of lesbians and gay men, as well as a history of gay immigration that dates at least to World War II (D'Emilio 1989b). A wave of lesbian and gay immigrants arrived in the Bay Area during the 1970s, when young people of all sexualities found themselves attracted by employment opportunities in the region's rapidly expanding service sector (FitzGerald 1986). Some came for the work, some for the climate, and some to be a part of "gay mecca." Others, of course, grew up in California.

Several San Francisco neighborhoods—Folsom, Polk Street, the Castro, Bernal Heights, parts of the Tenderloin, and increasingly the Mission—were recognized even by heterosexual residents as areas with high concentrations of gay men and/or lesbians.

|||||

The third tour bus in as many hours rolls through the Castro. I watch from behind the plate glass window of the donut shop, trying to imagine this neighborhood, so symbolic of "gay America," through tourist eyes. Every television reporter who covers AIDS seems to station herself somewhere on this block. The Castro used to be a place where gay men could come to cruise and enjoy one another, objects (if not always subjects) for themselves. Nowadays, says the man sitting next to me, when you see those buses coming around, you feel like you're in a museum or a zoo or something.

|||||

With its unique history and reputation as a gay city, San Francisco hardly presents a "typical" lesbian and gay population for study.[5] Yet the Bay Area proved to be a valuable field site because it brought together gay men and lesbians from very different colors and classes, identities and backgrounds. One estimate for 1980 put San Francisco's combined self-identified lesbian, gay, and bisexual population at 17 percent. Of those who placed themselves in one of these categories, 30 percent were women and 70 percent were men (DeLeon and Brown 1980).[6] Lesbians were a visible presence on both sides of the bay. In contrast to many smaller cities, the region supported an abundance of specialized organizations aimed at particular sectors of the gay population, from groups for people over or under a certain age to associations of individuals who played music or enjoyed hiking. With its multicultural population, the Bay Area also hosted a variety of social organizations, political groups, and informal gathering places for gay people of color.

Among lesbians and gay men in the country at large, San Francisco is known as a place that allows people to be relatively open about their sexual identities. Carol Warren (1977) has emphasized the need to be especially protective of respondents' identities when working with gay people, in light of the social stigmatization of homosexuality. Although I follow anthropological tradition by using pseudonyms throughout this study, I feel it is important to note that the vast majority of participants expressed a willingness to have their real names appear in print. Fear of losing employment and a desire to protect children's identities were the reasons offered by the few who requested assurances of anonymity. Unlike many studies of gay men and lesbians, this one assigns surnames to participants. In a Western context, introducing strangers by given names alone paradoxically conveys a sense of intimacy while subtly withholding individuality, respect, and full adult status from research participants. Because the same qualities are routinely denied to lesbians and gay men in society at large, the use of only first names can have the unintended consequence of perpetuating heterosexist assumptions.

|||||

While we sit at the bar watching women play pool, Sharon Vitrano is telling me about her experience walking home through the Tenderloin after one of the annual Gay Pride Parades. As she and a woman friend approached a group of men in front of a Mom-and-Pop grocery store, the two stopped walking arm in arm. On her mind, she says, were the tensions growing out of San Francisco's rapid gentrification, and escalating street violence linked to perceptions of gay people as wealthy real estate speculators. To Sharon's surprise and delight, one of the men shouted out, "Go ahead, hold hands! It's your day!"

|||||

In addition to the long hours of participant-observation so central to anthropological fieldwork, my analysis draws on 80 in-depth interviews conducted while in the field. Interview participants were divided evenly between women and men, with all but two identifying themselves as lesbian or gay.[7] Random sampling is clearly an impossibility for a population that is not only partially hidden or "closeted," but also lacks consensus as to the criteria for membership (Morin 1977; NOGLSTP 1986). In general, I let self-identification be my guide for inclusion.[8] Determined to avoid the race, class, and organizational bias that has characterized so many studies of gay men and lesbians, I made my initial connections through personal contacts developed over the six years I had lived in San Francisco previous to the time the project got underway.[9] The alternative—gaining entree through agencies, college classes, and advertisements—tends to weight a sample for "joiners," professional interviewees, the highly educated, persons with an overtly political analysis, and individuals who see themselves as central (rather than marginal) to the population in question.

By asking each person interviewed for names of potential participants, I utilized techniques of friendship pyramiding and snowball sampling to arrive at a sample varied in race, ethnicity, class, and class background. While the Bay Area is perhaps more generally politicized than other regions of the nation, the majority of interview participants would not have portrayed themselves as political activists. Approximately 36 percent were people of color; of the 64 percent who were white, 11 (or 14 percent of the total) were Jewish. Slightly over 50 percent came from working-class backgrounds, with an overlapping 58 percent employed in working-class occupations at the time of the interview.

At the outset I had intended to arrange second interviews with a portion of the sample, but decided instead to seek informal contexts for follow-up that would allow me to interact with participants as part of a group. Most of the direct quotations in this study are drawn from interviews, but some arose during dinner table conversations, birthday parties, a night out at a bar, or asides during a ball game. I strove not to select interview participants on the basis of the kind of experiences they claimed to have had. Individuals' characterizations of their personal histories ran the gamut from "boring" to "incredible," but I found these assessments a completely unreliable index of interest from an anthropological point of view.

Out of 82 people contacted, only two turned down my request for an interview. A few individuals made an effort to find me after hearing about the study, but most were far from self-selecting. The vast majority demanded great persistence and flexibility in scheduling (and rescheduling) on my part to convince them to participate. I believe this persistence is one reason this study includes voices not customarily heard when lesbians and gay men appear in the pages of books and journals: people who had constructed exceedingly private lives and could scarcely get over their disbelief at allowing themselves to be interviewed, people convinced that their experiences were uneventful or unworthy of note, people fearful that a researcher would go away and write an account lacking in respect for their identities or their perceptions.

To offset the tendency of earlier studies to focus on the white and wealthier sectors of lesbian and gay populations, I also utilized theoretic sampling. From a growing pool of contacts I deliberately selected people of color, people from working-class backgrounds, and individuals employed in working-class occupations.

|||||

What a busy day for a Friday, I think to myself, sinking into a chair after three back-to-back interviews. At the first apartment, stacks of papers had covered every counter, table, desk, and anything else approximating a flat surface. Before the interview began, Bernie Margolis, a Jewish man in his sixties, insisted on showing me his picture gallery. In one frame, a much younger Bernie stood next to Martin Luther King, Jr.; others held snapshots of children from a previous marriage and distinguished service awards from a variety of community organizations. Before I left, he asked me to proofread a political leaflet. From his Mission district flat I traveled up to the Fillmore to meet Rose Ellis, an African-American woman in her thirties. Laid off from her construction job, she was cooking a batch of blackeyed peas and watching soap operas when I arrived. After the interview, Rose asked me to play back part of the tape through her roommate's stereo system—so that she could hear what her voice sounded like. A little later I hurried home to interview Annie Sorenson, a young white woman who described herself as a "lesbian virgin" with few gay or lesbian friends. From the vantage point of an easy chair reflecting back upon the day, my initial reaction is to wonder what these three people are doing in the same book. Would they know what to say to one another if they met in chapter 4?

|||||

In any sample this diverse, with so many different combinations of identities, theoretic sampling cannot hope to be "representative." To treat each individual as a representative of his or her race, for instance, would be a form of tokenism that glosses over the differences of gender, class, age, national origin, language, religion, and ability which crosscut race and ethnicity. At the same time, I am not interested in these categories as demographic variables, or as reified pigeonholes for people, but rather as identities meaningful to participants themselves.

I concentrate here on the interpretive links participants made (or did not make) between sexual identity and other aspects of who they considered themselves to be, always with the awareness that identical symbols can carry very different meanings in different contexts. The tables in the appendix present demographic information on the interview sample, but—since this is not a statistically oriented study— merely to illustrate its diversity and provide descriptive information about participants.

Despite my efforts to incorporate differences, the sample remains weak in several areas, most notably the age range (which tends to cluster around the twenties and thirties), the inclusion of relatively few gay parents, and a bias toward fairly high levels of education.[10] Given the age-, gender-, and race-segregated structure of gay institutions and social organization, these results may partially have been a function of my own situation and identities. I was in my late twenties at the time of the study, had no children, and usually ran out of boxes to check when asked to number my years of education on forms or surveys. But the sample's deficiencies also indicate my emphasis during fieldwork, since its composition does not reflect other aspects of my identity as a white woman from a working-class background. I made the greatest effort to achieve breadth in the areas of present class, class background, and race/ethnicity.

In retrospect, I wish I had added age to this list of priorities. Judging from the gay men and lesbians in older age cohorts that I did interview, people who came out before the social movements of the 1950s–1970s may possess distinctive perspectives on the issue of disclosing their sexual identities to others, including relatives (cf. Hall 1978). Although those movements affected people of all ages who lived through that time period, older interview participants often cast their experiences in a comparative framework, distinguishing between what it meant to pursue same-sex erotic relations "then" and "now." Life experiences had made many acutely aware of the negative social and economic consequences that can follow from disclosure of a lesbian or gay identity. In her study of lesbians over 60, Monika Kehoe (1989) found that women who had married before they claimed a lesbian identity were likely to have maintained close ties with blood relatives (especially female kin) after coming out. Yet some of the same women had suffered ostracism at the hands of their heterosexual adult children.

To date there is conflicting evidence regarding the relationship between lesbian or gay identity and aging. Both the older gay men studied by Raymond Berger (1982b) and Kehoe's survey respondents reported loneliness and isolation, but their responses may have reflected the loneliness experienced by many people in the United States following retirement or the death of a partner. Further research needs to be conducted on the development of friendship networks among gay people over time, particularly given the high value historically placed on friendship by both lesbians and gay men. Do those networks expand, contract, or maintain their size as individuals grow older? Do gay people look more often to friendships, as opposed to other types of social relations, for support and assistance as they age? Are older gay men and lesbians participating in the discourse on gay families to the same extent as their younger counterparts? Since most existing studies compare lesbians to heterosexual women and gay men to heterosexual men within their respective age cohorts, there is also a need for research that contrasts the experiences of older lesbians and gay men.

|||||

"Are you a lesbian? Are you gay?" Every other day one of these questions greets my efforts to set up interviews over the telephone. Halfway through my fieldwork, I remark on this concern with the researcher's identity while addressing a course in anthropological field methods. "Do you think you could have done this study if you weren't a lesbian?" asks a student from the back of the classroom. "No doubt," I reply, "but then again, it wouldn't have been the same study."

|||||

As late as 1982, Raymond Berger experienced difficulty locating lesbians of any class, color, or creed for a study of older gay people. Concluding that lesbians had little in the way of a visible public community, he gave up and confined his book to men. While gay male institutions may be more apparent to the eye, lesbians have their own (actually quite accessible) organizations and establishments, most well-documented in local community newspapers. My point here is that lesbians remained invisible *to Berger;* for me, as a woman, finding male participants proved more of a challenge. Recent work in cultural anthropology has stressed the importance of recognizing the researcher as a positioned subject (Mintz 1979; Rosaldo 1989). In my case, being a woman also influenced how I spent my time in the field:

I passed more hours in lesbian clubs and women's groups than gay men's bars or male gyms.

Once I started to gain referrals, my lesbian identity clearly helped me lay claim to those bywords that anthropologists like to apply to relationships in the field when information is forthcoming: "trust" and "rapport." Many participants mentioned that they would not have talked to me had I been straight, and one or two cited "bad experiences" of having had their words misinterpreted by heterosexual researchers. In interviews with me people devoted relatively little time to addressing anti-gay stereotypes, and spoke freely about subjects such as butch/fem, gay marriage, sadomasochism (s/m), and drag queens—all topics controversial among gay men and lesbians themselves. Occasionally, of course, the larger context of eventual publication would intrude, and individuals would qualify their statements.

Presumptions of a common frame of reference and shared identity can also complicate the anthropologist's task by leaving cultural notions implicit, making her work to get people to state, explain, and situate the obvious. To study one's own culture involves a process of making the familiar strange, more the province of the poet or phenomenologist than of fieldworkers traveling abroad to unravel what seems puzzling about other societies. Early in the research my daily routine was structured by decisions about what to record. Everything around me seemed fair game for notes: one day I was living a social reality, the next day I was supposed to document it. Unlike anthropologists who have returned from the field to write ethnographies that contain accounts of reaching "their" island or village, I saw no possibility of framing an arrival scene to represent the inauguration of my fieldwork, except perhaps by drawing on the novelty of the first friend who asked (with a sidelong glance), "Are you taking notes on this?" [11] My task could not even be characterized as an exploration of "strangeness inside the familiar," a phrase used by Frances FitzGerald (1986) to describe her investigation of the gay Castro district. For me, doing fieldwork among gay and lesbian San Franciscans did not entail uncovering some "exotic" corner of my native culture but rather discovering the stuff of everyday life. [12]

||||||

After three rings I put aside the interview I've been transcribing and reluctantly head for the phone. It's my friend Mara calling for the first time in months. With a certain embarrassment, she tells me about the affair she's been having with a man. Everything is over now, she assures me, maintaining that the affair has no wider implications for her lesbian identity. "The reason I'm calling," she says half in jest, "is that I need an anthropologist. How would you like to ghostwrite a book about this whole thing? I'm going to call it My Year Among the Savages.*"*

|||||

During interviews I used coming-out stories as a point of departure for investigating issues of identity and relationships with blood or adoptive relatives. Such narratives are customarily related to and for other lesbians and gay men rather than for the benefit of a heterosexual audience. Coming-out stories had the advantage of representing a category meaningful to participants themselves, a category so indigenous that one woman asked, "Do you want the 33 or the 45 rpm version?"[13] Making new acquaintances was one type of occasion that often called for telling a coming-out story, and it seemed to me at times that my role as interviewer began to blend with the role of "lesbian friend of a friend."

|||||

In New York to do research at the Lesbian Herstory Archives, I notice that local news programs are dominated by coverage of the Statue of Liberty restoration project. "Miss Liberty" and "Lady Liberty," the newscasters call her. To people in the United States, "Mrs. Liberty" would sound like a joke.

|||||

A note on terminology is apropos here. I frequently refer to "lesbians and gay men" to remind readers of gendered differences and to undermine the all too common assumption that findings about gay men hold equally for lesbians. At times, however, I employ "gay" and "gay people" as generic terms that embrace both women and men. In the Bay Area, women themselves held different opinions regarding the application of these terms. Those who had come out in association with the women's movement were inclined to call themselves lesbians and reserve the word "gay" for men. Younger women, women who maintained social ties to gay men, and women with less connection to lesbian-feminism, were more apt to describe themselves as gay. In certain contexts a broad range of people employed "gay" as a contrasting parallel to the categories "straight" and "heterosexual."

Readers may also notice the conspicuous absence of the term

"American" throughout the text. A Latino participant playfully suggested the modifier "United Statesian" as a substitute that would demonstrate respect for residents of Central and South America—as well as Canada, Mexico, and the Caribbean—who also reside in the Americas name. I have elected to avoid such summary terms altogether, not only in deference to the linguistic claims of other peoples, but also because the label "American" is so bound up with nationalist sentiment ("the American way") that it defies limitation to a descriptive reference.

I have interchanged "African-American" with "black," "Native American" with "American Indian," and "Mexican-American" with "Chicano" and "Chicana." Preference for one or the other of these terms varied with regional origin, generation, political involvement, and personal likes or dislikes. In many contexts people referred to more specific racial and ethnic identities (Cuban-American rather than Hispanic, Chinese-American rather than Asian-American). Occasionally, however, they appealed to a collective racial identity defined vis-à-vis the socially dominant categories "white" or "Anglo." "Minorities" is clearly unsatisfactory for describing this collectivity, since white people represent the numerical minority in many parts of the Bay Area, not to mention the world as a whole. I employ "people of color" for lack of a better term, although the phrase remains problematic. Racial identity and skin tone do not always correspond to the color symbolism used to depict race in the United States. The term "people of color" can also reinforce racist perceptions of white as the unmarked, and so more generically human, category. White, of course, is also a color, and white people are as implicated in race relations as anyone else in this society.

Defining class is always a vexed issue, especially in the United States, where class consciousness is often absent or superseded by other identities (Jackman and Jackman 1983). Rayna Rapp (1982) has astutely observed that class is a process, not a position or a place. Class in this sense cannot be indexed by income or plotted along a sociological continuum from "upper" to "lower." Nevertheless, to convey the range of the interview sample, I have organized a rough classification of participants based on occupation (or parents' occupations, in the case of class background), following a Marxist interpretation of class as a relation to processes of production. Where the term "middle class" appears in the text, it is always in quotation marks to indicate its status as an indigenous term used by people I encountered during fieldwork, rather than an analytic category of my own choosing.

| | | | |

Leafing through the latest copy of a gay community newspaper, I come across a letter from a man angered by new governmental regulations that make it extremely difficult for gay people to become foster parents in Massachusetts. Asserting his right to parent, he has decided to sponsor a child abroad through the Foster Parents Plan.

| | | | |

In the following chapter I trace the ideological shift in which many lesbians and gay men began to portray themselves as people who seek not only to maintain ties with blood or adoptive relations, but also to establish families of their own. This vision resists more conventional views of family that locate gay people outside kinship's door. Because discourse on gay families critiques many of the procreative assumptions that inform hegemonic notions of kinship in the United States, it can yield insights into how the cultural domain of kinship becomes defined as its boundaries are drawn, contested, and redrawn. [14]

Unlike many studies of ideology and representation, this one sets out to account for the specific *content* of a discourse by posing the question: Why are gay families also called "families we choose?" Unlike purely symbolic analyses, this one situates narratives and representations in particular historical contexts, and grounds ideological change in lived experience. In place of a holistic analysis of some unified symbolic system, chapter 2 offers a glimpse of an emerging discourse that individuals enter in multiple, sometimes contradictory, ways. Although this section focuses on ideology, the larger analysis of which it is a part refuses to investigate signs apart from "the concrete forms of social intercourse" (Vološinov 1973:21).

| | | | |

My great-aunt has just returned from having dinner with my sister, her friends Ray and Joel (a gay couple), and Ray's parents. "It was just terrible," she tells me. "Can you believe that when Ray's lover served the salad he had made, Ray's father sat there and refused to eat it?"

| | | | |

Discourse on gay families has emerged in association with a particular set of sociohistorical and material conditions. Chapters 3 and 4, which focus on relations with what many lesbians and gay men call "straight family," begin to fill out this wider context. Highlighted here are the long-term impact of a gay movement that encouraged lesbians and gay men to disclose their sexual identities to heterosexual others, and the significance of this development for many gay people's perceptions of kinship relations. My subject matter dictated the emphasis on narrative in these chapters. Disclosing a lesbian or gay identity to "biological" or adoptive relatives is considered a very personal (not to mention nervewracking) experience, the type of situation in which an anthropologist would almost never be present. In this section my objective is not to reduce coming out to a static developmental process by abstracting stages or defining a trajectory (cf. Coleman 1982; Ponse 1978). Rather, I am interested in understanding how persons in the process of taking on a new, ostensibly sexual, identity find themselves talking as much about kinship as sexuality.

|||||

Several lesbians and gay men are sprawled across my living room floor, gathered to watch another made-for-TV movie about the lives of gay people. Once the show comes on, laughter punctuates its dialogue in places the producers surely never intended. During the commercials, my guests express outrage that these movies always depict gay people in relation to blood relatives, ignoring the lovers, friends, and gay families most "real" protagonists would have.

|||||

Chapter 5 examines the "families we choose" side of the symbolic opposition between straight and gay families. Changes in the conceptualization of the relation between friends and lovers, along with challenges to the vision of a unified gay community, appear here as additional historical antecedents that have helped to shape the contemporary discourse on gay families. This portion of the analysis does not present a community study in the traditional sense, but one that treats community as a cultural category implicated in the renegotiation of kinship relations.

|||||

Shortly before officially beginning fieldwork, I attend a ritual celebration of the bond between two lesbian lovers. The two have created their own ceremony, and make it clear that they are seeking support and recognition for their relationship, not the sanction of church or state. Milling about in the crowd afterward, I notice that many of the heterosexuals are busy comparing notes on their own weddings, while the major topic of conversation among the lesbians and gay men seems to be how lucky the hosts are to have parents and other "biological" relatives present for the ceremony.

| | | | |

In chapter 6 I pause to take a closer look at lesbian and gay lovers in committed relationships. Recent scholarly work on gay couples draws heavily on psychological theories which characterize gay relationships as ties that primarily reflect back upon the self. By critiquing the assumption that partners with a common gender identity participate in a relation of sameness, I argue that the use of mirror imagery to describe gay couples reinforces stereotypes of gay men and lesbians as narcissistic, self-absorbed, irresponsible, and wealthy. The analytic utility of the mirror metaphor is limited by its insensitivity to many subtleties of lesbian and gay relations, and by its implication that gay people lack truly social relationships, much less kinship ties.

| | | | |

During the first few months of fieldwork, I ask an interview participant in his early thirties for contacts and introductions. Peter Ouillette seems to be stalling for time. Finally he explains, "I really want to help you out . . . it's just that I hate going through my address book. So many of my friends have died."

| | | | |

Becky Vogel and I are sitting in a cafe, talking over cappuccino about her plans to have a child through alternative insemination. "I'm on the lookout for boys," she laughs, reveling in the irony of such a statement. "Do you know any Jewish men who want to coparent?"

| | | | |

Chapter 7 investigates the rising interest in lesbian and gay parenting at a time when AIDS has had a major impact on gay men in the United States. Within the wider discourse on kinship, the lesbian baby boom represents a partial reincorporation of biology into chosen families. At the same time, through cooperation in alternative insemination and coparenting arrangements, lesbians and gay men have challenged the centrality of heterosexual intercourse and a two-person, "opposite" gender model of parenthood to kinship relations.

| | | | |

At the weekly strip show in one of San Francisco's lesbian bars, Tough Love is making her farewell performance. While friends and admirers

throw long-stemmed roses, kisses, and dollar bills toward the stage, the
dancer stands tall under the spotlight with tears flowing down her face.
As the lights and music fade, the audience gives her a standing ovation.
My companion, who spent the summer training to be a bartender in a
strip joint that catered to a heterosexual male clientele, turns to me in
amazement: "This is so different than I thought it would be. She's got
respect!" The next morning an acquaintance calls to ask how I can sit
through anything so "male-identified."

| | | | |

In the final chapter I consider the political implications of a discourse on gay kinship, including the ongoing debate about whether
gay families represent assimilation to a heterosexual (or, as some
would argue, bourgeois) model. After exposing the inadequacy of a
rhetoric of model and paradigm, sameness and difference, pro-family
and anti-family for evaluating the significance of families we choose, I
suggest new ways to think about whether a family-centered discourse
bears the potential to change prejudicial perceptions of gay people as
it transforms the practice of kinship.

TWO | EXILES FROM KINSHIP

> Indeed, it is not so much identical conclusions that prove minds to be related as the contradictions that are common to them.
> —ALBERT CAMUS

Lesbian and gay San Francisco during the 1980s offered a fascinating opportunity to learn something about how ideologies arise and change as people lock in conflict, work toward reconciliation, reorganize relationships, establish or break ties, and agree to disagree. In an apartment on Valencia Street, a young lesbian reassured her gay friend that his parents would get over their initially negative reaction if he told them he was gay. On Polk Street, a 16-year-old searched for a place to spend the night because he had already come out to his parents and now he had nowhere to go. While two lovers were busy organizing an anniversary party that would bring blood relations together with their gay families, a woman on the other side of the city reported to work as usual because she feared losing her job if her employer should discover that she was mourning the passing of her partner, who had died the night before. For every lesbian considering parenthood, several friends worried about the changes children would introduce into peer relationships. For every eight or nine people who spoke with excitement about building families of friends, one or two rejected gay families as an oppressive accommodation to a heterosexual society.

Although not always codified or clear, the discourse on gay families that emerged during the 1980s challenged many cultural representations and common practices that have effectively denied lesbians and gay men access to kinship. In earlier decades gay people had also fought custody battles, brought partners home to meet their parents, filed suit against discriminatory insurance policies, and struggled to maintain ties with adoptive or blood relations. What set this new

21

discourse apart was its emphasis on the kinship character of the ties gay people had forged to close friends and lovers, its demand that those ties receive social and legal recognition, and its separation of parenting and family formation from heterosexual relations. For the first time, gay men and lesbians systematically laid claim to families of their own. Subsequent chapters explore the sociohistorical circumstances and material conditions that have shaped this discourse. Here I examine the ideological transition that saw "gay" and "family" change from mutually exclusive categories to terms used in combination to describe a particular type of kinship relation.

IS "STRAIGHT" TO "GAY" AS "FAMILY" IS TO "NO FAMILY"?

For years, and in an amazing variety of contexts, claiming a lesbian or gay identity has been portrayed as a rejection of "the family" and a departure from kinship. In media portrayals of AIDS, Simon Watney (1987:103) observes that "we are invited to imagine some absolute divide between the two domains of 'gay life' and 'the family,' as if gay men grew up, were educated, worked and lived our lives in total isolation from the rest of society." Two presuppositions lend a dubious credence to such imagery: the belief that gay men and lesbians do not have children or establish lasting relationships, and the belief that they invariably alienate adoptive and blood kin once their sexual identities become known. By presenting "the family" as a unitary object, these depictions also imply that everyone participates in identical sorts of kinship relations and subscribes to one universally agreed-upon definition of family.

Representations that exclude lesbians and gay men from "the family" invoke what Blanche Wiesen Cook (1977:48) has called "the assumption that gay people do not love and do not work," the reduction of lesbians and gay men to sexual identity, and sexual identity to sex alone. In the United States, sex apart from heterosexual marriage tends to introduce a wild card into social relations, signifying unbridled lust and the limits of individualism. If heterosexual intercourse can bring people into enduring association via the creation of kinship ties, lesbian and gay sexuality in these depictions isolates individuals from one another rather than weaving them into a social fabric. To assert that straight people "naturally" have access to family, while gay people are destined to move toward a future of solitude and loneliness, is not only to tie kinship closely to procreation, but also to treat gay men and lesbians as members of a nonprocreative species set apart from the rest of humanity (cf. Foucault 1978).

It is but a short step from positioning lesbians and gay men somewhere beyond "the family"—unencumbered by relations of kinship, responsibility, or affection—to portraying them as a menace to family and society. A person or group must first be outside and other in order to invade, endanger, and threaten. My own impression from fieldwork corroborates Frances FitzGerald's (1986) observation that many heterosexuals believe not only that gay people have gained considerable political power, but also that the absolute number of lesbians and gay men (rather than their visibility) has increased in recent years. Inflammatory rhetoric that plays on fears about the "spread" of gay identity and of AIDS finds a disturbing parallel in the imagery used by fascists to describe syphilis at mid-century, when "the healthy" confronted "the degenerate" while the fate of civilization hung in the balance (Hocquenghem 1978).

A long sociological tradition in the United States of studying "the family" under siege or in various states of dissolution lent credibility to charges that this institution required protection from "the homosexual threat." Proposition 6 (the Briggs initiative), which appeared on the ballot in California in 1978, was defeated only after a massive organizing campaign that mobilized lesbians and gay men in record numbers. The text of the initiative, which would have barred gay and lesbian teachers (along with heterosexual teachers who advocated homosexuality) from the public schools, was phrased as a defense of "the family" (in Hollibaugh 1979:55):

> One of the most fundamental interests of the State is the establishment and preservation of the family unit. Consistent with this interest is the State's duty to protect its impressionable youth from influences which are antithetical to this vital interest.

Other anti-gay legislative initiative campaigns adopted the slogans "save the family" and "save the children" as their rallying cries. In 1983 the *Moral Majority Report* referred obliquely to AIDS with the headline, "Homosexual Diseases Threaten American Families" (Godwin 1983). When the *Boston Herald* opposed a gay rights bill introduced into the Massachusetts legislature, it was with an eye to "the preservation of family values" (Allen 1987).

Discourse that opposes gay identity to family membership is not confined to the political arena. A gay doctor was advised during his residency to discourage other gay people from becoming his patients, lest his waiting room become filled with homosexuals. "It'll scare away the families," warned his supervisor (Lazere 1986). Discussions of dual-career families and the implications of a family wage system usually render invisible the financial obligations of gay people who support dependents or who pool material resources with lovers and others they define as kin. Just as women have been accused of taking jobs away from "men with families to support," some lesbians and gay men in the Bay Area recalled coworkers who had condemned them for competing against "people with families" for scarce employment. Or consider the choice of words by a guard at that "all-American" institution, Disneyland, commenting on a legal suit brought by two gay men who had been prohibited from dancing with one another at a dance floor on the grounds: "This is a family park. There is no room for alternative lifestyles here" (Mendenhall 1985).

Scholarly treatments are hardly exempt from this tendency to locate gay men and lesbians beyond the bounds of kinship. Even when researchers are sympathetic to gay concerns, they may equate kinship with genealogically calculated relations. Manuel Castells' and Karen Murphy's (1982) study of the "spatial organization of San Francisco's gay community," for instance, frames its analysis using "gay territory" and "family land" as mutually exclusive categories.

From New Right polemics to the rhetoric of high school hallways, "recruitment" joins "reproduction" in allusions to homosexuality. Alleging that gay men and lesbians must seduce young people in order to perpetuate (or expand) the gay population because they cannot have children of their own, heterosexist critics have conjured up visions of an end to society, the inevitable fate of a society that fails to "reproduce."[1] Of course, the contradictory inferences that sexual identity is "caught" rather than claimed, and that parents pass their sexual identities on to their children, are unsubstantiated. The power of this chain of associations lies in a play on words that blurs the multiple senses of the term "reproduction."

Reproduction's status as a mixed metaphor may detract from its analytic utility, but its very ambiguities make it ideally suited to argument and innuendo.[2] By shifting without signal between reproduction's meaning of physical procreation and its sense as the perpetuation of society as a whole, the characterization of lesbians and gay men as nonreproductive beings links their supposed attacks on "the family" to attacks on society in the broadest sense. Speaking of parents who had refused to accept her lesbian identity, a Jewish woman explained, "They feel like I'm finishing off Hitler's job." The plausibility of the contention that gay people pose a threat to "the family" (and, through the family, to ethnicity) depends upon a view of family grounded in heterosexual relations, combined with the conviction that gay men and lesbians are incapable of procreation, parenting, and establishing kinship ties.

Some lesbians and gay men in the Bay Area had embraced the popular equation of their sexual identities with the renunciation of access to kinship, particularly when first coming out. "My image of gay life was very lonely, very weird, no family," Rafael Ortiz recollected. "I assumed that my family was gone now—that's it." After Bob Korkowski began to call himself gay, he wrote a series of poems in which an orphan was the central character. Bob said the poetry expressed his fear of "having to give up my family because I was queer." When I spoke with Rona Bren after she had been home with the flu, she told me that whenever she was sick, she relived old fears. That day she had remembered her mother's grim prediction: "You'll be a lesbian and you'll be alone the rest of your life. Even a dog shouldn't be alone."

Looking backward and forward across the life cycle, people who equated their adoption of a lesbian or gay identity with a renunciation of family did so in the double-sided sense of fearing rejection by the families in which they had grown up, and not expecting to marry or have children as adults. Although few in numbers, there were still those who had considered "going straight" or getting married specifically in order to "have a family." Vic Kochifos thought he understood why:

> It's a whole lot easier being straight in the world than it is being gay. . . . You have built-in loved ones: wife, husband, kids, extended family. It just works easier. And when you want to do something that requires children, and you want to have a feeling of knowing that there's gonna be someone around who cares

about you when you're 85 years old, there are thoughts that go through your head, sure. There must be. There's a way of doing it gay, but it's a whole lot harder, and it's less secure.

Bernie Margolis had been sexually involved with men since he was in his teens, but for years had been married to a woman with whom he had several children. At age 67 he regretted having grown to adulthood before the current discussion of gay families, with its focus on redefining kinship and constructing new sorts of parenting arrangements.

I didn't want to give up the possibility of becoming a family person. Of having kids of my own to carry on whatever I built up. . . . My mother was always talking about she's looking forward to the day when she would bring her children under the canopy to get married. It never occurred to her that I wouldn't be married. It probably never occurred to me either.

The very categories "good family person" and "good family man" had seemed to Bernie intrinsically opposed to a gay identity. In his fifties at the time I interviewed him, Stephen Richter attributed never having become a father to "not having the relationship with the woman." Because he had envisioned parenting and procreation only in the context of a heterosexual relationship, regarding the two as completely bound up with one another, Stephen had never considered children an option.

Older gay men and lesbians were not the only ones whose adult lives had been shaped by ideologies that banish gay people from the domain of kinship. Explaining why he felt uncomfortable participating in "family occasions," a young man who had no particular interest in raising a child commented, "When families get together, what do they talk about? Who's getting married, who's having children. And who's not, okay? Well, look who's not." Very few of the lesbians and gay men I met believed that claiming a gay identity automatically requires leaving kinship behind. In some cases people described this equation as an outmoded view that contrasted sharply with revised notions of what constitutes a family.

Well-meaning defenders of lesbian and gay identity sometimes assert that gays are not inherently "anti-family," in ways that perpetuate the association of heterosexual identity with exclusive access to kinship. Charles Silverstein (1977), for instance, contends that lesbians and gay men may place more importance on maintaining family ties than heterosexuals do because gay people do not marry and raise children. Here the affirmation that gays and lesbians are capable of fostering enduring kinship ties ends up reinforcing the implication that they cannot establish "families of their own," presumably because the author regards kinship as unshakably rooted in heterosexual alliance and procreation. In contrast, discourse on gay families cuts across the politically loaded couplet of "pro-family" and "anti-family" that places gay men and lesbians in an inherently antagonistic relation to kinship solely on the basis of their nonprocreative sexualities. "Homosexuality is not what is breaking up the Black family," declared Barbara Smith (1987), a black lesbian writer, activist, and speaker at the 1987 Gay and Lesbian March on Washington. "Homophobia is. My Black gay brothers and my Black lesbian sisters are members of Black families, both the ones we were born into and the ones we create."

At the height of gay liberation, activists had attempted to develop alternatives to "the family," whereas by the 1980s many lesbians and gay men were struggling to legitimate gay families as a form of kinship. When Armistead Maupin spoke at a gathering on Castro Street to welcome home two gay men who had been held hostage in the Middle East, partners who had stood with arms around one another upon their release, he congratulated them not only for their safe return, but also as representatives of a new kind of family. Gay or chosen families might incorporate friends, lovers, or children, in any combination. Organized through ideologies of love, choice, and creation, gay families have been defined through a contrast with what many gay men and lesbians in the Bay Area called "straight," "biological," or "blood" family. If families we choose were the families lesbians and gay men created for themselves, straight family represented the families in which most had grown to adulthood.

What does it mean to say that these two categories of family have been defined through contrast? One thing it emphatically does *not* mean is that heterosexuals share a single coherent form of family (although some of the lesbians and gay men doing the defining believed this to be the case). I am not arguing here for the existence of some central, unified kinship system vis-à-vis which gay people have distinguished their own practice and understanding of family. In the

United States, race, class, gender, ethnicity, regional origin, and context all inform differences in household organization, as well as differences in notions of family and what it means to call someone kin.[3]

In any relational definition, the juxtaposition of two terms gives meaning to both.[4] Just as light would not be meaningful without some notion of darkness, so gay or chosen families cannot be understood apart from the families lesbians and gay men call "biological," "blood," or "straight." Like others in their society, most gay people in the Bay Area considered biology a matter of "natural fact." When they applied the terms "blood" and "biology" to kinship, however, they tended to depict families more consistently organized by procreation, more rigidly grounded in genealogy, and more uniform in their conceptualization than anthropologists know most families to be. For many lesbians and gay men, blood family represented not some naturally given unit that provided a base for all forms of kinship, but rather a procreative principle that organized only one possible *type* of kinship. In their descriptions they situated gay families at the opposite end of a spectrum of determination, subject to no constraints beyond a logic of "free" choice that ordered membership. To the extent that gay men and lesbians mapped "biology" and "choice" onto identities already opposed to one another (straight and gay, respectively), they polarized these two types of family along an axis of sexual identity.[5]

The chart below recapitulates the ideological transformation generated as lesbians and gay men began to inscribe themselves within the domain of kinship.

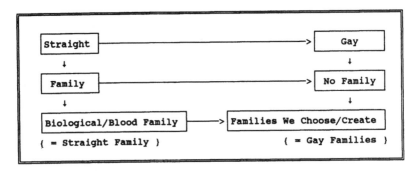

What this chart presents is not some static substitution set, but a historically motivated succession.[6] To move across or down the chart is to move through time. Following along from left to right, time appears as process, periodized with reference to the experience of coming out. In the first opposition, coming out defines the transition from a straight to a gay identity. For the person who maintains an exclusively biogenetic notion of kinship, coming out can mark the renunciation of kinship, the shift from "family" to "no family" portrayed in the second opposition. In the third line, individuals who accepted the possibility of gay families after coming out could experience themselves making a transition from the biological or blood families in which they had grown up to the establishment of their own chosen families.

Moving from top to bottom, the chart depicts the historical time that inaugurated contemporary discourse on gay kinship. "Straight" changes from a category with an exclusive claim on kinship to an identity allied with a specific kind of family symbolized by biology or blood. Lesbians and gay men, originally relegated to the status of people without family, later lay claim to a distinctive type of family characterized as families we choose or create. While dominant cultural representations have asserted that straight is to gay as family is to no family (lines 1 and 2), at a certain point in history gay people began to contend that straight is to gay as blood family is to chosen families (lines 1 and 3).

What provided the impetus for this ideological shift? Transformations in the relation of lesbians and gay men to kinship are inseparable from sociohistorical developments: changes in the context for disclosing a lesbian or gay identity to others, attempts to build urban gay "community," cultural inferences about relationships between "same-gender" partners, and the lesbian baby boom associated with alternative (artificial) insemination. Later chapters will explore the significance of each of these developments for the emergence of a discourse on gay families. If Pierre Bourdieu (1977) is correct, and kinship is something people use to act as well as to think, then its transformations should have unfolded not only on the "big screen" of history, but also on the more modest stage of day-to-day life, where individuals have actively engaged novel ideological distinctions and contested representations that would exclude them from kinship.

DECK THE HALLS

Holidays, family reunions, and other celebrations culturally categorized as family occasions represent everyday arenas in which people in the Bay Area elaborated discourse on kinship. To attend was to catch a glimpse of history in the making that brought ideological oppositions to life. During the season when Hanukkah, Christmas, New Year's, and Winter Solstice converge, opportunities abounded to observe the way double-sided contrasts like the one between straight and gay families take shape. Meanings and transformations appeared far less abstract as people applied and reinterpreted them in the course of concrete activities and discussion. Their emotional power suddenly became obvious and inescapable, clearly central to ideological relations that have been approached far too cognitively in the past.

In San Francisco, gay community organizations set up special telephone hotlines during the holidays to serve as resources for lesbians and gay men battling feelings of loneliness or depression. At this time of year similar feelings were common in the population at large, given the tiring, labor-intensive character of holiday preparations and the pressure of cultural prescriptions to gather with relatives in a state of undisturbed happiness and harmony. Yet many gay people considered the "holiday blues" a more acute problem for themselves than for heterosexuals because disclosure of a lesbian or gay identity so often disrupted relations with straight relatives. The large number of gay immigrants to the Bay Area ensured that decisions about where to spend the holidays would make spatial declarations about family ties and family loyalties.

As Terri Burnett, who had grown up on the East Coast, saw it:

> Most people move out here so that nobody will find out. And then they're out all over the place here, but they would *never* go back home. That's one of the reasons why we see so many people depressed at Thanksgiving and Christmas. Because they can't be themselves. They have to go back to households in which they pretend to be all these other people. It's living a schizophrenic existence. And so many people here in San Francisco live a total lie. And this is supposed to be the liberation haven.

For those whose sexual identity was known to biological or adoptive relatives, conflicts over gaining acknowledgment and legitimacy for relationships with lovers and others they considered gay family was never so evident as on holidays. When Chris Davidson planned to return to her childhood home in the Bay Area for the holidays, she worried about being caught in the "same old pull" between spending time with her parents and time with her close lesbian friends. That year she had written her parents a letter in advance asking that they confront their "possessiveness" and recognize the importance of these other relationships in her life. Another woman regarded her parents' decision to allow her lover in their house to celebrate New Year's Day together with "the family" as a sign of growing acceptance. Some people had decided to celebrate holidays with their chosen families, occasionally inviting relatives by blood or adoption to join the festivities. One man voiced pride in "creating our environment, our *intimate* environment. I have an extended [gay] family. I have a lot of friends who we have shared Christmas and Thanksgiving with. Birthdays. Just as you would any other extended family."

In the field I spent Christmas eve with my lover and six other lesbians. All of us were known to the two women who had invited us to their home, but neither my lover nor I had met any of the others previously. Earlier in the year, my partner and I had begun to develop a multistranded family relationship with our hosts, Marta Rosales and Toni Williams.

That night the eight of us had gathered together to combine support with celebration at a potentially difficult time of year, goals that each woman seemed to weigh differently in accordance with her total kinship situation. Everyone was conscious of how the holiday was supposed to proceed: "extended family" would assemble in one place, momentarily putting aside the cares of day-to-day life in favor of eating, reminiscing, enjoying, exchanging gifts, and catching up on family gossip. We were also acutely aware that such gatherings help define family membership, just as purposeful exclusion on holidays can alienate family ties.

Different backgrounds and political orientations did not prevent us from raising similar questions about such occasions. If your parents or siblings reject you because you are a lesbian, does spending the holidays with gay family offer an equal, second-best, or better alternative? What do you miss about celebrating with straight family? Is there anything *to* miss? Would it be a good idea to bring a lover to visit biological or adoptive relatives for the holidays? If she decides to come along, is it worthwhile to try to explain why your "friend" is so important to you? If you have a partner and are lucky enough to have both straight families accept you, whose relatives should you spend the holiday with? How accepting would they have to be to invite them to spend a holiday at your home?

This was the first Christmas Marta and Toni had spent "alone together," a phrase each kept repeating as though the wonder of it would never sink in. Other years they had made the trip to southern California, where both maintained ties to blood kin. The two of them planned to spend a quiet Christmas morning in their own apartment, but wanted to share their mixed sense of excitement and loss with a group of their closest friends the evening before. As though to provide a counterpoint to the emotions Toni and Marta were experiencing, one of their guests left before dinner to catch a plane to New York City where her parents lived. Although she intended to stay there only overnight, due to work obligations, she wanted to be with her family for the holiday.

Her departure triggered a passionate debate about why she would want to do such a thing. "Her mother's crazy—totally nuts," one of the women who knew her reported. "She's never gonna have a good time there. I don't see why she's going." Another complained that parents expect their gay kids to do all the traveling, continuing to treat them as single whether or not they have a partner. "They might ask a lover to come along, if they're accepting," someone commented. "Yeah, but you still have to go there—it's hard to get them to come here." One after another, women spoke about how they had always "gone home" with high expectations (for love, understanding, a "good connection" with relatives), only to have their hopes shattered within the first few hours. Rhetorically, someone asked why we keep trying, why we keep going back. Another woman entered the conversation to question the tendency to continue calling the place where a person grows up "home." "As far as I'm concerned," she said, "*this* is home." A sense of shared experience filled the room with brief silence, drawing this group of relative strangers close.

With dinner in the oven, Toni and Marta joined us to add their stories about the frustrations of Christmas past when they had shuttled back and forth between relatives in the southern part of the state. Most of Marta's relatives knew they were lovers and often invited them to visit, but Toni's parents had forbidden Marta to enter their house after discovering the lesbian nature of their relationship years ago. Marta was feeling proud of her lover for "standing up" to her parents for once: "She says, 'I'm not going home, 'cause Marta and I want to spend Christmas together. And the day you guys can have her home for Christmas, I'll be home.' " "Still," Toni said to the group at large, "don't you miss being with them? Your parents and all?" "Sure," responded a woman who was out to her biological family and found spending time with them relatively unproblematic. "Like hell," came the quick rejoinder from a woman sitting in the corner near the fireplace. "Forget it, let's eat," said another. "Then let's open the presents!" As the group drifted toward the room at the back of the apartment where a long table had been set up, the conversation turned to the scents of cinnamon and roast turkey wafting in from the kitchen. Moments later we were sitting down, our glasses raised in a toast. "To being here together." And the refrain: "Together."

When a celebration brought chosen relatives into contact with biological or adoptive kin, family occasions sometimes became a bridge to greater integration of straight and gay families. Those who felt rejected for their sexual identities, however, could experience holidays as events that forced them to ally with one or the other of these opposed categories. The feeling was widespread that, in Diane Kunin's words, "[gay] people have to make some really excruciating choices that other people are not faced with." Because contexts such as holidays evoked the more inclusive level of the opposition *between* two types of family, they seldom elicited the positive sense of choice and creativity associated with gay families. Instead, individuals too often found themselves faced with the unwelcome dilemma of making an either/or decision when they would have preferred to choose both.

KINSHIP AND PROCREATION

Since the time of Lewis Henry Morgan, most scholarly studies of familial relations have enthroned human procreation as kinship's ultimate referent. According to received anthropological wisdom, relations of blood (consanguinity) and marriage (affinity) could be plotted for any culture on a universal genealogical grid. Generations of field-workers set about the task of developing kinship charts for a multitude of "egos," connecting their subjects outward to a network of social others who represented the products (offspring) and agents (genitor/ genetrix) of physical procreation. In general, researchers occupied themselves with investigations of differences in the ways cultures arranged and divided up the grid, treating blood ties as a material base underlying an array of crosscultural variations in kinship organization.

More recently, however, anthropologists have begun to reconsider the status of kinship as an analytic concept and a topic for inquiry. What would happen if observers ceased privileging genealogy as a sacrosanct or objective construct, approaching biogenetic ties instead as a characteristically Western way of ordering and granting significance to social relations? After a lengthy exercise in this kind of bracketing, David Schneider (1972, 1984) concluded that significant doubt exists as to whether non-Western cultures recognize kinship as a unified construct or domain. Too often unreflective recourse to the biogenetic symbolism used to prioritize relationships in Anglo-European societies subordinates an understanding of how particular cultures construct social ties to the project of crosscultural comparison. But suppose for a moment that blood is not intrinsically thicker than water. Denaturalizing the genealogical grid would require that procreation no longer be postulated as kinship's base, ground, or centerpiece.

Within Western societies, anthropologists are not the only ones who have implicitly or explicitly subjected the genealogical grid to new scrutiny. By reworking familiar symbolic materials in the context of nonprocreative relationships, lesbians and gay men in the United States have formulated a critique of kinship that contests assumptions about the bearing of biology, genetics, and heterosexual intercourse on the meaning of family in their own culture. Unlike Schneider, they have not set out to deconstruct kinship as a privileged domain, or taken issue with cultural representations that portray biology as a material "fact" exclusive of social significance. What gay kinship ideologies challenge is not the concept of procreation that informs kinship in the United States, but the belief that procreation *alone* constitutes kinship, and that "nonbiological" ties must be patterned after a biological model (like adoption) or forfeit any claim to kinship status.

In the United States the notion of biology as an indelible, precultural substratum is so ingrained that people often find it difficult to take an anthropological step backward in order to examine biology as symbol rather than substance. For many in this society, biology is a defining feature of kinship: they believe that blood ties make certain people kin, regardless of whether those individuals display the love and enduring solidarity expected to characterize familial relations. Physical procreation, in turn, produces biological links. Collectively, biogenetic attributes are supposed to demarcate kinship as a cultural domain, offering a yardstick for determining who counts as a "real" relative. Like their heterosexual counterparts, lesbians and gay men tended to naturalize biology in this manner.

Not all cultures grant biology this significance for describing and evaluating relationships. To read biology as symbol is to approach it as a cultural construct and linguistic category, rather than a self-evident matter of "natural fact." At issue here is the cultural valuation given to ties traced through procreation, and the meaning that biological connection confers upon a relationship in a given cultural context. In this sense biology is no less a symbol than choice or creation. Neither is inherently more "real" or valid than the other, culturally speaking.

In the United States, Schneider (1968) argues, "sexual intercourse" is the symbol that brings together relations of marriage and blood, supplying the distinctive features in terms of which kinship relations are defined and differentiated. A relationship mediated by procreation binds a mother to a daughter, a brother to a sister, and so on, in the categories of genitor or genetrix, offspring, or members of a sibling set. Immediately apparent to a gay man or lesbian is that what passes here for sex per se is actually the *hetero*sexual union of two differently gendered persons. While all sexual activity among heterosexuals certainly does not lead to the birth of children, the isolation of heterosexual intercourse as a core symbol orients kinship studies toward a dominantly procreative reading of sexualities. For a society like the United States, Sylvia Yanagisako's and Jane Collier's (1987) call to analyze gender and kinship as mutually implicated constructs must be extended to embrace sexual identity.

The very notion of gay families asserts that people who claim nonprocreative sexual identities and pursue nonprocreative relationships can lay claim to family ties of their own without necessary recourse to marriage, childbearing, or childrearing.[7] By defining these chosen families in opposition to the biological ties believed to constitute a straight family, lesbians and gay men began to renegotiate the meaning and practice of kinship from within the very societies that had nurtured the concept. Theirs has not been a proposal to number gay families among variations in "American kinship," but a more comprehensive attack on the privilege accorded to a biogenetically grounded mode of determining what relationships will *count* as kinship.

It is important to note that some gay men and lesbians in the Bay

Area agreed with the view that blood ties represent the only authentic, legitimate form of kinship. Often those who disputed the validity of chosen families were people whose notions of kinship were bound up with their own sense of racial or ethnic identity. "You've got one family, one biological family," insisted Paul Jaramillo, a Mexican-American man who did not consider his lover or friends to be kin.

> They're very good friends and I love them, but I would not call them family. Family to me is blood. . . . I feel that Western Caucasian culture, that it's much more broken down, and that they can deal with their good friends and neighbors as family. But it's not that way, at least in my background.

Because most individuals who expressed this view were well aware of the juxtaposition of blood family with families we choose, they tended to address gay kinship ideologies directly. As Lourdes Alcantara explained,

> I know a lot of lesbians think that you choose your own family. I don't think so. Because, as a Latin woman, the bonds that I got with my family are irreplaceable. They can't be replaced. They cannot. So my family is my family, my friends are my friends. My friends can be *more important* than my family, but that doesn't mean they are my family. . . . 'Cause no matter what, they are just friends—they don't have your blood. They don't have your same connection. They didn't go through what you did. For example, I starved with my family a lot of times. They *know* what it is like. If I talk to my friends, they will understand me, but they will never feel the same.

What Lourdes so movingly described was a sense of enduring solidarity arising from shared experience and symbolized by blood connection. Others followed a similar line of reasoning (minus the biological signifier) when they contended that a shared history testifies to enduring solidarity, which can provide the basis for creating familial relationships of a chosen, or nonbiological, sort.

In an essay on disclosing a lesbian or gay identity to relatives, Betty Berzon (1979:89) maintains that "from early on, being gay is associated with going against the family." Many people in the Bay Area viewed families as the principal mediator of race and ethnicity, drawing on folk theories of cultural transmission in which parents hand down "traditions" and identity (as well as genes) to their children.[8] If having a family was part of what it meant to be Chicana or Cherokee or Japanese-American, then claiming a lesbian or gay identity could easily be interpreted as losing or betraying that cultural heritage, so long as individuals conceived kinship in biogenetic terms (cf. Clunis and Green 1988:105; Tremble et al. 1989). Kenny Nash had originally worried that coming out as a gay man would separate him from other African-Americans.

> Because I related to the black community a lot as far as politics, and . . . unfortunately, sexual politics in some parts of the black movement are not very good. Just as there is this continuing controversy about feminism and black women in the women's movement. It's a carryover, I think, into [ideas] about gay people, gay men and lesbians. Because there are some people who think of [being gay] as the antithesis of building strong family institutions, and that's what we need: role models for people, bringing up children, and all that stuff.

Condemnations of homosexuality might picture race or ethnicity and gay identity as antagonists in response to a history of racist attributions of "weak" family ties to certain groups (e.g., blacks), or in response to anything that appeared to menace the legacy of "strong" kinship bonds sometimes attributed to other categories of people (e.g., Latinos, Jews). In either case, depicting lesbian or gay identity as a threat to ethnic or racial identity depended upon the cultural positioning of gay people outside familial relations. The degree to which individuals construct racial identity *through* their notions of family remains a relatively unexplored aspect of why some heterosexuals of color reject gay or lesbian identity as a sign of assimilation, a "white thing."

Not all lesbians and gays of color or whites with a developed ethnic identity took issue with the concept of chosen families. Many African-Americans, for instance, felt that black communities had never held to a strictly biogenetic interpretation of kinship. "Blacks have never said to a child, 'Unless you have a mother, father, sister, brother, you don't have a family' " (Height 1989:137).[9] Discourse and ideology are far from being uniformly determined by identities, experiences, or historical developments. Divergent perceptions of the relation between family ties and race or ethnicity are indicative of a situation of ideological flux, in which procreative and nonprocreative interpretations vie with one another for the privilege of defining kinship. As the United States entered the final decade of the twentieth century, lesbians and gay men from a broad spectrum of racial and ethnic identities had come to embrace the legitimacy of gay families.

FROM BIOLOGY TO CHOICE

Upon first learning the categories that framed gay kinship ideologies, heterosexuals sometimes mentioned adoption as a kind of limiting case that appeared to occupy the borderland between biology and choice. In the United States, adopted children are chosen, in a sense, although biological offspring can be planned or selected as well, given the widespread availability of birth control. Yet adoption in this society "is only understandable as a way of creating the social fiction that an actual link of kinship exists. Without biological kinship as a model, adoption would be meaningless" (Schneider 1984:55). Adoption does not render the attribution of biological descent culturally irrelevant (witness the many adopted children who, later in life, decide to search for their "real" parents). But adoptive relations—unlike gay families—pose no fundamental challenge to either procreative interpretations of kinship or the culturally standardized image of a family assembled around a core of parent(s) plus children.

Mapping biological family and families we choose onto contrasting sexual identities (straight and gay, respectively) places these two types of family in a relation of opposition, but *within* that relation, determinism implicitly differentiates biology from choice and blood from creation. Informed by contrasting notions of free will and the fixedness often attributed to biology in this culture, the opposition between straight and gay families echoes old dichotomies such as nature versus nurture and real versus ideal. In families we choose, the agency conveyed by "we" emphasizes each person's part in constructing gay families, just as the absence of agency in the term "biological family" reinforces the sense of blood as an immutable fact over which individuals exert little control. Likewise, the collective subject of families we choose invokes a collective identity—who are "we" if not gay men and lesbians? In order to identify the "we" associated with the speaker's "I," a listener must first recognize the correspondence between the opposition of blood to choice and the relation of straight to gay.

Significantly, families we choose have not built directly upon beliefs that gay or lesbian identity can be chosen. Among lesbians and gay men themselves, opinions differ as to whether individuals select or inherit their sexual identities. In the aftermath of the gay movement, the trend has been to move away from the obsession of earlier decades with the etiological question of what "causes" homosexuality. After noting that no one subjects heterosexuality to similar scrutiny, many people dropped the question. Some lesbian-feminists presented lesbianism as a political choice that made a statement about sharing their best with other women and refusing to participate in patriarchal relations. In everyday conversations, however, the majority of both men and women portrayed their sexual identities as either inborn or a predisposition developed very early in life. Whether or not to act on feelings already present then became the only matter left to individual discretion. "The choice for me wasn't being with men or being a lesbian," Richie Kaplan explained. "The choice was being asexual or being with women."

In contrast, parents who disapproved of homosexuality could convey a critical attitude by treating gay identity as something elective, especially since people in the United States customarily hold individuals responsible for any negative consequences attendant upon a "free choice." One man described with dismay his father's reaction upon learning of his sexual identity: "I said, 'I'm gay.' And he said, 'Oh. Well, I guess you made your choice.' " According to another, "My father kept saying, 'Well, you're gonna have to live by your choices that you make. It's your responsibility.' What's there to be responsible [about]? I was who I *am*." When Andy Wentworth disclosed his gay identity to his sister,

> She asked me, how could I *choose* to do this and to ignore the health risks . . . implying that this was a conscious, 'Oh, I'd like to go to the movies today' type of choice. And I told her, I said, 'Nobody in their right mind would go through this *hell* of being gay just to satisfy a whim.' And I explained to her what it was like growing up. Knowing this other side of yourself that you can't tell anybody about, and if anybody in your family knows they will be upset and mortified.

Another man insisted he would never forget the period after coming out when he realized that he felt good about himself, and that he was

not on his way to becoming "the kind of person that they're portraying gay people to be." What kind of person is that, I asked. "Well,
you know, wicked, evil people who *decide* that they're going to be
evil."

Rather than claiming an elective gay identity as its antecedent, the
category "families we choose" incorporates the meaningful *difference*
that is the product of choice and biology as two relationally defined
terms. If many gay men and lesbians interpreted blood ties as a type
of social connectedness organized through procreation, they tended
to associate choice and creativity with a total absence of guidelines for
ordering relationships within gay families. Although heterosexuals in
the Bay Area also had the sense of creating something when they
established families of their own, that creativity was often firmly
linked to childbearing and childrearing, the "pro-" in procreation. In
the absence of a procreative referent, individual discretion regulated
who would be counted as kin. For those who had constructed them,
gay families could evoke utopian visions of self-determination in the
absence of social constraint. Of course, the contextualization of choice
and creativity within the symbolic relation that opposes them to blood
and biology itself lends a high degree of structure to the notion of gay
families. The elaboration of gay kinship ideologies in contrast to the
biogenetic symbolism of straight family illustrates the type of structured relation Roman Jakobson (1962) has called "the unexpected
arising from expectedness, both of them unthinkable without the
opposite."

Certainly lesbians and gay men, with their range of backgrounds
and experiences, did not always mean the same thing or advance
identical cultural critiques when they spoke of blood and chosen
families. Ideological contrasts utilized and recognized by all need not
have the same significance for all.[10] Neither can an examination of
ideology alone explain why choice should have been highlighted as an
organizing principle of gay families. Only history, material conditions, and context can account for the specific content of gay kinship
ideologies, their emergence at a particular point in time, and the
variety of ways people have implemented those ideologies in their
daily lives. In themselves, gay families comprise only a segment of the
historical transformation sequence that mapped the contrast between
straight and gay first onto "family/no family," and then onto "biological family/families we choose." Gone are the days when embracing a

lesbian or gay identity seemed to require a renunciation of kinship. The symbolic groundwork for gay families, laid during a period when coming out to relatives witnessed a kind of institutionalization, has made it possible to claim a sexual identity that is not linked to procreation, face the possibility of rejection by blood or adoptive relations, yet still conceive of establishing a family of one's own.

| # COMING OUT TO "BLOOD" RELATIVES

He launched his anathemas surely and quietly. He did not allow himself to be carried away by emotion nor did he try to carry away his public: North Americans do not like to hear displays of passions they do not share.
—JOSÉ MARTÍ DESCRIBING WENDELL PHILLIPS

Nervously, the young man explained that he was about to leave for a visit with his family and had decided to tell his parents he was gay. "I need to ask for your prayers and support," he said, looking around the congregation before resuming his seat. The setting for his remarks was a service at the Metropolitan Community Church (MCC) in San Francisco's Castro district. By the 1980s the Bay Area was hosting a variety of religious organizations directed primarily to lesbians and gay men, including MCC, the synagogue Sha'ar Zahav, and a local chapter of the Catholic group Dignity, as well as gay Buddhist, Pagan, and New Age spiritual gatherings. After the first speaker finished, a man across the aisle rose to give thanks for the love and acceptance shown by his parents when he had come out to them two years earlier. "I want to rejoice with you that they can be here with us today," he added, turning to the middle-aged woman and man at his side. A chorus of "Amens" filled the room.

Aside from AIDS, no other topic encountered during my fieldwork generated an emotional response comparable to coming out to blood (or adoptive) relatives. When discussion turned to the subject of straight family, it was not unusual for interviews to be interrupted by tears, rage, or a lengthy silence. "Are you out to your parents?" and "Are you out to your family?" were questions that almost inevitably arose in the process of getting to know another lesbian or gay person.

Claiming a gay identity in the presence of parents or siblings frequently involved an anxiety-filled struggle to bring speech about sexual identity (if not sex) into the cultural domain of "the family." Coming out to a biological relative put to the test the unconditional love and enduring solidarity commonly understood in the United States to characterize blood ties. Stories that told of coming out to a particular relative marked "acceptance" with explicit affirmations of love and kinship. Conversely, "rejection" could entail severance of family ties previously held to be inalienable. In this sense, coming out to biological kin produces a discourse destined to reveal the "truth" not merely of the self, but of a person's kinship relations. At the end of what many lesbians and gay men imaged as a long journey to self-discovery, when I tell you "who I (really) am," I find out who you (really) are to me.

DISCLOSING SEXUAL IDENTITY

When police raided New York City's Stonewall Inn in June 1969, the bar became the symbolic birthplace of a gay movement after patrons used physical force to "fight back."[1] Only in the wake of gay liberation did deliberately disclosing one's sexual identity to biological or adoptive relatives become *structured* as a possibility and a decision for self-identified lesbians and gay men in the United States. According to the historical periodization that separates "old gay" from "new gay," homosexuals in the days before Stonewall did not dare reveal their sexual identities to others for fear of criminal prosecution, incarceration, and loss of employment.

The meaning of coming out has shifted steadily over the years, gradually assuming its current dual sense of claiming a lesbian or gay identity for oneself and communicating that identity to others.[2] Originally those others were likely to have been gay acquaintances, not straight relatives. As one man in his sixties put it, what was termed "coming out" in the 1950s would be called "strictly closetry" today. At that time coming out signified a person's entrance into the "gay world," which could involve frequenting a gay bar or revealing one's sexual identity to a few close friends who were also "in the life."[3] In New Orleans during the 1950s, for example, Doris Lunden's lover's father "took us to a place called The Starlet Lounge once, which was a gay bar that I later came out into" (Bulkin 1980:26). As late as 1976, Barbara Ponse (1976:331) observed, "The family's awareness of the gay self usually occurs through observation of cues rather than by direct disclosure on the part of the lesbian."

Most people perceived little to gain and everything to lose by claiming a gay identity in a heterosexual context. Terri Burnett, who witnessed the purge of lesbians from the armed forces during the McCarthy era, remembered:[4]

> In the fifties, people were not just sort of walking around jumping up and down. We were being prosecuted. Being thrown in jail. Having your record stamped 'Known Homosexual.' . . . I mean, there was a lot of reason why people were not just thrilled to come out. If you were thought to be a person who was a lesbian or a gay person, you could be fired from your job, and there would be no question that you would never find another one. Unless, of course, you wanted to be a cook in a fry store or something.

A more immediate reason to conceal sexual identity from family members in particular was the threat of institutionalization. According to Harold Sanders, in his sixties at the time of the interview:

> If you think it was rough in the 1950s . . . the 1920s, you just didn't talk about anything about [being] gay. On this side of the Atlantic. You could in Paris. But if you did here, you ended up in an insane asylum. Your family would sign you in for your own good. They could get you into there. That's something that cannot be now. You couldn't do anything about it. . . .
>
> People did get away with things. But, again, there was a lot of treachery. People would have a change of heart—then they would tell all. . . . You didn't know: your best friend might decide for your own good that you needed some help. . . . What you'd be doing if you came out, you'd be declaring yourself fit for the insane asylum.
>
> The background in this, in the remote distance, was Hitler. We did know something about what Hitler was doing. Because he started, you know, on a health drive, to purge Germany of the unhealthy people. Began with handicapped people, and he gradually got around to gay people. I can remember a sickening feeling when I heard that people were being taken to the SS. . . . It was terrifying. And there was nobody you could talk to about it, because of this treachery thing.

Although some older gays welcomed the heightened visibility and the encouragement to come out (in the sense of "going public") associated with the gay movement, others experienced these changes as stressful or even threatening after years of remaining closeted to avoid the more obvious manifestations of oppression (Dunker 1987; Hall 1978; Kehoe 1989).[5] In a sense, too, the contrast between "old gay" and "new gay" minimizes the extent to which oppressive conditions still prevail. Laws that criminalize homosexual acts remain on the books in approximately half of the states, and while these laws are selectively enforced, the 1986 *Bowers v. Hardwick* decision by the U. S. Supreme Court underscores their viability. That decision upheld a lower court ruling that convicted a Georgia man for consensual homosexual acts performed in the privacy of the defendant's bedroom. The Supreme Court held that in this case a state law criminalizing sodomy overrode any right to privacy on the part of the defendant.

Meanwhile, some gay men and lesbians linked a documented rise in anti-gay violence during the 1980s to the introduction of domestic partner legislation and the popular association of AIDS with gay people. In 1989, physical and verbal attacks against lesbians and gay men reported to Community United Against Violence (CUAV), a San Francisco-based community organization, increased by approximately 100 incidents over the previous year (Olmstead-Rose 1990); 1987 had witnessed a corresponding increase in the degree of violence associated with such incidents. From 1984 to 1985 reports of assaults rose 89 percent, and by 1985, the number of clients served by CUAV had increased 62 percent over the preceding year. Although the actual number of such attacks is difficult to assess because many cases go unreported, this issue has received recognition as a growing national problem: in 1986 the House Judiciary Committee's Subcommittee on Criminal Justice held its first hearings on antigay violence; 1990 saw the passage of the Hate Crimes Statistics Act, which provided for data collection on crimes that target individuals because of their sexual orientation (Bull 1988; McKnight 1986; Roe 1985; White 1986).

Many gays in their teens continue to worry about being "locked up" in juvenile detention or psychiatric facilities, a fear not without foundation for those who come out before attaining legal majority. To further complicate the issue, some individuals did elect to reveal their sexual identities to relatives well before the advent of the gay movement. Taken together, these observations qualify the notions of unilinear progress, liberation, and steadily increasing openness implicit in the old gay/new gay antithesis.[6]

Fully 73 percent of respondents to a 1985 *Los Angeles Times* poll viewed homosexual sex as "wrong" (down only slightly from 76 percent in 1973). As Kenneth Burke (1941) has pointed out, the moral judgment, "It is wrong," is actually a variant of the command, "Don't do it!" Almost 90 percent claimed they would be "upset" if their children grew up to be lesbian or gay (Balzar 1985).[7] In view of such persistent disapproval, why has disclosure of a gay identity to blood and adoptive relatives gone from being largely out of the question before the 1960s to very much *the* question for lesbians and gay men at present?[8]

During the early 1970s, activists valorized coming out to heterosexuals as a strategy designed to gain political power and promote self-respect. Sometimes called the "Harvey Milk philosophy," after the first openly gay person to be elected city supervisor in San Francisco, coming out to others provided an important but limited tactic for countering heterosexism and building a gay movement.[9] (Visibility obviously has not caused racial and gender oppression to vanish in the United States; on the contrary, visibility has supplied the symbolic scaffolding for practices that perpetuate racism and sexism.) Although few interview participants spoke of coming out to biological or adoptive relatives as a political expedient, remarks such as, "I really *should* come out to them," and, "If I don't come out, how will things ever get better?" testified to the continuing influence of this ethical imperative. Equally important in elevating coming out to its current status as an ever-present possibility was the eclipse of jail and asylum as the principal sites for institutional intervention into the lives of gay people. Another contributing factor was the sense—fostered by public debate and media portrayals of the social movements and counterculture of the 1960s–70s—that moral standards applied to sexual behavior had entered a period of flux.[10] This folk theory of change made measures such as the passage of gay rights ordinances and the removal of homosexuality from the American Psychiatric Association's list of mental illnesses susceptible to interpretation as signs of the dissolution of any social consensus that would stigmatize homosexuality (Bayer 1981). Reactions to disclosure of a gay identity could then be expected to vary from person to person and relative to relative. Even if you were a gay man or lesbian who read the *Los Angeles Times* in 1985, the extension of discourse on homosexuality into new arenas and the formulation of that discourse in modes that emphasized dissent might have encouraged you to treat the outcome of disclosure as a gamble and a risk.

Many lesbians and gay men in the Bay Area were willing to bet on the one-in-four chance that they would be accepted. Because a more public discourse had opened up new forums for contesting heterosexism, many also believed that, by presenting alternative constructions of what it means to be gay, they might persuade relatives to move from a position of rejection to acceptance. During this period, coming out began to be defined situationally and imaged by degrees, appearing as a continuous process of disclosing sexual identity. Rather than occupying some absolute position "in" or "out" of the closet, an individual could be out to some people but not others, or out at school while closeted at work (K. Jay 1978; Newton 1979). It was in this context that lesbians and gay men in the 1980s called upon one another to explain why they had or had not come out to blood and adoptive relatives.

By this point in time coming out to others required a direct statement that acknowledged gay identity: a variation on the order of "Aunt Rochelle, I'm a lesbian," or, "Yeah, Dad, I like women." This statement might be euphemistically phrased, but nonverbal hints intended to convey the same information—bringing gay friends to your parents' house, hoping your brother would notice the double bed in the studio apartment you shared with a lover—did not qualify. Annie Sorenson was a white woman in her thirties who maintained that she had not come out to her parents:

> I'm friends with Walter and his lover Paul, and my mother knows them, and she did ask me once. She just asked me once, you know. "You shouldn't be hanging around with people like that. People will think you're queer, too." And I said, "Well . . ." Then she said, "You aren't, are you?" And I said, "Well, what do you think?" (laughs) And she never answered.

Those who had come out often reported seeking verbal confirmation to prevent relatives from "explaining away" their identity or practicing "denial" by refusing to admit something already known. Otherwise they might have found themselves in Bob Korkowski's situation as a teenager.

> I kept this [nude photographs of men and erotic stories] all in a little box that I was very careful about hiding. One day I got

home from school and my mother called me into the room, and there was this box. So, in a way I was really relieved; I remember crying. . . . [Years later] when I finally told her, I think I was 18. She reacted as if she had no idea that it was true.

For a statement of sexual identity to be classified as coming out, a gay or lesbian subject must be its author. Discovery did not count, though individuals sometimes wished relatives would figure it out to avoid the anxiety entailed in the act of disclosure. A commonly narrated experience involved coming out to someone with fearful anticipation, only to be told that the listener "knew it all along." However, a man who believed his mother "knew" would not say he had come out to her unless he had explicitly acknowledged his gay identity in her presence. The importance placed on taking the initiative in disclosure was also evident in an ethic that discouraged one gay person from coming out for another, at least without permission.[11]

Coming out is structured in terms of a conceptual opposition between hiding (or lying) and honesty, an opposition elaborated through spatial imagery that situates the self within a social landscape. Implicit in most of the coming-out stories I heard was a division between an authentic inner self and a surface presentation directed toward an outer world. Other people, including relatives to whom an individual had come out, were assumed to replicate this organization of body and mind: "[My parents] couldn't have been more supportive. On the outside. I don't know what they were feeling inside." Passing for heterosexual offers a paradigmatic instance of this split between interior knowledge and the superficial appearance perceived by others, what Barbara Macdonald (1983:4) has described as "the experience of having the reality of your own life—your joy or your grief—unconfirmed by the reality around you." Coming out bridges this gap by ripping off the mask (in the Enlightenment sense) to reveal hidden truths.[12] The visceral, unpredictable character of this experience can be seen in the words of a woman who described coming out to her husband and children after years of marriage as "throwing out my insides": "I'd try to say, 'This is really me. This is all of me. And will anybody be left liking me?' "

This image of a core self, while privileged as a source of knowledge and crystallized as an essential being somewhere deep inside the body, is subject to division into conflicting or collaborating parts (Foucault

1973; M. Z. Rosaldo 1983).[13] Implicit in the notions of self-esteem and self-acceptance is a reflexivity that makes the self the simultaneous subject and object of an act or thought process (M. Rosenberg 1979). Once a person had claimed a lesbian identity, she was said to have come out to herself, just as she might come out to relatives, friends, or employers. Subjective identification as a lesbian was presumed to have occurred through an internal dialogue in which she "came to terms" or "made peace" with herself. Self-acceptance could facilitate unification of the inner self, but without disclosure to others this self would remain trapped in the private, interior space known as the closet.

The stress of monitoring every word and action entails bringing unstated assumptions about gender and heterosexual relations into constant focus in order to orchestrate passing for heterosexual (Newton 1979).[14] Kevin Jones, a young black man who worked as a printer at the time of his interview, emphasized, "I can't picture myself being 55 years old and still being under that. It just eats at you. Not enough to make you do it [come out], but it's always hanging over you. Always." Another man remembered his years in the military as a time when "I felt like I wasn't one whole person, trying to please two separate groups" (those who knew and those who did not).

In coming out, a person acts to create a sense of wholeness by establishing congruence between interior experience and external presentation, moving the inner into the outer, bringing the hidden to light, and transforming a private into a social reality. The closet symbolizes isolation, the individual without society, a stranger even to self. Its imagery is consistent with the atomistic conceptions of a society in which individuated actors must struggle to communicate and gain legitimacy for private truths. In the process of coming out, a person hopes to leave behind the extreme self-consciousness alluded to by the man who joked that he came out to his parents because he was tired of remembering to edit pictures of his lover out of his slide shows.

Most of the people interviewed believed that deception has a negative effect on social relationships, undermining the trust considered a prerequisite for "close" connections. They experienced unspoken truths as things that come between people, barriers that introject "distance" into relationships. One ideal for negotiating relationships was to be "up front" about things by bringing secrets "out into the open." If, however, a person anticipated a bad reaction to disclosure, he or she often refrained from coming out to that particular relative. Some feared material consequences like institutionalization, violence, kidnapping, child custody suits, or loss of financial support. "My father is the type of individual that will hop on the first plane out here with a shotgun," said one man, who grappled with what has been termed "legitimate paranoia" whenever he considered telling his father. I met several people who had experienced physical retaliation when they came out to parents while still living at home. One man reported beatings at the hands of his brother for being an "embarrassment to the family." Others felt protective of relatives, worrying that someone in poor health might have a heart attack or "nervous breakdown" at the news. The objective of concealment was often to shield the self or the relative from pain and violence in the belief that it takes two intact persons to make a relationship, however limited that relationship might be.

The ambivalence and uncertainty frequently associated with a decision to come out arise because disclosure entails far more than the cultural conviction that a person can liberate or explicate the self through confession (cf. Foucault 1978). What became clear from talking to hundreds of lesbians and gay men is that they expected coming out to yield insights into relationships. Would kin ties prove genuine? Could familial love endure? What kind of power dynamics might be uncovered in the process?

Not everyone was willing to put kinship relations to this test. As one woman described it, the decision to conceal her sexual identity from her parents was motivated by "not wanting to know the truth, sort of like maybe if I don't tell them, then I won't be disillusioned." Others, however, expressed regret over never having come out to relatives who had died. In retrospect they believed disclosure would have "strengthened" bonds with the departed, or at the very least yielded an accurate assessment of where the two parties stood vis-à-vis one another.

Those who had resolved to risk the loss of a relationship by coming out offered similar rationales, contending that little would be left to forfeit if a relative refused to acknowledge one's "real" self. Philip Korte considered his skepticism about the permanence of blood ties a personal departure from dominant cultural understandings, but many gay men and lesbians in San Francisco shared his attitude:

If you can't be honest with somebody, then what kind of relationship are you really salvaging? What are you giving up if they react badly and they're gone? What have you really lost? Now families, I know, are different—for some people, not for me.

CATEGORICAL UNDERSTANDINGS (OR, IT'S ALL RELATIVE)

Before making the decision to come out to a particular relative, people typically isolated criteria they hoped would give them some indication of what sort of response to expect. Aside from offering a rationale for making the decision, such evaluations mitigated the anxiety of wondering whether they would encounter rejection that could lead to termination of a valued relationship. A therapist who served a primarily lesbian and gay clientele described this interplay between uncertainty and prediction: "Most people do not know what's going to happen to them if they do [come out]. They only think they do." When people attempted to predict the outcome of disclosure, their judgments generally reflected cultural assumptions about gender, power, and specific categories of kinship relations.

Although "closeness" was perhaps the most commonly invoked criterion upon which to base the decision, individuals used it to argue both for and against coming out. A close relationship might be cited as grounds to anticipate acceptance, or as a factor that magnified the potential for dire consequences with so much "at stake" in a relationship. Some came out first to the relatives they considered closest, some last, others not at all—but whatever the decision, close relatives represented key figures in the decision-making process.

"Closeness" and "distance" are terms that incorporate geographic, socioemotional, and genealogical dimensions (Schneider 1968). An intimate relationship with someone regarded as "immediate" family, a sibling with whom a person feels he or she has nothing in common, and a "distant" cousin who doubles as a friend, illustrate three possible combinations of these different senses of closeness. When people contemplated coming out to a relative they generally took both emotions and genealogy into account, performing a kind of cultural calculus to determine the best course of action.

Because most people considered disclosure a prerequisite for intimacy and a way of bridging emotional distance, coming out became one context in which they could create or destroy closeness even as they invoked it to explain the course of events. Bob Tremble and his associates (1989:257) have argued that "when the love of children and the value of family ties are strong, nothing, including homosexuality, will permanently split the family." But no method exists to measure the strength of social ties; indeed, "strength" is a quality inferred largely with hindsight, as relatives affirm or deny kinship in the aftermath of disclosure.

Parents typically occupied the emotional epicenter of coming out.[15] In response to the generic question, "Are you out to your family?" people usually discussed parents first. In unsolicited comments, they also employed "family" as an equivalent for mother and/or father. The dyadic quality of this emotional focus is suggested by the name of the national support group PFLAG, which stands for "Parents and Friends of Lesbians and Gay Men," rather than "parents and relatives" or "relatives and friends." When an individual raised by a grandmother or anyone other than a biological parent considered coming out to straight family, the person who had assumed responsibility for childrearing usually became a focus of concern, suggesting that it was the relation of social parent to child rather than genealogical relationship per se that assumed significance in this context.

Both gay men and lesbians tended to depict mothers in general (though not necessarily *their* mothers) as more likely to "understand" than fathers. Gender came into play here in the form of cultural notions which assigned feelings to women and reason to men, and which credited women with responsibility for the maintenance of "family life." Expectations of motherly understanding and fatherly disapproval were also evident in the surprise some people registered when they described a father who had been "supportive" or a mother who became upset at news of a child's gay identity.

Philip Korte drew on notions of gender and closeness to develop an interpretive rationale for having ignored popular wisdom by coming out to his father first. The motivational strategy he outlined did not rest on qualities attributed to fathers in any essentialist sense, but rather on a view of himself as a positioned subject who, as a male, could initiate a "man-to-man" talk. "I had always been closer to my mother. Logically, she would of been the one to go to. But for some reason, this felt like man's business (laughs). It was just so serious. Dad was the one you went to with the real serious stuff." Regardless of whether particular parents' reactions fulfilled or countered expectations, when both biological parents were alive and known, their adult children tended to interpret the parents' responses in ways that carried and perpetuated gendered distinctions.

Siblings in general were presumed to be more accepting than either fathers or mothers. If brothers and sisters had not yet reached adolescence, people usually postponed coming out to them. But individuals who had deliberately avoided coming out to parents while still living at home had often disclosed sexual identity to a sister or brother in the same household. Although siblings might feel obliged to profess more understanding than parents, this did not necessarily make them less heterosexist. One woman said she learned this the hard way when her sister spent months staring at her and crying after learning of her lesbian identity. Another man still felt the hurt of coming out to a brother who said everything was "okay" but asked him not to visit his children.

When discussing coming out, people often contrasted parents and siblings as representatives of different generations. Their assumption seemed to be that younger relatives would prove more "progressive" and older adults less knowledgeable or sophisticated.[16] In addition to subscribing to a social evolutionism in which the passage of time becomes synonymous with progress and historical advance, these characterizations referred back to the impression that attitudes toward sexuality are changing because discourse on homosexuality now permeates a range of public forums. "I wasn't born into that world and neither was my family," remarked a lesbian in her forties.

Younger gays who had come out to their parents sometimes hesitated to disclose their sexual identity to grandparents, despite the feelings of affection and closeness that often characterized those relationships. Although often framed in terms of age, this reluctance to come out to grandparents had less to do with number of years lived and more to do with making generations into symbols of particular historical periods, since some individuals' grandparents were members of the same age cohort as others' parents. As Werner Sollors (1986) has pointed out, generation is fundamentally a metaphorical rather than an explanatory concept. Cultural differences also affected this relative evaluation of generations. One Native American man named his elders as the persons most likely to be sympathetic because the latter sometimes had knowledge of "traditional" *berdache* institutions that incorporated elements of gender-blending and same-sex sexuality.[17]

As with other categories of kin, expectations about the way a grandparent would react to disclosure did not dictate a course of action. Lourdes Alcantara, an immigrant from Latin America, decided to come out to her senile grandmother, reasoning that even if her *abuelita* told other family members, no one would believe her. One man had a grandfather who, as a Christian evangelist, seemed an unlikely candidate for acceptance. He told the grandfather anyway, not because he anticipated understanding, but because he decided that without honesty the relationship would not mean much: "The alternative is, you just sit around waiting for people to die so you can be yourself." In another case a grandmother contradicted expectations by demonstrating more acceptance than a man's parents. With much laughter, the man described a scene in which his grandmother attempting to calm his mother by exclaiming, "Felicia, get over it!"

Those who had children usually planned to tell them "someday," but varying philosophies prescribed the optimal time for disclosure. Some believed it better to wait until children were "old enough to understand"; some recommended telling them at a very young age to affirm the "natural," everyday reality of being gay; others advised coming out to children well after puberty to avoid influencing their sexual identities. No standardized expectation of acceptance or rejection by children seemed to exist, although gay parents described deep fears of repudiation by their children, not unlike the anxiety they felt when they contemplated coming out to their own parents. Those who had already come out to their children cited a range of reactions, from a nine-year-old son who thanked his mother for being honest to a daughter in high school who refused to discuss the subject. One woman told the story of her teenage son, who joked that now they could go to the malls together and "check out" women. On the hopeful side, a therapist with a large gay clientele knew of no child who had completely cut off relations with a lesbian or gay parent. Monika Kehoe (1989), however, reported mothers whose adult children had rejected them after learning of their lesbian identity.

Other believed predictors of acceptance or rejection included education, travel, religion, and occupation. Relatives in show business, a father who had worked with interior decorators, an aunt who had attended college, and a father who, as a musician, was often "on the road," were all offered as examples of family members likely to be understanding. Relatives with these attributes—like relatives assigned to the kinship categories discussed above—who did not conform to expectations were portrayed as anomalies: "Despite being well-educated" or "despite having been around," so-and-so had a "bad reaction." In the process these indicators became self-confirming, exceptions that appeared to prove the rule in a manner consistent with cultural notions of gender relations and family ties.

FAMILY—WHICH FAMILY?

Before considering how the historical developments that made coming out to relatives a major preoccupation simultaneously shaped gay kinship ideologies, I want to take a closer look at what lesbians and gay men in the Bay Area had in mind when they talked about their straight families. The standardized "American family" is a mythological creature, but also—like its reified subsidiaries ("the" black family, "the" gay family)—an ideologically potent category. Feminist scholars have critiqued deployment of "the family" as a normative construct by analyzing how households vary in composition, organization, and representation. [18] In practice, notions of family bring sexual identity into relationship with other types of identifications, including race and class.

Not surprisingly, people of color, whites with strong ethnic identities, and people who considered themselves working class were the ones who most frequently drew connections between sexual identity, race, class, ethnicity, and kinship. Their theories about the ways these identities have an impact on coming out fell into three general areas: (1) emphasis on family as a solidary unit rather than a collection of members, (2) contrasts between "close" families attributed to people of color and the working class, versus white and managerial-class families described as "fragmented," and (3) distinctions between the unconditional love believed to characterize families from the speaker's own background and the contingent love assigned to families in dominant social categories. In most cases the people who voiced these theories identified themselves with a background defined by opposition to attributes and practices they labeled "white," "Anglo," "American," or "middle class."

Individuals whose ethnic identifications ranged from German-American to Cuban-American spontaneously linked these identities to efforts by relatives to keep news of lesbian or gay kin "within the family" (cf. Hidalgo and Christensen 1976–1977). The theory of a family with sharply defined boundaries that separate it from the "outside world," a family willing to accept gay relatives as long as knowledge of their sexual identity remained within those boundaries, surfaced when I spoke with Marvin Morrissey, an African-American man employed as a technician:

> I find among a lot of Latinos, they says their parents don't mind who they sleep with, but they're just worried to death that the neighbors will find out. See? Puerto Rican kids who park their cars out, haul way 'cross town and walk to a gay bar, so that their uncles and aunts won't see the car parked near one and jump to the assumption that they're in there. That's closer to the black experience than the fact that they've got this big hang-up about who you sleep with and what you do in bed.

Individuals sometimes cast this dynamic in class terms, tracing such concerns to pressures to "make something of yourself." In these descriptions relatives were reported to believe that coming out to persons outside "the family" would sabotage hopes for upward mobility.

Clearly no common "tradition" can account for similar theories advanced by people claiming such varied cultural identities. Rather, the individuals who made this type of argument articulated their own identities by drawing a symbolic contrast between Latino (or working-class, or Chinese-American) families portrayed as solidary units presumed to transmit class and ethnicity, and white (or "middle-class" or "American") families depicted as piecemeal assemblies of roles and relationships. Whites from a managerial/entrepreneurial class background also described embarrassment directed toward them by relatives, but unless they had a strong ethnic identification, they tended to attribute their relatives' reaction to the personal characteristics of the individuals involved instead of race or class.

Some working-class people and people of color claimed they came from "tighter," "warmer," or "larger" families, citing this "difference" to bolster contradictory arguments that coming out was either easier or more difficult for individuals from their particular background. According to Simon Suh, a Korean-American man:

> This is really generalizing, but everyone says Asian families tend to be very close-knit. Everyone knows what everyone else is doing. . . . So of course everyone watches what they do. I don't know whether I believe that, but I do somehow think that Asian people do have a harder time coming out, both to themselves and to others.

Individuals sometimes credited historical circumstances for bringing about such solidarity, as when Jews asserted that the Diaspora and Holocaust had made Jewish families especially determined to stay close.

A man who said he came from an "extended" family sighed, "That's a lot of people to tell!" Balancing this view was the alternate belief that coming out is simpler in an "extended" family because a larger group offers more relatives from which to choose, increasing the probability of finding what one person called an "Auntie Mame" who will understand. At issue here, of course, is not some absolute number of genealogical relations, but how individuals draw the boundaries of family and the numbers they consider close relatives or active members.

The third folk theory contended that families among people of color are characterized by unconditional love, in contrast to white families that make love contingent upon behavior.[19] Frank Maldonado, a Chicano from a working-class background with a civil service job, formulated this belief in terms of personal experience: "I've seen more white gay men give up their families, or be thrown out of their families, than I have Latinos. I think my mother's attitude is real typical: 'I don't want to see it, I don't want to talk about it. You're my son, you're my daughter. I love you.' "

A functionalist argument parallel to Carol Stack's (1974) account of kinship in black communities frequently accompanied variations on this theory presented by African-American gays.

> Some of the blacks have had rough times with their grandmothers or their religious aunts or whatever. Or if they came from small towns. But when push comes to shove, they're all in the same boat, and get off in a hostile environment. I have never heard of

the levels of brutality among my black gay friends that I've heard among whites when they came out. I never! . . . Being kicked out at 13. . . . Or being shipped off to an insane asylum. Well, I remember one black man saying: if somebody's gonna do that, it's gonna be the general authorities that will do it.

And in the words of Tyrone Douglas, an African-American in his twenties from a working-class background:

In the Black community, I think there's things you can be that are worse than gay. I don't think it's regarded as the most horrible thing, overall. . . . Always there was bigger things to be worried about. Like having a job, or like drugs. . . . People always say this: as long as you're doing something with your life, or making something out of yourself, that's fine. Then your business is your business. It's fine; who cares. What's worse is, is to be just another bum on the street. That's really the mentality. Or be a thief, or a drug dealer, or something like that, that's really wrong. To be that, and be straight—it's really better if you're gay and halfway together.

But other lesbians and gays of color refuted this theory, citing experiences of being "kicked out" by relatives, or an initial apprehension that rejection *could* have followed disclosure. Yoli Torres, who was Puerto Rican, told a story of seeking refuge with her grandmother when she was 15, after her mother told her to "leave until you get your senses together." Terri Burnett, a black woman who had married and borne children before coming out, believed the fear of similar consequences had shaped her earlier life choices. She described herself at age 25:

Oh, I knew I was a lesbian. In fact, everybody in the world—apparently, after I spoke with my mother and my sister—everybody knew that I was a lesbian. They just forgot to tell me. What they forgot to tell me was that they weren't going to reject me because of it. Instead of me having to go through seven years of psychiatrists, and being threatened with electric shock therapy, and drinking myself into oblivion, I could have been a lot happier. It could have been a lot different. . . . had I known that my mother would still have loved me, and my sister and brother and everybody else would not have thrown me out, I would have been very different.

Being thrown out and losing familial love were also common fears and experiences among white gay people who had grown up poor or working-class. The lack of any necessary connection between class or ethnicity and unconditional love was equally evident in comments like those of Arturo Pelayo, a Nicaraguan-American who saw his mother's acceptance as a unique aspect of her character, though he could have explained her reaction as the consequence of race, economic necessity, or "tradition":

> My mom was exceptional. She's a single parent, right, and she came to a country where she didn't know the language and she brought up all these kids and everything, and all that she ever worried about was that we became "yuppies"—you know, the upwardly mobile—but she never said anything to me about my being gay. It was always make sure you did your rosary, make sure you did this and that.

Do working-class people, people of color, and whites with strong ethnic identifications have any more or less reason to fear being disowned and rejected when they come out to relatives? The relative incidence of acceptance and rejection in various groups, including differences in what is perceived as acceptance or rejection, is a matter for further research. Such differences may indeed exist, though functionalist explanations are inadequate to account for them.

Here my concern is to understand kinship as it is implicated in the meaningful constitution of gay and lesbian selves. What many people in the Bay Area presented were interpretive accounts that *credited* characteristics like unconditional love to race, class, or ethnicity (mediated through families). While it is significant that they drew connections between coming out and other aspects of their identities, they also linked these categories in contradictory ways—believing, for example, that the "close-knit" families attributed to certain categories of people on the basis of racial identity both facilitate and hinder disclosure. The emergence of coming out to others as a historical practice and possibility ensured that lesbian- and gay-identified people of all colors and classes would occupy a common cultural ground, insofar as the revelations entailed in disclosure called into question the enduring solidarity customarily associated with blood relations.

CONDITIONAL LOVE

"Have I got a story for you!" became a phrase I grew accustomed to hearing during interviews. And occasionally, someone who had heard I was doing this study would approach me to say, "I have a friend who's got a *great* story." As I discovered after a few months in the field, "great" had little to do with happy endings. "Good" coming-out stories could be extremely positive when describing the process of "self-discovery" that led to adoption of a lesbian or gay identity. When the same "good" stories turned to the subject of coming out to kin, however, they tended to revolve around traumatic incidents. The protagonist was institutionalized, threatened with electroshock therapy, kicked out of the house, reduced to living on the street, denied an inheritance, written out of a will, battered, damned as a sinner, barred from contact with younger relatives, shunned by family members, or insulted in ways that encouraged him or her to leave. Shaping these narratives were cultural notions of what makes a good story (drama, coherence, climax) coupled with assumptions about what makes an individual coming-out experience prototypical.

It was very common for people to compare their own coming-out experiences with stories they had heard, stories that presented being rejected as an average, unexceptional occurrence. Rejection covered a gamut of reactions, from disapproval of homosexuality to love made contingent upon renunciation of gay identity. To the extent that an individual understood love to define kinship, he or she experienced the loss of one as the loss of the other. Being disowned also encompassed the withdrawal of love, but made the termination of kinship much more explicit. Graphic symbols such as denying a person entrance to a relative's home, sitting *shiva* (performing a mourning ritual as though the person had died), and turning pictures of the lesbian or gay relative to face the wall, informed the protagonist that she or he would no longer be treated as part of the family.

Sometimes relatives in these stories accompanied their actions with verbal statements that disavowed kinship (e.g., "You're not my son"). Context inevitably conditioned responses to my questions about kinship. If I asked, "What is your relationship with your father like?"

people recognized the category "father" and usually proceeded to talk about the person they believed to be their genitor, stepfather, or male adoptive parent. But in the context of narratives in which individuals framed their own categories, some of the same people said they had "no father," "no mother," or "no family." The possibility of rejection was so much in the foreground for people considering coming out that acceptance often became a residual category embracing everything from grudging toleration to confirmations of love and a positive pride in gay identity.

Among interview participants, the symbolic weight accorded rejection was disproportionate to the numbers who actually reported being disowned or rejected after coming out. Out of 80 interviewees, 27 (roughly one-third) recounted stories in which incidents they labeled as rejection constituted a focal point.[20] Yet the vast majority reported *fears* of being disowned and losing family, even when rejection did not ensue. "I don't know why I thought they were gonna reject me," said one man, "but I was scared to death." Individuals who regarded their straight family as accepting often wondered why I wanted to talk with them, since they believed they had "boring" stories, or even "no story" at all. The same people tended to view their coming-out experiences as exceptional. Asides incorporated into their narratives included, "I was lucky. My brother was very supportive," and, "Well, they didn't disown me."

Many individuals who had come out to themselves while still adolescents were careful to establish financial independence and separate residence before coming out to parents, "just in case" (cf. Fricke 1981). Brian Rogers, a photographer, had decided to tell his parents only after living away from New England for two years, "because even if they do react negatively, I don't need them. I'm sufficient on my own. I guess I was afraid that they were gonna cut me off or something. So I wasn't gonna tell them until I was absolutely sure that I could take care of myself." A man in his forties recalled explaining to his mother why he hadn't come out to her sooner:

She said, "How early did you know?" And I said, "Oh, late grade school. High school for sure." She said, "Why didn't you tell me?" I said, "Well, we're talking about the 1960s, and even now people get disowned, thrown out of the house, committed, given electroshock therapy." She said, "Well, I wouldn't have reacted like that." And I said, "You go tell a fifteen-year-old kid [that]. People usually don't come out to their parents at that time. . . ." I said, "I'm not taking the chance of losing everything."

Several who had come out to relatives as teenagers were subjected to physical and verbal abuse, in addition to the almost standardized penalties mentioned by the last narrator.

In most people's eyes, the emotional threat of "losing love" matched and even surpassed the potential for devastating material consequences.

> I didn't come out and tell my parents, certainly, because I was still living at home, and I still needed them. . . . As long as your parents didn't know that part of you, they wouldn't reject you . . . I had been working since I was 15½ at my godparents' deli. So I didn't feel like I was dependent on them economically. It was more of a mental pull, to stay and to be loved.

If these accounts often equated "family" with "love," they presented "disown" and "hate" as their contraries: "Leaving the home, I was finally free. . . . So I thought, well, I'd better tell them before they hear it. And I didn't need them as a support system. So I figured if my worst fear came true, they disowned me or hated me . . ."

Although being disowned is specific by definition to the parent-child relationship and can only be initiated by the parent, rejection travels both ways. Some gay men and lesbians had rejected relatives when they encountered abuse, when they grew tired of being asked to change their sexual identities, or when they no longer felt loved for who they "really" were. "I guess coming out to [my mother] really meant losing her," said Jeanne Riley.

> She was not willing for me to be out. . . . To her, it was just this social embarrassment, and she doesn't want to deal with it. She does not want to know for nothing about it, and if I'm willing to be quiet and pretend I'm not who I am, then she's willing to accept me. . . . I haven't spoken to her in about three years.

In another instance, after an adolescent's parents discovered a letter from her lover, they left a typewritten note on the door telling her she was "mentally disturbed." The woman packed her things and left.

Most individuals gave relatives more time to adjust. But if rejection became protracted, with relatives continuing to "deny" a person's identity or withhold love, gay people sometimes "gave up on"—by giving up—their straight families.

Because the experience of a split self accompanies passing for straight in this culture, people in the process of coming out asked not only, "Will they still love me?" but also *which* self the other claimed to love. Would parents and siblings, aunts and uncles, cousins and grandparents still care for someone once they knew that person's "true," essential, interior reality? The injunction that love should characterize kin ties can make coming out sufficient to undermine basic presumptions about the character of kinship and the permanence of blood relations. Mark Arnold, for example, phoned his mother one evening to let her know he was planning to return "home" for a visit:

> The next day I got a call from my father saying, "You're homosexual. You're diseased, and I don't want you back in the house. . . ." I hung up, and I was really hurt. Kind of numb. I was numb for a long time. We weren't close as a family, but even though you're not close, it's such a connection that it was really affecting me. And I was surprised how much it affected me.

In an era when nearly every lesbian and gay man considers coming out, the unconditional love recognized as both symbol and substance of kin ties has come under intense scrutiny by almost every gay-identified person. This dynamic operated to some degree even for those who did not anticipate being disowned: "I don't have the type of family that I really felt would reject me. They're not that type of people. I couldn't even conceive of it. *Although you know you're risking that.*" [my emphasis] In coming-out stories, kin terminology very often underscored avowals of continuing love: "I love you—I'm your mother," or, "You're still my sister." But even as such statements reaffirmed kinship, they implicitly ceased to take for granted the old adage that family is forever.

DISCURSIVE LOCATIONS

Foucault (1978) has described the historical production of discourse about sexuality within the specialized domains of medicine, psychiatry, the courts, and the confessional. While coming out to blood relatives retains the form of disclosure, it also represents a re-situation of such discourse, bringing speech about sexuality into the realm of family. Stories told by those who had claimed a lesbian or gay identity after the 1960s often displayed this shift. In these narratives, relatives send the protagonist to a religious adviser or psychiatrist. After ascertaining the individual's satisfaction with her or his sexual identity, the professional sends the person home and asks parents or siblings to come in for counseling. This humorous twist displaces the appropriate context for discourse on sexual identity from the confessional and therapist's office back to the family that originally attempted to exorcise speech about sexuality. Implicit in this turnabout is a condemnation of institutionalized gay oppression mediated by medicine, religion, and kinship.[21]

Memories of talk about sex within the domain of straight family centered on snickers and hushed conversations shared with siblings or cousins, together with the proverbial lecture about "the birds and the bees"—a presentation that skirted the issue of nonprocreative sex (heterosexual or homosexual). Most people maintained that their parents had rarely discussed sex, and many cited this silence as a factor that made them hesitate to come out.

Significantly, the discourse on sexuality that coming out initiates within families has much more to do with kinship than with sex per se. To speak of sexuality without speaking of sex is possible in part because at this historical moment, homosexuality is organized in terms of identity rather than acts (Foucault 1978; McIntosh 1981; Weeks 1977). The heart of coming out involves laying claim to a label understood to reflect back on total personhood. Occasionally a listener might ask, "Just what is it that you *do*?" but a person coming out generally would not volunteer information about sexual activities.[22]

> I can recall when I came out to my parents, just under two years ago, being real concerned because I felt [they would think] coming out . . . was all about sex, and it would make them uncomfortable. And I wanted to come out, but also say that we don't have to discuss the specifics of how I have sex. Because that's not part of coming out.

A lesbian or gay identity could be realized as much in the course of the telling as the feeling or the doing. "As long as it was just inside of me it wasn't real," one woman explained. According to Tyrone Douglas, "Saying it and coming out to my family was really, in a way, saying it for myself." Disclosure turns out to be not simply a matter of producing truths about the self through confession in the Foucauldian sense, but of establishing that self's lesbian or gay identity as a *social* "fact."

What is spoken belongs to the social arena, demanding attention, discussion, and response. Control is implicit in the very characterization of coming out to others as a decision, as though subjects had the power to determine what others know and the conditions of their knowing. With a story about his former lover, Jorge Quintana commented on the assumption that individuals control their environment.

> Guillermo's father died, and then he couldn't accept the fact that his father didn't know that he was gay. And his mother confessed, "Look. You lived with Jorge for fourteen years. We knew you were gay." Which was another blow to him. You see, he thought he has kept it a secret.

The moral of this anecdote is that remaining closeted offers only an illusory sort of control, one likely to prove inadequate for preventing others from filtering a person's identity through their notions of homosexuality as deviance.[23]

Gay men and lesbians are well attuned to stereotypes of homosexuality, having faced many in the process of claiming their own identities. Coming out, as one woman characterized it, is like "saying to somebody that you are the scum of the earth in their eyes." But by endeavoring to frame and control this discourse, people challenged portrayals of homosexuality as sin, sickness, or a "phase." The goal was to attain a measure of self-determination through self-definition.

By the 1980s, satisfaction with a lesbian or gay identity and lack of any desire to change had become idealized prerequisites for coming out to others. "I have to feel okay about myself when I tell them," explained one man, "so they have no choice but to feel okay about me." Individuals applied the criterion of self-acceptance to distinguish between confessional and other modes of "truth telling." Harold Sanders offered an example of how not to come out to one's children:

> One time, when I left New York, I had had what was then called a "moral conversion." I told them about how wicked I had been. That's not much of a coming-out talk. I don't think I ever did

have the talk that they should have had: tell them who I am at a time when I feel good about it.

Most people preferred to disclose their identities face-to-face, feeling that this method conveyed honesty, courage, and forthrightness.[24] By preventing relatives from avoiding the topic, it also opened an important forum for renegotiating interpretations of gay identity. Contrast the situation in which one person comes out for another: gossip, rumor, and the innuendo that proliferates around matters of secrecy ensue, making it all the more difficult to confront heterosexist assumptions. Rather than positioning themselves as helpless victims of rejection, most people attempted to move relatives along the path to acceptance by contesting negative impressions of what it means to be gay or lesbian.

The idea of going up to someone and bluntly stating, "Hi, I'm gay," without further elaboration elicits laughter from a lesbian or gay audience. "The problem wasn't in telling [my mother]," said Simon Suh. "It was just thinking of the right way, the right way to say it. You don't want to just blurt it out." In view of the widespread condemnation of homosexuality in the United States, coming out "right" translated into reassuring relatives that sexual identity is no one's "fault"; refuting impressions about living a tragic or lonely life; and putting gay identity in the context of friendship, "community," and chosen families.

TAKING IDENTITY, TALKING KINSHIP

I have seen some very articulate people at a loss for words when they encountered what they regarded as typical heterosexual objections to coming out: "Why do you have to talk about it? It's your own business. Why flaunt it?" The symbolic mediation of kinship by sexuality in the United States is one factor that explains why lesbians and gay men cannot confine their identities to the bedroom, why they resist the accusation that coming out flaunts sexuality by violating culturally constituted boundaries between public and private domains. For while sex may not be an everyday topic of discussion in settings like workplaces, schools, churches, and synagogues, references to kinship are omnipresent.

"How's your husband?" "What did you do over the weekend (and

who did you do it with)?" "Are you married?" "Where are you
spending the holidays?" All are common enough questions that arise
in small talk between individuals who may not be very well ac-
quainted. Every time a lesbian or gay man faces a question like this,
she or he must decide how forthcoming to be about sexual identity.
Implicitly, these questions call upon gay people to disclose ties to
partners, friends, children, and others they may consider kin, which
in turn entails contesting biogenetic and legalistic notions of what
kinship is all about. Because sexuality brings people into relationship,
its implications can never be contained within the parameters of identity or some ideally privatized sphere.

Ties to lovers and other gay kin magnify the difficulty and stress of
remaining closeted. "You know what's horrible?" remarked a friend I
made in the course of fieldwork.

> Valentine's Day. Anything like that. Because it's like, "Look
> what I got for Valentine's Day. So-and-so sent me a card." And
> here Toni would buy me flowers, and she bought me a gift. . . .
> They'd say, "Marta, you're always in a good mood." I felt like
> saying, "That's because I'm in love." And I never could say that
> to [my coworkers]. I never could.

Even if they know a person is gay, relatives and acquaintances can
fabricate a very loud silence by avoiding the type of "personal" questions they routinely direct to everyone else.

Although some gay people in the Bay Area felt that coming out to
acquaintances was not worth the trouble or risk, almost all viewed
disclosure to straight family as desirable. Even individuals who had
minimized contact with relatives over the years shared this desire to
come out, at least to parents and siblings. Yet the pursuit of honesty
can apply to any valued relationship, whether classified as kin or non-
kin. Why should they have perceived blood relations as a separate
case?

Because it represents the past, straight family—like old friends
made long before coming out—presents the best and most critical
audience for disclosure. A self-defined lesbian preparing to come out
to others has been busy redocumenting her identity with respect to a
new set of relevances, generally recasting the autobiographical "I" as
the story of an essential and timeless lesbian self (Frye 1980; T.S.
Weinberg 1978). Relatives who "knew her when" wield the power to

confirm or contest autobiographical reconstructions that portray her lesbian identity as something there all along but only recently discovered.

Perhaps most important, coming out to blood family offers a unique opportunity to clarify kinship relations. If the loss of love, and with it kinship, represented the worst fear for most people contemplating disclosure, their highest hopes often focused on securing recognition for their chosen families. In retrospect the moment of disclosure might appear as a first step toward integrating straight family with the gay families that are families we choose. In this sense, coming out could have as much to do with growing up and establishing family ties as what people "do in bed."

For those who had not previously married, coming out sometimes doubled as a declaration of independence and adulthood.[25] To the extent that individuals equated disclosure with "being themselves," coming out shared with growing up the sense of an individual set against society, developing a unique personality in the course of learning to "take charge" of his or her own life. "What do you mean when you say being out allows you to be yourself?" I asked a lesbian in a club one night. She replied, "If I feel like doing a certain something, I'm gonna do it." This link between claiming an autonomously defined sexual identity and seeking recognition as an adult was perhaps epitomized by the story another woman told of coming out to her mother in a bar after buying drinks to celebrate the narrator's twenty-first birthday.

Acknowledgment of a child's gay identity can be accompanied by the consciousness that a transition into full adult status is at issue. "In my family," said Sean O'Brien,

> there's actually a whole story, which I usually tell people. My sister Sharon, who is the oldest sister, married when she was about 18. She married a black man. And among Irish Catholics in the Bronx, you don't marry black men. When I came out to my parents, my mother's response was to immediately see the connection between me coming out as a gay man and my sister marrying William. And she said, "When Sharon married William, I realized that I can't control you kids. That each one of you is gonna find your love wherever you can, and I can't control that. And I accept that. And I still love you."

To the extent that people in the United States image themselves as autonomous agents, redefinition of self becomes something that must be accomplished in relative isolation before being communicated to others. Stories recounted by people who had come out in their late teens or early twenties often described moving out of their parents' homes about the time they adopted a lesbian or gay identity. Differences in class background affected the new setting: some came out in the military, some in college dormitories, and others on the street. But whether this move involved traveling three blocks, switching counties, or traversing the continent, many portrayed it as an attempt to gain a measure of independence by establishing distance from blood relations. Barry Isaacs, for example, believed that relocating facilitated "coming to terms" with his identity: "I wasn't in my home town. I could do or be anything I wanted." Others, however, experienced leaving home as more obstacle than aid to coming out. According to one woman's interpretation of "Latino culture," leaving home could mean leaving family behind, a move she considered likely to disrupt a Latina's sense of self.

In some cases both parents and their adult children seemed to view disclosure as a bid to renegotiate power in a relationship. Richie Kaplan remarked that her mother "would say on the one hand, 'Who is influencing you to be a lesbian?' and on the other hand, I had an iron will that wouldn't bend. Which could be interpreted as meaning I wouldn't listen to her, 'cause she didn't want me to be a dyke." Blaming other relatives for "causing" someone's gay identification— most commonly by attributing it to improper childrearing—represents another form of withholding full adult status by asserting control over an individual's self-definition. A father contends his son "turned out" gay because his wife worked; a sister recalls that her brother never got along with their father; a mother blames herself because her second husband beat the children; a brother believes his sister would never have been a lesbian if their parents had not divorced. Each of these arguments betrays the influence of now discredited psychological theories that proferred universal—if contradictory—etiologies for homosexuality. But relatives also cling to these explanations because the power to do implies the power to undo.

Charlyne Harris, a black woman in her twenties, said her mother considered homosexuality a sin.

I talked to her about a week ago. She said, "Are you still involved in that stuff?" (laughs) And I said, I said, "What stuff?" She said, "You know, are you still messing around with women?" And I said, "Yeah." And she just said, "Oh. I just wanted to know." . . . She checks in hoping that one day I'll say, "No." 'Cause it's hard for her, too.

Contending that someone is not "really" gay implicitly challenges that person's maturity in a society where children are often supposed not to "know their own minds."

The connection between coming out and the validation of adulthood seemed to have less to do with chronological age than with cultural understandings that defined adulthood in relation to marriage. Dick Maynes, a 63–year-old white man who had never married, lost a prestigious and well-paying job after revealing his sexual identity to an employer. He had written his mother a coming-out letter just a year before being interviewed.

Not beating her over the head with the gay issue, but more affirming my sense of self as an adult. I got a letter from her that was just nasty. When I look back on it now, it was a kind of "how dare you be a grownup, be someone I can't control." So I wrote back and said essentially, "I have grown up into a strong man," that I've been through my own version of hell. "And if you can't treat me accordingly, then I guess we don't have anything to say to each other."

Stephen Richter, a white man in his fifties, had come out to his parents after living on his own for ten years. In Stephen's account of their response, his father employed words like "spoiled" and raised the issue of economic support to emphasize Stephen's position as the child in the relationship.

My father's [letter] was one of telling his son that he was very spoiled and that he'd given me a great deal. I'd never had to worry about a roof over my head and a meal in my stomach, etc. etc. etc. And he did not care for my lifestyle, and he did not care for my friends. Well, of course, he didn't even know any of my friends, but that's his choice of words. And so I wrote a letter right back. . . . I said, "Yes, indeed, I am a homosexual. And

I've never given you any grief. I've supported myself since I'm eighteen. I'm a good person—I believe myself to be a good person." In those days I was still somewhat patriotic, and I said, "I'm a good citizen."

Because straight relatives generally assume that closeted lesbians and gay men are single, they can remain oblivious to many committed relationships their gay relative maintains. "I didn't realize until after I came out to my parents," said Louise Romero. "Always having to hide, it kind of caught up with me all of a sudden. I thought, god, I hate having to hide my feelings for this woman." In this context, it becomes understandable why many people based the timing of a decision to come out on such developments as having a lover, deciding to coparent a child, or encountering a crisis that affected a family of friends.

In a related attempt to clarify kinship relations, some people came out to their parents while they were single in order to make it clear that they did not plan to acquire conventional families of their own. Kevin Jones reasoned, "At least if I tell them exactly where I am, then they don't have to put all these hopes and aspirations of me getting married and having kids and all that." Other single gay men and lesbians described bringing friends and people they considered chosen family to meet blood or adoptive relatives. But some, when asked if they were out to parents or other straight relatives, responded, "No. Well, see, I'm not in a relationship, and I've never been in a serious relationship, so . . ." One person explained his decision to postpone coming out this way: "I haven't lived with anybody, and there hasn't been somebody who has been a constant in my life—a relationship. I'd consider doing it in that case."

Andy Wentworth felt that his relationship with his mother was steadily deteriorating. His mother knew all about his job as a carpenter, which she viewed as a step down in the world, but nothing of his success at building a five-year relationship with another man. "She sees my life as going nowhere," he exclaimed, "but the emotional side has gone everywhere!" If Andy were to come out to his mother, he would be serving notice that his straight family no longer occupied the primary focus of his loyalty and love. His hope would be not only to strengthen the relationship with his mother, but also to have her acknowledge bonds that linked him to his lover and several other close friends.

SELECTION AND REJECTION

The historically recent practice of coming out to blood relatives brought one type of discourse on sexuality into the familial domain, highlighting notions of kinship embedded in contemporary understandings of sexual identity. In an era when nearly all lesbians and gay men consider coming out to biological kin, many in the Bay Area had reached the tacit conclusion that elements of choice rather than inevitability contribute to the maintenance of blood ties. The fear of losing relatives acted as powerfully as the actual experience of being disowned to erode their faith in the permanence and unconditional love usually attributed to those ties. Disclosure became a process destined to uncover the "truth" of kinship relations.

Because positive responses to coming out reaffirmed a kinship at least momentarily threatened, they quietly imported choice into the notion of blood family. Once chosen, blood ties joined friendships and erotic ties as something to "work for" and "fight for," rather than something to take for granted. The accepting relatives described in coming-out stories argue that "blood is blood," offer reassurances of love, and address their gay relatives using kinship terminology. When a break with biological kin occurs in the narratives, both parties are likely to speak of relations as "lost"—a metaphor that leaves the door open to finding them again sometime in the future. Even when parents disown a child, they may agree to renew the kinship tie if the child adopts a heterosexual identity. This rhetoric of lost and found invokes choices made—to keep, to throw away, and perhaps to pick up once again.

Like erotic relations, bonds symbolized by blood prove terminable precisely because they are selectively perpetuated rather than "naturally" given. A degree of choice always enters into the decision to count (or discount) someone as a relative. Knowingly or unknowingly, individuals set about editing their "family trees" by arranging relatives along a continuum defined by poles of closeness and distance (Schneider 1968). After coming out to themselves, for example, some people reported subjecting blood ties to new scrutiny in a search for gay relations. Great-aunts, second cousins once removed, and blood relatives who might otherwise be considered genetically or emotionally distant in an ego-centered accounting of kinship suddenly assumed prominence as gay or lesbian forebears.

To a great extent, these generalizations about choice held equally for gays and heterosexuals in the Bay Area. Gay interpretations of kinship did not contest the faith that some indelible biogenetic grid exists somewhere "out there," traceable by anthropologists if not by every lay person. Their conceptions of biological or straight family rested upon culturally generalized notions of blood and love as the symbolic grounds of kinship, incorporating the imagery of roots and genes that supplies key organizing metaphors for kinship in the United States. While the meaning of categories like love varied in context as individuals brought those notions into relation with other aspects of their identities (e.g., ethnicity), the possibility of betrayal engendered by mutual or unilateral rejection in the aftermath of disclosure could not but raise the specter of alienated kinship ties.

Of course, heterosexuals can also be disowned. But when straight people encounter rejection by relatives, that rejection arises on a case-by-case basis, generally in response to something done rather than something fundamental to their sense of self. Self-identified lesbians and gay men, in contrast, experience rejection as an ever-present possibility structured by claiming a stigmatized sexual identity.

For gay people, biology and choice have become ideologically salient as categories structuring kinship, through the lived experience of making decisions to disclose their sexual identities or to remain closeted. Put another way, the experience of contemplating disclosure and facing the potentially devastating effects of rejection has added new dimensions of meaning to these symbolic constituents of kinship for lesbians and gay men. Although gay people in the Bay Area did not treat blood, choice, or creation as symbols in the way an anthropologist might, coming out tended to bring "choice" to the center of awareness and make it explicit as a significant facet of kinship relations that are ostensibly given in biology and nature. It is therefore no coincidence that selectivity became the organizing principle of gay families, or that when gay families emerged they were also called families we choose.[26]

Most lesbians and gay men are initially shocked to realize that genetic inheritance, love, and kinship are not "naturally" allied. Although permanent estrangement from biological or adoptive relatives seems to be the exception rather than the rule, any collection of coming-out narratives will bear testimony to the wounds inflicted by the lines, "*My* son/*my* daughter could never be gay!" and "You're no daughter/son of *mine*!" In an inversion of the well-known fairy tale, those who come out find themselves called upon to explain how it is that a duck could have come from a family of swans. Sadly enough, stories and experiences have demonstrated to most lesbians and gay men that the identity presumed by blood ties can indeed be sundered by the species difference depicted in the historical construction of homosexuality as perversion.

| # KINSHIP AND COHERENCE: TEN STORIES

Is there really a reality within you? If there's one inside me, there's got to be one in you. So let us work to make this a reality together, instead of apart.

—DOROTHY BOLDEN
In Nancy Seifer, *Nobody Speaks for Me!*

Coming-out stories contextualize a specific autobiographical moment within what Alfred Kazin (1979) has called "the epic of personal struggle, a situation rather than a plot." In both spoken and written coming-out narratives, a dominant theme emerges: after an extended odyssey of self-discovery leading to identification as a lesbian or gay man (frequently accomplished in great isolation), the protagonist endeavors to win a degree of understanding from a straight society represented by blood or adoptive relatives.[1] The portions of these narratives that describe changes in sexual identity and the sections that treat coming out to other people present very different organizing questions. "Who am I?" wonders the protagonist in the former, while characters in the latter are more likely to raise the cry of the jeremiad: "How long, oh lord, how long?" However well a lesbian or gay man may plan the moment of disclosure, she or he confronts the possibility of rejection while clinging to the hope of being delivered from heterosexism by finding a niche of acceptance in a forbidding land.

Rather than chronicling a purely informational exchange, stories about coming out to others convey the suspense engendered when revelation of the narrator's sexual identity puts an established social tie to the test. More often than not, that tie involves relations of kinship. These narratives typically condense a series of events into a single moment of truth in which blood relatives either renew or sever familial ties. Regardless of which reaction ensues, both parties to the disclosure take their biogenetic link as a given and continue to treat it as a "natural fact." At the same time, however, the fear of being disowned that so often accompanies coming out carries with it a potential for distinguishing the social tie of kinship from this biogenetic connection. In the specific context of coming out, blood ties may be reduced conceptually to mere material substance with little bearing on future kinship, making the enduring quality of kin ties something to be established in practice through verbal affirmations and signs of love. The drama and emotional anticipation hinges on the unresolved issue of whether solidarity will endure as the familial character of a tie comes into question.

Coming-out stories sound and read more like travelogues of what it can mean to reveal a gay identity than testimonials to exemplary conduct or how-to guides for people contemplating disclosure. No special category of person specialized in telling these stories. While individuals sometimes linked sexual identity to gender, race, age, class, religion, or ethnicity in the course of a given narrative, coming out remains one of the few experiences that consistently crosscuts these identities. Although people related these stories in a variety of contexts, they generally shared them only with other lesbians or gay men.

In casual conversation, coming-out stories arose in the course of getting to know new friends and lovers or as a way of laying claim to "community" membership (cf. Frye 1980). In keeping with essentialized and self-referential conceptions of identity in the United States, every individual was expected to have her or his own story. The narrator represented all lesbians or gay men only in the sense that every gay person faces decisions about disclosing a stigmatized sexual identity to potentially antagonistic others.

Although many people had encountered acceptance after coming out to their straight families, they tended to summarize positive experiences with brief statements: "My parents were fine about it." In contrast, the most elaborated stories chronicled experiences of hostility, misunderstanding, and rejection. The dramatic tension encapsulated in these narratives resonates with the nervousness and apprehension displayed by people building their resolve to come out to a particular relative. Standing before the twin doors of acceptance and rejection, they hesitate, wondering whether the Lady or the Tiger will emerge.

In most instances coming-out narratives go beyond the epic struggle of rising up to conquer adversity in a heterosexist society. The protagonist appears as a heroic figure with a definite task to accomplish:

demonstrating continuity of self to secure continuity of kinship. If the potential for disruption of kinship was the central problematic facing individuals as they came out, establishing a coherent self while downplaying the novelty of one's gay identity offered a strategy for working toward maintaining biological ties as kin ties.

In a society where heterosexuality was the presumption and procreation the most accessible framework for configuring family relations, homosexuality appeared as a shift in identity, as movement from a heterosexual norm. A relative's first reaction was often to question this "change." Could this be a case of self-delusion? A "phase"? The person coming out frequently responded by presenting gayness as an essential identity, something that had been there all along but was only recently recognized, a development that made sense of past experiences, like pieces of a puzzle falling into place. Because homosexuality in the United States is now most commonly understood as an identity that infuses the entire self (as opposed to an activity in which any self can participate), a person could most easily establish consistency by arguing that he or she had always been gay.

This is not to deny that some people and lesbians regarded their lesbian or gay identity as a decision rather than a discovery. Many more described coming out as a process that had modified or even transformed their self-perception. But in the context of coming out to relatives, portraying continuity of self served to counter the implication that being gay transforms a person into something alien, deviant, or monstrous. As Kevin Jones said: "Afterwards, I told [my parents], 'I'm still the same person. I'm still 5'11". Still black, still 180 pounds. I haven't changed at all. So there's no sense in acting different, 'cause I haven't changed.' " To assert coherence is to deny species difference, to claim a place in kinship as one's parents' child.

There are indications that biographical continuity can be equally important to blood kin attempting to come to terms with a relative's sexual identity. Carolyn Griffin (1986:16) found that "accepting" parents "often reported that they had a moment when they realized that this child of theirs, labeled a 'social reject,' is the same child they held in her arms as an infant." Responding to disclosures of a lesbian or gay identity with a phrase like, "You're still the same you," becomes a token of acceptance. In Margie Jamison's words:

I've never understood [how] people always say, 'This is my son. He's no longer my son,' and, 'This is my daughter. She's no longer my daughter. You know what has happened.' Nothing's happened! Nothing has changed! That's the thing I've never understood. Nothing has changed. I'm still me. I've not turned into a monster.. I've not turned into anything. And that's the thing: I'm not *turned* into anything. I have *always* been.

The insistence on being the "same person" in these heartfelt yet totally conventionalized statements draws on deeply cultural notions of self hood as a matter of being rather than doing, of consistency rather than absolute transfiguration.[2] In a situation where the shared substance symbolized by blood might prove insufficient to guarantee kinship, coming out to straight family was often aimed at eliciting signs that would confirm family ties. But in order to undercut any grounds for renegotiating our relationship, I must first show you that the "me" you loved all along is still the same "me."

In 1959, Gina Pellegrini was born into an Italian-American family on the East Coast. Her father worked as a musician while her mother held a variety of jobs in service industries. By the time she was 15 or 16, Gina had a steady lover her own age. Although Gina came out to her lover's parents after a few months, she never made a decision to tell her own parents about her partner or her gay identity.

> I had a fight with my stepdad, so I got kicked out of there. And he just dropped me off at my dad's house, lock, stock, and barrel. That was it. Then I had a fight with my dad about . . . he didn't like the people I was hanging out with. . . . So then, after that, my mom got custody again, and that's when she found out that I was gay. And then she sent me to someplace. Oh, first I went to a foster home. And I got kicked out of there 'cause they found out I was gay. And then I went to . . . oh, after that they put me in a girls' home. And for some reason I got kicked out. It was in a girls' home; there was about 15 girls, young girls there. And they thought it would be . . . "detrimental" was one word they used. They just didn't know how to cope with it.

Too often the material side to kinship relations gets lost in discussions of changing identity and cultural notions of self. Gina's story underscored the precarious economic and legal position of people who come out while still minors. This young woman's best efforts could not prevent her parents from throwing her out and allowing her to be shuffled from institution to institution. Although Gina portrayed herself as active, engaged, and willing to fight, because of her age her parents controlled the situation. Eventually she took her parents to court and had herself declared an "emancipated minor," a legal status that allowed her to live independently and determine her own residence.

Gina's parents "discovered" her gay identity, rather than allowing her to take the initiative in coming out to them. As in so many coming-out stories, relatives (by both blood and adoption) appear as the agents of disrupted kinship: her stepfather ends their argument by physically ejecting her from the house, while her mother requests intervention by state authorities. The irony of being placed in an exclusively female institution was not lost on Gina, but became overshadowed by mixed feelings of hurt and anger.

Gina presented her sexual identity to me as a timeless, essentialized fact. "I was gay," she said—not "I became gay," "I decided I was gay," or even "I had just come out." Establishing a coherent personal history was not at issue in her story, in part because Gina did not contest her parents' interpretation of what it meant to be gay or ask them to reconsider terminating the relationship. The reportage style of her narrative ("I did this, then I did that, then something else happened . . . ") presented events in an unusually abbreviated form. Before the interview Gina had mentioned that these experiences were very difficult for her to discuss; in this case, the lack of elaboration testified to the deep emotional impact of being kicked out. At the social gatherings where coming-out stories were exchanged, this type of story would present a morality tale that defined the pole of rejection, warning listeners of the discontinuities that disclosure can introduce into blood and adoptive relationships. The intensity of Gina's break with her parents came through in her phrase, "lock, stock, and barrel." It remained unclear from the narrative—and unclear in Gina's mind—whether she continued to regard her parents as family afterwards, or whether she viewed the break as a sign of kinship lost.

Scott McFarland's emerging gay identity also became known to his mother while he was in high school. Although he had lived in the Bay Area for more than ten years, Scott was born and raised in a small Appalachian town, and his father died while he was young. A white man in his thirties, Scott identified more with his Southern origins than with any racial or ethnic classification. The two of us sat around my kitchen table for several hours one day trading stories about our coming-out experiences. If the tape recorder had not been turning, we probably would not have considered our encounter an interview.

I had decided to skip school one day to go to the local mental hospital. I had to tell somebody about this and get some help. What *really* was the problem was this dismal family situation. I didn't know it. I just assumed . . . somehow I got it all mixed up, and I thought, well, the way for me to feel better in my life is to deal with this issue of being gay. Which I didn't have words for. But I went over to the hospital. This is in high school. And I tried to talk to them, and they let me sit there for four hours, at which point the receptionist—I never got beyond the reception-ist—came out and said, "You'll have to bring your mother along before we'll be able to talk to you."

That was terrible. And I couldn't at that point go back to school. I suppose it was my most Russian afternoon. In all the Russian novels, the Russians are walking across bridges—in Mos-cow, there's all these bridges. I remember I walked all day from one bridge over the river up to the other and back . . . .

When I got home that night, naturally they called Mom to say that I hadn't come to school. You were supposed to call in. She was very hysterical . . . She dragged me all over the house, smacking me around and stuff, and I finally told mother why I had been [to the hospital], and her reaction was that it would be better to be dead. She explained this very carefully to me.

I was *desperate*, I was just desperate at that point. I thought, well, I can't go to the hospital and get help. I can't take what's going on here. I don't know what to do. So I thought, well, I will try a suicide attempt, and we'll see what comes of that. And I remember thinking that if I take a bunch of pills, someone will *have* to help me. It will *have* to be taken out of the hands of this horrible situation here. So that's what I did. I took a bunch of pills. I had no idea what they were. And I drank a few bottles of iodine that I'd found. . . . And I told my mom that I'd done it. Then she said, "Well, I hope that you left some for me." That was her only comeback. And I said, "Well, no, I didn't" (laughs). And I thought, "Well, that's it. I just thought I'm gonna get help, and so what's gonna happen is I'll *die* from this." I went up and I went to bed.

I woke up three days later. . . . It's all very groggy and confused in my memory. But the upshot of the whole thing is, my mother had gotten up the next morning and made sure that no one disturbed me, and gotten everyone and taken off for a little long weekend vacation. And when they got back, my oldest sister cleaned me up, and we never talked about it. We *never* talked about it. It was never brought up again. It's still very hard for me to talk about these things, but I can do it, so I'm very proud of that.

Scott's story depicted a situation somewhere between coming out and being found out, since his mother extracted the disclosure under duress. Like Gina Pellegrini, Scott experienced the extreme vulnerability of individuals who come out to themselves while still dependent upon adults for financial support and protection. Scott's only ally proved to be an older sister, in accordance with categorical understandings that anticipate greater acceptance from siblings than from parents. The large population of homeless people in San Francisco included a number of young gay and lesbian runaways who faced a similar lack of perceived alternatives in the lives they had left behind.

Under the influence of the medical model ("homosexuals are sick"), Scott originally viewed death as a better option than going on with life as a gay man. Dying can signify the dissolution of blood ties in the United States: accordingly, parents who had disowned a child often employed the rhetoric and ritual of death (cf. Schneider 1968). Some Jewish lesbians and gay men had had relatives sit *shiva* for them.[3] Not uncommon in coming-out stories were statements by relatives such as, "It's like he was never born," and, "As far as I'm concerned, my daughter is dead." For a mother to have wished the death of a child she had nurtured and brought into life symbolically turned back the hands of time, attempting to negate not only the relationship but Scott's very existence.

By the time of our talk, Scott took pride in his ability to give words to experiences that contradicted his understanding of what "family life" was supposed to be like. That pride extended to his decision to articulate his gay identity (another unmentionable) to his mother, and his mother's attempt to silence this discourse first through death and then by refusing to discuss any of the events surrounding Scott's disclosure. Against this backdrop of violence and murder by default, arriving at my apartment to tell the tale constituted an accomplishment in itself.

For Scott the autobiographical act of telling his own story had played as great a part in remaking his identity as the experience of coming out (cf. Stone 1982). Like the phoenix rising, Scott pictured himself reborn into a new identity through the confrontation with his mother. Images of death and rebirth highlighted the discontinuities of a transfigured self, leaving Scott standing alone at the story's conclusion. As he moved toward his own future, Scott put this particular blood tie behind him, abandoning efforts to gain his mother's acceptance by demonstrating coherence of self. From his trial by fire, a new person had emerged.

In his thirties at the time of the interview, Rafael Ortiz had also attempted to kill himself as a teenager. He was raised near his present home in the predominantly Latino Mission District of San Francisco, and made a point of telling me that he seldom traveled to gay sections of the city. Although his parents separated when he was a boy, he grew up in close contact with a number of aunts, uncles, and cousins who lived in the neighborhood. Rafael attributed his suicide attempt to his youthful fear that living as a gay man would mean being "locked up" and "having no family."

I moved into my dad's, and I told him that I tried to commit suicide—I wouldn't tell him why. And he told me, two weeks prior to that, he sat me down and said if I was ever to turn the other way—this is my father, who is an ex-boxer—that "it would be okay, son." I just shied away from that. I moved in there, and I told him, "Will you tell my mother?" And so . . . well, he didn't.

And so I called my aunt over, who is the black sheep of the family, to talk about it. I knew I could tell her, 'cause she had been married to a black man and had three kids from a black man, and ever since then she was dirt. I mean, that's the kind of family I come from. So I called Aunt Lupe over, and I said, "Lupe, I'm this and that. Now I have this boyfriend." So she told my mother, who was hysterical. And then my mother told all my brothers and sisters. That's how my cousins and everybody found out. . . . Then the next time I saw them, I remember walking into the house, and everybody's looking at me like I had just come out of my grave or something. But we didn't talk about it.

Though Rafael mentioned his suicide attempt in passing, his story focused on decisions about disclosing his gay identity. The grave metaphor in the closing scene once again tied coming out to the imagery of death, with Rafael rising from the burial that would have been the consequence of his self-destruction. But Rafael's father, unlike Scott's mother, demonstrated acceptance by offering him a place to stay and affirming the kinship tie between them. When he reassured Rafael that it would be okay to "turn the other way," his father made a point of calling him "son." Rafael also highlighted the fact that his father had been a boxer—a symbol of masculinity—knowing that most gay listeners would take this profession as a sign of someone likely to be homophobic. This aside framed his story as a tale of reversed expectations, making the unconditional form of his father's acceptance appear all the more remarkable.

Interracial marriage, like death, is another recurring theme in coming-out narratives.[4] Because Rafael's aunt had been shunned and marginalized by relatives, he reasoned that they occupied structurally similar positions within "the family" and decided to come out to her first. Significantly, the silence of other blood kin in the story did not apply to the topic of homosexuality. After listening to her son's disclosure, Rafael's mother maneuvered not to stifle but to control the discourse by telling other relatives herself. Without authoring these revelations, Rafael found it difficult to initiate discussions in which he could project positive interpretations of his sexual identity. Following through on the analogy between Rafael and his aunt, relatives seemed to regard him as another errant sheep: disdained, but still within the family fold.

For Amy Feldman, who grew up in New York City, relations with her parents were similarly distant at the time she decided to come out. Unlike Scott McFarland and Rafael Ortiz, however, she was not prepared to paper over her parents' attitudes with silence. The living room where I interviewed Amy was furnished with the basics: a dilapidated couch and easy chair, with a cardboard carton that once had held a television now serving as an end table. Her stories were detailed and intense, often interrupted by tears or laughter. When she decided to come out to her parents, Amy had not seen them since the time her father hit her with a baseball bat.

I did come out to my parents. It's a kind of humorous story. It goes like this: I hadn't seen them for 2½ years. It was a very conscious decision on my part. My brother kept calling me; I saw my brother. My brother knew I was a lesbian, because my brother came over to my house and walked in on me and my lover making love in the living room. So he knew. And so I said, "So, you know." So he goes, "So I know." So I says, "So how do you feel?" And he said, "You're still my sister." I said, "Good thinking, guy! Glad you feel that way, you know? I'd hate to lose you!" He said, "Don't tell Mommy and Daddy."

My brother kept calling me to go see my father. I couldn't see my father. There was no way I could see my father. They were still threatening to divorce. They were still going through this bullshit. Then finally my cousin, my mother's sister's son, was getting bar mitzvahed out in New Jersey. And I was invited to the bar mitzvah. So, I had been with my lover Sandy for two years. We were living together for a year. We had the house, the car, the dogs, the whole nine yards. So I decided to go to the bar mitzvah.

They picked me up and they told me they're getting divorced. They're really getting divorced. That they don't want the family to know about it, all this stuff. They're gonna tell them after the bar mitzvah. They don't want to ruin—good Jews that they are, they don't want to ruin the good times with the family. So we drive to New Jersey; they're talking about they're getting divorced and how they're not supposed to tell the family, and all this stuff. All right. We go to the bar mitzvah, have a very nice time, dance, drink, whatever. Drank a little, whatever, smoked pot. You better believe I smoked a lot of pot then, fucking dealing with my parents for the first time in 2½ years! Talked to my cousins. My cousins kind of got a hit that I was a lesbian, but I didn't know how to confront it, I didn't deal with it, I just let it go.

So driving home—I worked at the Palladium theater in New

York, and they were gonna drop me off at work on the way home from New Jersey. We're driving home and getting closer to Manhattan. My father starts asking me these questions. "So, Amy, what have you been doing for the last 2½ years of your life," you know? "Oh, I've been working and in school for a while. I go out, I go dancing, I have friends. I've been doing a little theater." "Oh really? What have you been doing? Specifically, where have you been going dancing?" "I've been going to Club 57, I've been going to Ice Palace, the Duchess, Peaches."

He's driving in the car, and then we're going down 14th Street in Manhattan. And 14th Street is a two-way street, two lanes on each side of the road. And we're driving in the left lane going eastbound on 14th Street. And he says, "So, uh, Amy, uh, aren't those, uh, gay clubs?" And my brother's sitting in the back going, "Don't say it, Amy! don't say it!" I'm like, "Yes. Those are gay clubs, yeah. Uh-huh." "Uh, Amy, uh, are you gay or what?" You know? My brother said, "Amy, don't say it!" And I said, "Yeah, I'm a lesbian. I'm gay."

Well, we went across 14th Street sideways. Two lanes one way, two lanes back, two lanes one way, two lanes back. "You're *what*? You're fucking gay? What's wrong with you? You're a fucking queer?" And going on, and on. And my mother turned around, and she goes, "What are you trying to do, spite me or something?" And I said, "Mother, I really never think of you when I'm making love to a woman." And she was like, "Huh! I'm really disappointed!" And started saying all this stuff. Well thank god, I was getting out at the next corner. I got out at the next corner, and I said, "You sit on it, folks. You swallow it. 'Cause that's the way it is." I slammed the door and I went on my way. I got inside the Palladium and I was shaking. I was shaking like a fucking leaf.

The impression of a continuous and timeless lesbian self emerged clearly from Amy's interview. In her story, a "settled" relationship with a lover emphasized her commitment to a lesbian identity. That commitment was magnified by possession of the trappings of the stereotypically "all-American" family: "the house, the car, the dogs, the whole nine yards." Sandwiched between the invitation to a relative's bar mitzvah and Amy's decision to attend, this passage credited the tie to a lover as the immediate reason for coming out. Amy's resolution to disclose her lesbian identity to her parents on a family occasion likewise framed kinship, rather than sexuality per se, as the domain in which coming out would take place.

Amy's brother's discovery set up an opposition in the narrative between parents who had remained ignorant of her sexual identity and a sibling very much "in the know." Although her brother affirmed their kinship tie with the comment, "You're still my sister," Amy's response recognized the possibility of "losing" him as a sibling. "Good thinking," she added, wryly acknowledging her brother's willingness to search for a congruence between cultural constructions of sexuality and kinship that would allow their relationship to continue. When Amy's parents announced their own secret—a divorce—it not only prefigured Amy's revelation but also extended the theme of severed kinship ties.

In describing the journey to the bar mitzvah, Amy linked sexual identity to family and ethnicity by sarcastically asserting that a "good Jew" does not "ruin the good times with the family." Although she reported waiting until after the event to communicate her potentially disturbing news, Amy tacitly placed herself in the category "bad Jew" by revealing her lesbian identity in the car. As it unfolded, the interaction between daughter and father contradicted Amy's stated intention to take the initiative in disclosure. While Amy's characterization maintained fidelity to the model of what constitutes coming out, her story ended up doing something rather different from what it initially announced it would do. Contrary to listeners' expectations, Amy's father had to extract the information from her, piece by torturous piece. Her brother's repetitions of the phrase, "Don't say it!" after each small disclosure allowed the dramatic tension and sense of struggle to build. Even after her father deduced that his daughter had been frequenting gay clubs, the denouement hinged on Amy's acknowledgment of the gay character of those bars and on her specific statement of lesbian identity.[5]

Amy's mother insisted upon viewing her daughter's identity solely in relation to herself, as something adopted "to spite me." In an unusual but deliberate attempt to disconcert her mother, Amy abruptly shifted the focus of discussion from identity to sex. The success of her comeback depended on its veiled allusion to incest, and marked a shift in tone from humor to anger that carried through to the end of the story. Meanwhile, her father's erratic driving symbolized the violence and danger that can greet such disclosures. By the conclusion, Amy's shaking and swearing conveyed the emotional toll of what had transpired. She rejected her parents without giving them an opportunity to further reject or injure her. After getting out of the car and slamming the door, Amy went on her way to a paying job that underscored her independence and self-sufficiency. With this parting gesture, she completed a symbolic differentiation from her blood family, giving spatial representation to the emotional distance that would continue to separate Amy from her parents.

When Jerry Freitag, a white man who was raised Lutheran, came out to his parents, he shared Amy Feldman's nervous anticipation. Although his father worked in a blue-collar trade and his mother was a secretary, Jerry had followed a path of upward mobility to a position as a market analyst. The condominium he shared with his lover Kurt was filled with new but not inordinately expensive furniture. While we spoke, he played absent-mindedly with a young kitten that insisted on being included in the interview.

> I knew I was moving to California at the time, and I knew I was gay. And I knew if I didn't tell them before I left, that I would never tell them. Once 3,000 miles were between us, it would just be too difficult for me to talk to them about it. So I went over one night, and I hemmed and hawed for about an hour. We were sitting at the kitchen table. And then finally I just let it spill out. I said, "I'm gay." Or "homosexual," or something. My father clutched his heart, and my mother starts crying.
>
> My father thought I was gonna tell them that I was in love with a black girl and marrying a black girl. At this point, I was living with a woman when I told them. And I had brought the woman over to the house a couple of times. And she was Jewish. And my mother says, "We're just finally getting used to the idea that you'll probably marry a Jew. Now this!"
>
> My parents are very Protestant-oriented. When I first became friends with Kurt, they were upset that he was Catholic. "We shouldn't be associating with Catholics." I mean, they said a lot of things. My father said he wished I was a murderer. That he could deal with that better, than a son who was homosexual.

Geographic distance about to be introduced into a relationship became the motive for Jerry's attempt to reduce emotional distance by coming out to his parents. Gathering together around the kitchen table in the evening situated the encounter in a familial setting that emphasized their common working-class background. When his disclosure "spilled out," "truths" about his identity moved across a semiotic landscape: away from his inner self, past his superficial appearance, and out into the world with the explicit statement, "I'm gay."

Jerry's parents responded as though homosexuality was the worst conceivable disaster that could have befallen their son. Interracial and interreligious marriages had comprised their list of imagined horrors, but their son's declaration jarred them out of this procreative, heterosexual framework. Conventionalized references to a mother's tears and a father clutching his heart have great cultural resonance in the United States, where the heart represents the corporeal seat of love and emotion. In this context, the specter of cardiac arrest suggested the possible termination of the father-son relationship. Jerry did not perceive his father to have denied kinship, since his father continued to refer to him as a son. But the allusion to the father's death by heart attack paralleled the final phrase in which his father compared Jerry to a murderer, making his son the metaphorical agent of any break in their relationship. As Jerry later commented, this was the one line in all his parents' responses that "really got to me."

The analogy of interracial marriage, mentioned by both Jerry Freitag and Rafael Ortiz, condemns an individual for relating to a different category of person, but comparison to a murderer condemned Jerry himself for being a member of a stigmatized category. Though his father never questioned the coherence of Jerry's selfhood, his reaffirmation of their kinship tie coexisted with expressions of disgust.

Louise Romero grew up just outside San Francisco, not far from the place where Jerry Freitag had made his new home. Because her kin lived in what is now the western United States well before Mexico attained its independence, she considered herself "Brown" or "Hispanic" but not "Mexican-American." Louise maintained active relationships with many of her biological relatives, some of whom lived nearby. Pictures of nieces and nephews dotted her living room.

It hurt a lot coming out. I came out, and decided to tell my mother and my sisters, because every time I'd come over to visit, they'd have boyfriends there. My sister would invite me over to dinner and have this guy there, try to fix me up, and that was really hard. So finally I told her, and it turned out she was the most homophobic. She freaked out. She even had my sister paged at a football game, high school football game, to come home 'cause she had to tell her something. Which I find out later. . . .

Me and my sister, we never were close. When I decided to tell her, it was just like forget it, it was just the wrong move. So I thought I better talk to Mom. Mom kind of freaked out. She said, "You weren't born with a penis," and she started cleaning the house madly (laughs). It was really weird. I said, "Yeah, I know, Mom." And then my brother thought it was sacrilegious. They all thought I should go to church more. They brought the priest over. It was a real mess.

Louise explained her motive for disclosure as a wish to clarify her kinship status. As long as her mother and sisters saw her as a single heterosexual, eligible for marriage, they would continue to place her in awkward social situations by playing matchmaker.

Her narrative reinforced prevailing understandings of what makes a "good" coming-out story by focusing primarily on events that threatened to disrupt family relationships. The characterization of coming out as a "mess" at the conclusion of the story referred back to the "hurt" of the opening line, creating the impression that coming out for Louise had meant experiencing unqualified rejection (cf. H. Sacks 1974).[6] Only after several minutes of follow-up questioning did Louise reveal that she had considered her father fairly accepting from the moment she came out to him. "My father never treated me any different [after he knew]," she told me. Different treatment would have implied recognition of a change in Louise that affected their relationship; by treating her as he had in the past, he recognized continuity in her as a person. Yet Louise's father remained noticeably absent from the narrative, because Louise's story was about perceived discontinuities in identity that had threatened relationships with her mother and sister.

Her sister's alarm following the disclosure contradicted the categorical expectation that siblings will be more supportive than parents. When Louise evaluated her tie to this sister as "never close," it was another way of saying that nothing had changed in their relationship. In this case consistently negative interactions testified to continuity of self. Louise's mother responded to her disclosure with an anatomical and gender-crossing definition of homosexuality: the lesbian as pseudo-male. By "cleaning the house madly," her mother took refuge in a "proper" activity for women, intended perhaps as an oblique rebuke to Louise. Portraying homosexuality as a matter of gender identity rather than sexual identity (genitalia being a key symbolic ground of gender in the United States) allowed the mother to contend that her daughter's lesbianism represented a case of "mistaken" identification. Since Louise did not have a penis, she should have realized that no change in personhood had occurred. Louise, however, insisted on presenting herself simultaneously as a lesbian *and* the same person, leaving the conflict with her mother and the status of their relationship unresolved.

Misha Ben Nun was raised near San Francisco in a family that placed greater value on the cultural than the religious aspects of their Judaic heritage. At the time of the interview her parents had explicitly disowned her, a development that framed her story and focused her attention on the parent-adult child relationship. As long as she remained a lesbian, Misha's parents refused to consider her their daughter. Should she one day find a boyfriend and marry, they had promised to embrace her within "the family." During the events described in the narrative, Misha was staying at her parents' home for a few days while recovering from minor surgery. The story opened with Misha's mother, who made her living as a mental health professional, playing the part of a therapist.

> So then she changes, and tells me how disgusting my life is, and how I've created all this pain and suffering in her life. There's something about, definitely, pain and suffering that gets to me, but is also so typical of Jewish families. And goes on to basically give me this lecture about how I should be changing my life, and they can't stand it any more, and they're getting to the end of their patience. That I'll be a failure. That I am destroying my life, and I just can't see it, because I'm so much involved in—they very much think that gay culture in San Francisco is a cult. And once you get into it, you can't get out, because the only people that you have, your only friends, are people in the gay community. . . . That's why I thought they were gonna kidnap me.

'Cause I thought, well, if they think it's a cult, then they probably think they can kidnap me.

And then my father enters. And my mother says, "Oh, we're just having a family therapy session. Why don't you join?" My father's like, "I think I'll leave." "No! This is really serious, David. Why don't you join. Sit down," she says, "tell her how you feel about her life." And he proceeds to tell me how disgusting I am, and that I'm making my life miserable, and how can I be so naive to do this. And all these really horrible things. And I was basically caught. There I was. I was stranded. I couldn't even walk [due to the surgery]. I didn't have a car. So I called up my housemates, and said, "I'm taking the train, pick me up."

It was in an hour, and I had my father drive me down to the train station. During the trip down, he kept asking, "Well, have you considered now? Have you touched a man, or kissed a man, in the last five years? Do you ever think about men?" All this stuff that's really gross. Ugh, really sickening. "Well, I don't know if I can love you unless you . . . " Basically, the message is, "We can't love you unless you fuck a man." And it's so bizarre to me! It's so alien. It's so strange, that that is the ultimate criteria for love. . . .

The real painful stuff is that—I mean, I didn't have family in this country besides my immediate family. Either they died in the war, or died in concentration camps, or they're in Israel. So there was this sense when we were growing up that we were it. And *we* were gonna continue the family, and we were gonna create this family in this country. But we were *it*, and you rely on each other. 'Cause no one else will be there, and people will turn against you, and you can't trust anyone in this country anyway. Just being fed all that stuff. So being disowned was so —I mean, I think it's gonna be horrendous for any person, but particularly because I felt like I didn't have an extended family to go to. My siblings were not supportive.

But there was all of a sudden a realization that [my parents] fed [me] a line: that they would always be there. They always talked about unconditional love, and how important that was. This real sense that they were a family and were a unit and would work out *anything*. Survivors, that we were all survivors. That not only my father was, but we were, and we could survive anything together as long as we were together. So what did it mean, if they disowned me?

One way of denying continuity of self to justify a break in kinship is to split the self into parts and label one part as more "true" or "real" than the others. Misha's parents did not argue that she had somehow "turned into" a lesbian, which would have admitted temporal discontinuity, but rather that she did not know her own mind because she had been influenced by gay friends. Given her parents' analogy between gay community and religious cults, Misha's fear of being kidnapped did not seem far-fetched. Stories were widespread in San Francisco about cult members who had been kidnapped by relatives and forced into "deprogramming" or behavior modification therapies. Earlier in the century, a strikingly similar rationale was offered to justify institutionalization as a response to disclosures of homosexuality. "I knew of people who had *been* whisked away," said Harold Sanders, speaking of the 1940s. "And it was always explained, 'Well, he really wasn't himself.' "

The possibility of "losing love" confronts all lesbians and gay men when they come out to biological or adoptive relatives, but Misha interpreted that threat in the context of her Jewish identity and family history. Because so many of her relatives had died or were murdered during World War II, she grew up with a sense of having a limited number of blood relations. Her own coming-out experience prevented Misha from arguing (as some Jewish gays and lesbians did) that the Diaspora and the Holocaust have made it next to impossible for Jewish children to be disowned. Instead, the expectation of unshakable solidarity that she attributed to "Jewish culture" heightened her sense of betrayal at being rejected by her biological parents.

By referring to the community she had found in San Francisco, Misha attempted to move the discussion in the direction of friendship and kinship, but her father insisted on reducing sexual identity to a matter of sex. When her father elevated (hetero)sexual activity to a signifier of sexual identity by asking Misha if she had had sex with a man, he mixed erotic with nonerotic forms of love. Misha perceived this as an inappropriate and "bizarre" equation: a father's love for his daughter should not have anything to do with sex, and certainly should not be made contingent upon it. Yet her father's comment is revealing because it strikes at the procreative heart of what many gay people mean when they speak of straight or biological family. Although incest prohibitions constitute as they distinguish categories of blood and marriage relations in the United States, both types of ties refer back to the symbolism of biological procreation through heterosexual intercourse.

Unlike many of the men and women introduced in this chapter, Misha saw little promise of any evolution toward acceptance by her parents. In her story she portrayed herself more as observer than actor, increasing the sense of a hopeless situation. Her physical dependence after surgery seemed to make it easier for her parents to cast her in the childlike role of someone who did not understand her own best interests. The only hint of self-determination in the narrative arose when she turned away from blood family toward her housemates in San Francisco. After years of struggle, Misha felt she would have to look elsewhere to find family.

The extremely oppressive consequences that Misha Ben Nun described as the aftermath of disclosure define the genre of coming-out stories to such an extent that stories which end happily tend to incorporate a surprising turn of events in order to play on fears of a disastrous break with parents or siblings. Al Collins was a white man who had grown up in South Carolina, where his father owned a small business and his mother worked at home. In a good year, he netted a substantial income from his job as a car salesman. When I interviewed Al, he was involved in a committed relationship he called a gay marriage.

> [Coming out] was a pretty heavy situation. Because I had made the decision in my mind that I was going to tell [my family] when I got out of the air force. And so I went back home and I was having problems of how exactly I was going to do it. And just incidentally one day we had a little situation came up where my whole family was there, and we were sitting and the TV was on, and this announcement came on TV where the local college in my area had about six gay students who were trying to organize a gay council and my whole town was in an uproar. And my father stood up and announced, "Oh god, give me my fucking shotgun and I'll go out there and blow those queers away."
>
> And it just hit me. And I stood up and I told my dad, "Yeah,

you better watch who you're pointing the gun at, 'cause you might shoot somebody who you don't want to." And he knew what I meant and he says, "What are you talking about, boy?" And I said, "Dad, I'm gay," and he goes, "What!" and started yelling and screaming, and my mother kind of twinged (laughs), and both my sisters started laughing because I was like a practical joker at home, and they thought that I was kidding. And from that point on we learned to accept each other.

My mother was the first to actually accept it that everything was okay, and my father took me out and we jumped in the truck and went out and drank whiskey. And I'm not much of a drinker, but to him this was how he had to handle it, so we went out and we both got drunk together and it turned out ironically that my father was really more in tune to the gay life than I had ever even dreamed of. It turned out that he had a close friend that he was in the navy with—they were friends for years, and then this guy, who was very close to him, he found out he was gay. So he kind of was worried and understanding at the same time. But now there's no problem whatsoever.

And I think it was a really good step for them as well as for me because they've learned about that it's not bad to be gay. I've turned around their whole idea of what a gay person really was. Up until that point my father had always heard that a gay person was bad and dirty and probably effeminate and a night creature that comes out nights when no one else is looking! And it changed his whole perception of what it was.

Al, like Amy Feldman, portrayed coming out as a premeditated decision. His story "works" because it contains a twist that plays on the violence, death, and fear of being disowned that are standard imagery in descriptions of coming out to biological relatives. The opening line set up this twist by encouraging listeners to group this narrative with the "heavy" coming-out stories that chronicle ruptured family ties. The television news report of gay student organizing located the tale in an era of expanding media coverage and a dissolving consensus regarding homosexuality. As Al continued, he established a Southern setting with his usage of "boy" alongside a string of hackneyed symbols of rural white Southern life ("shotgun," "truck," "whiskey").

Al credited his mother with being the first to come to terms with his sexual identity, but his story focused on the father-son tie. As in Louise Romero's narrative, the relationship threatened by disclosure occupied center stage. Although his father knew what Al meant when his son called his bluff, he forced Al to confirm his sexual identity with the explicit verbal statement considered central to coming out. Going out drinking together established the two as peers in a "man-to-man" relationship. The reference to whiskey, a "hard" liquor, underlined this gender solidarity even as the context of drinking invoked notions of adulthood in a nation that places age restrictions on alcohol sales.

By the story's conclusion, the drinking scenario had implicitly refuted the father's effeminate stereotype of gay men. Rather than allow his parents to grieve over some incomprehensible transfiguration of their son's activities and sense of self, Al encouraged them to revise their interpretation of the entire category "homosexual." Attributes like masculinity that they had long associated with their son need not contradict his new identity or imply any change in Al as a person. In the end, the parallel between the son coming out to himself in the air force and the father recalling his friendship with a gay navy buddy became a bridge to understanding and acceptance.

Danny Carlson, a Native American man, had pursued a similar course of trying to reconcile his parents to his gay identity through persistent efforts and education. When he was a teenager, Danny's "immediate family" moved from a small town in rural California to the Paiute reservation. His story unfolded in the context of describing reservation life.

It's just Indian people. There are so few of us, we know each other. So I figured, hey, I'll *have* to tell my parents. Like I said, in high school, I *knew*. I was really, really sexually active, and I had a boyfriend—two boyfriends who were in the city. And then I met my *love;* it went on for seven years. So I figured I should be honest, at least, with them. If not shock them. Well, that wasn't my plan.

I went home back to the rez, and I told them that I was gay. Of course they didn't know what I meant. They felt that I was just going through a phase. Or, "You'll still get married." Freaked them out. They kicked me off the ranch. Kicked my boyfriend off, off the ranch. Cried all the way back to the city. And it took them about six months to come around.

   My sister, at that time, she lived here in the city. And she went home, and she got on their case. She said, "He's our blood. How could you just . . . he's my brother, and if you're gonna 86 him, then you might as well 86 me, too." She's always been by my side. So, after six months, my mom came down [to the city] before my dad. And she cried, and she said, "What did we do wrong?" She felt bad. She felt guilty. I said, "Nothing! Nothing. You didn't do nothing wrong." Then my dad, even up to this point, he *still* hasn't accepted it.

Danny's account offered another glimpse into the renegotiation of the meaning of gay identity that so often accompanies coming out. His parents initially attempted to refute his sexual identification by calling it a phase in order to reassure themselves that marriage and a family of procreation lay ahead in Danny's future. When they kicked him off the ranch, their unstated message seemed clear: Get out and don't return until you move on to the next "phase," and get back to being the person we know.

Danny attributed his decision to come out to three factors: the material conditions of reservation life (which incorporated an interpretive link to race, culture, and history), the desire to preempt discovery by relatives, and the more immediate circumstance of having a lover. What distinguished the relationship with his latest partner from ties to previous boyfriends was the addition of love to sex. This combination transformed both the relationship and its proper domain, bringing it into the realm of kinship for Danny and prompting the disclosure to his biological family. Since his boyfriend was present on the occasion Danny chose to come out to his parents, it seems likely that Danny had hoped to gain recognition for the relationship as well as acceptance for his sexual identity.

   To argue for the permanence of the bond that joined them, Danny's sister invoked the symbolism of shared blood. In one breath she named Danny her brother to reaffirm kinship, and opposed the horizontal axis of sibling ties to the generational axis represented by parent-child relationships. By positioning herself alongside her brother as members of a sibling set, she buttressed her contention that disowning him would invalidate the link between shared substance (blood) and kinship, making her own tie to the parents equally subject to termination. Not surprisingly, Danny retrospectively emphasized the closeness and continuity in his relationship with his sister.

Movement between the reservation and the city, between American Indian and white environments, opened and closed the story. This narrative flow brought the past—represented by the reservation and Indian "ways" as well as by blood family—forward into Danny's present. In joining these two parts of Danny's life, this narrative progression also validated his self-definition as a "go-between" who helps his people cope in a white world. After the interview Danny mentioned with pride that when he returns to the reservation, nephews and nieces who once teased him for effeminate mannerisms now call him "Uncle," which he valued as a token of inclusion and respect.

The child of a salesman and a bookkeeper, Vince Mancino was born to Italian-American parents in the suburb of a large Midwestern city. He moved to San Francisco at the height of the wave of lesbian and gay immigration during the 1970s. Although he grew up Roman Catholic, after coming out he became active in the Metropolitan Community Church. The friend who gave me Vince's name described him as a quiet person, but during the interview he had a lifetime of things to say.

> After about after a year I was in San Francisco, my mother called to explain that they'd be in San Francisco in a week. She said, "Surprise!" And I said, "Well, I have a surprise for you, too." And the first day, I went to their hotel room and I told them that I was gay. I had worked up this long dissertation. Looking back now, it was just silly. And my mother said, "So tell us something we don't know." And my father said, "Yeah, I guess I always knew but didn't want to admit it." So for the first day, everything was wonderful and "how could you ever think we would love you any less?"
>
> The second day, I guess it really sunk into them, and it changed to "it's okay for other people's sons to be gay, but you're really not." So it was not okay for their son to be gay—they knew I wasn't. . . . What they said is that they see that I had some really nice friends here, and because they were also gay, because they were gay, I just *thought* that I was gay because I wanted to identify with them. I said, "Dad, it does not work that way."

My father said what I needed was seven days and seven nights with a good woman. It was very hard not laughing. And I said, "Dad, that might even be a pleasurable experience, but it wouldn't change what I felt in my heart." He said, "If you only knew the touch of a woman, you'd know the truth." I said, "Dad, if you only knew the tenderness of a man, you would know the truth." He said, "That's disgusting." I said, "If you accept nothing else, for your own peace of mind, accept that I will not change." I said, "It took me 22 years to come to the point of acceptance that I have." That I did not expect him overnight to understand. But I did expect him to try.

So the following Christmas when I came back to Oakdale to visit, he said, "I know this really good woman." I said, "Dad, I know this really good man." So he didn't speak to me for a couple of days after that. Next Christmas, we repeated the same scene. And then one day in my apartment about five years ago—it was right here, just walking into the kitchen—I just stopped, and I realized that I did not need for my parents to accept me. And I said out loud, "Mom, Dad, I don't need for you to accept me any more. It would be nice, but I don't need it."

And when I went home for Christmas that year, it was as if everything had changed. I guess what it was, is they sensed, for the first time, that *I* was comfortable with who I am. Because it was okay for me, it was okay for them. And they talked about, "Well, this is how you are. We just want you to be happy."

At one point my aunt dropped in and said, "When are you going to get married?" My mother said, "Um . . . well . . . uh, my son, he uh . . . he doesn't date girls." And that's all she said! And Christmas morning I opened up one gift, and it was an electric blanket with dual controls! I said, "Mom, this is wonderful, but what am I gonna do with dual controls?" She said, "Eh —you never know." I just shook my head, not believing. I was very surprised.

Vince's story subverted genre conventions by showing his parents regressing from initial acceptance to denial and rejection. Claiming they had known all along, his parents initially imparted a continuity to Vince's self-definition that even he had not insisted upon. Their subsequent feelings of dismay led them to search for another way to challenge perceived discontinuities in his sense of self. After maintaining that *their* son could never be gay, they traced the error of his ways to a "mistaken" identification with (gay) friends over (straight) family. Like Louise Romero's mother, Vince's parents were prepared to continue the relationship, but only after discounting his claim to a new identity. In their view, Vince had chosen the wrong way to differentiate from his family of origin and grow into adulthood.

Time after time, Vince addressed his father as "Dad," emphasizing kinship in the belief that his father would eventually try to move toward acceptance. But his father, like Misha Ben Nun's, insisted on treating gayness as a matter of sex alone, ignoring related aspects of identity and kinship. The imagery of "seven days and seven nights" alludes to God's creation of the "natural" world in Genesis and the exemplary pairing of man with woman in the story of Adam and Eve. In response Vince advanced an independent interpretation of gay identity with the statement, "It does not work that way," meaning that acts of straight sex in the absence of identity do not a heterosexual make.

Unlike Jerry Freitag, who came out to his parents before moving away, Vince told me he felt he needed distance to establish his independence, "just in case [my parents] reacted badly." In his story dual surprises set up a metaphor of exchange, which Vince used to try to place his relationship with his parents on an egalitarian footing. At first his parents attempted to reassert their authority by defining Vince's identity for him. The turning point in the relationship and in the narrative came with Vince's realization that he no longer needed his parents' approval. It is significant that this moment of enlightenment occurred on his own territory, in the residence he had established away from his parents' home. Accepting himself as an adult and a gay man facilitated his parents' acceptance, reflecting the belief that these two processes parallel one another, and that "truths" must originate from the inner self of the person coming out.

With phrases like "how you *are*," Vince's parents finally acknowledged his gay identity to be fundamental to his selfhood. When his mother responded to the aunt who was not privy to Vince's identification, she used the term "son," reaffirming the enduring and kin character of their blood tie in a way she could not have accomplished with his proper name or a personal pronoun. The extent of her acceptance was, of course, signified by the presentation of the electric blanket—an accessory for Vince's home and more specifically his bed, a standardized location for sexual activity in the United States.

At the time of the events related in the story, Vince was single, but without dual controls the gift would not have conveyed the same message of acceptance. His mother's response to Vince's surprise on opening the package ("Eh—who knows?") plays on the mythic figure of the mother who is always urging her children to marry. In contrast to Danny Carlson and Amy Feldman, whose immediate impetus for coming out involved a bid to gain recognition for preexisting ties to lovers, Vince found himself amazed because his mother went out of her way to foster the potentiality of such a tie. Her comment placed the gift in the context of future kinship: finding a gay partner and building a relationship that melds sex with love. Though such relationships are not for everyone, Vince could hardly have done a better job of explaining how lesbian and gay sexualities can become embedded in families we create.

| # FAMILIES WE CHOOSE

Friendship is an upstart category, for it to usurp the place
of kinship or even intrude upon it is an impertinence.
—ELSIE CLEWS PARSONS

Every Thursday night in the cityscape that framed
my experience of "the field," my lover and I had dinner with Liz
Andrews. The three of us juggled work schedules, basketball practice,
and open-ended interviews around this weekly event. Occasionally
these gatherings meant candlelight dinners, but more often Thursday
found us savoring our repast in front of the TV. The first few weeks
of gourmet meals gave way to everyday fare with a special touch, like
avocado in the salad or Italian sausage in the spaghetti sauce.

Responsibility for planning, preparing, and subsidizing the meals
rotated along with their location, which alternated between Liz's
home and the apartment I shared with my lover. At only one point
did this egalitarian division of labor and resources become the subject
of conscious evaluation. Liz offered to pay a proportionately greater
share of a high-ticket meal, reasoning that she had the largest income.
In the ensuing discussion, reluctance to complicate "power dynamics"
in the group resolved the issue in favor of maintaining equal contributions.

After supper we might play cards, trade anecdotes about mutual
acquaintances, describe recent encounters with heterosexism, discuss
world politics or the opening of a new lesbian strip show, exchange
recipes, explain how we would reorganize the Forty-Niner offensive
lineup, or propose strategies for handling the rising cost of living in
San Francisco. Or we might continue watching television, taking
advantage of commercial breaks to debate that perennial enigma: "What
do heterosexual women see in Tom Selleck, anyway?" While we grew
comfortable with argument and with differences in our class back-

grounds, age, and experiences, we tended to assume a degree of mutual comprehension as white women who all identified ourselves as lesbians.

After a few months of these dinners we began to apply the terms "family" and "extended family" to one another. Our remarks found a curious counterpart in a series of comments on changes in the behavior of Liz's cat. Once an unsociable creature that took to hiding and growling from the other room when strangers invaded her realm, now she watched silently from beneath the telephone table and even ventured forth to greet her visitors. Not that she does that for everyone, Liz reminded us: clearly we were being taken into an inner circle.

In retrospect, the incipient trust and solidarity imaged in this depiction of a world viewed through cat's eyes appears as one of several elements that combined to make Thursdays feel like family occasions. The centrality of the meal—sharing food on a regular basis in a domestic setting—certainly contributed to our growing sense of relatedness. In the United States, where the household is the normative unit of routinized consumption, many family relationships are also commensal relationships. Although we occupied separate households, we interpreted the option of independent residence as a feature distinguishing gay families from straight, one that qualified "our" kind of family as a creative innovation. In truth, this contrast may have been a bit overdrawn. Moving to the same neighborhood had prompted the routinization of the weekly dinner meetings, and I personally enjoyed walking over to Liz's apartment when it was her turn to cook. These evening strolls underlined the spatial contiguity of our households while allowing me to avoid the seemingly interminable search for a parking space in San Francisco.

Efforts to encourage a low-key atmosphere framed our interactions during supper as everyday experience rather than a guest-host relationship. It was not uncommon for any one of us to leave immediately following the meal if we were tired or had other things to do. Conversation, while often lively, seldom felt obligatory. Also facilitating the developing family feeling was a sense of time depth that arose after the arrangement had endured several months, a dimension augmented by a ten-year friendship between Liz and myself.

On some occasions other people joined our core group for activities, events, and even Thursday night get-togethers. Once Liz asked two gay male friends to dinner, and another time—with somewhat more anticipation and formality—the group extended an invitation to Liz's parents. When her parents arrived a guest-host relationship prevailed, but Liz, my lover, and I became the collective hosts, preparing and serving the food and making sure that her parents were entertained. One could imagine other possible alignments: for example, Liz and her parents busy in her kitchen while my lover and I waited to be served. The differentiation of activities and space presented a graphic juxtaposition of the family Liz was creating with the family in which she had been raised. By introducing my lover and me to her parents in the context of a Thursday night meal, Liz hoped to bridge these two domains.

About the time that the three of us began to classify ourselves as family, we also began to provide one another with material assistance that went beyond cooking and cleaning up the dinner dishes. When one of us left on vacation, another volunteered to pick up the mail. After Liz injured her foot and decided to stay at her parents' house, I fed the cat. On street cleaning days Liz and my lover moved each other's vehicles. Liz offered me the use of her apartment for interviews or studying while she was at work. "Emotional support" accompanied this sort of assistance, exemplified by midweek phone calls to discuss problems that could not wait until Thursday. Our joint activities began to expand beyond the kitchen and living room, extending to the beach, the bars, political events, restaurants, a tour of Liz's workplace, and Giants games at Candlestick Park.

Faced with the task of analyzing this type of self-described family relationship among lesbians and gay men, my inclination while yet in the field was to treat it as an instance of what anthropologists in the past have termed "fictive kin." The concept of fictive kin lost credibility with the advent of symbolic anthropology and the realization that all kinship is in some sense fictional—that is, meaningfully constituted rather than "out there" in a positivist sense. Viewed in this light, genes and blood appear as symbols implicated in one culturally specific way of demarcating and calculating relationships. Under the influence of Continental philosophy, literary criticism, and an emerging critique of narrative form in ethnographic writing, anthropological monographs—like the kinship structures they delineated—came up for review as tales and constructions, inevitably value-laden and interpretive accounts (Clifford 1988; Clifford and Marcus 1986; Geertz

1973; Marcus and Fischer 1986; Rabinow 1977). Although the category "fictive kin" has fallen from grace in the social sciences, it retains intuitive validity for many people in the United States when applied to chosen families. From coverage in the popular press to child custody suits and legislative initiatives, phrases such as "pretended family relations" and "so-called family" are recurrently applied to lesbian or gay couples, parents, and families of friends.

The very concept of a substitute or surrogate family suffers from a functionalism that assumes people intrinsically *need* families (whether for psychological support or material assistance). Commentators who dispute the legitimacy of gay families typically set up a hierarchical relationship in which biogenetic ties constitute a primary domain upon which "fictive kin" relations are metaphorically predicated. Within this secondary domain, relationships are said to be "like" family, that is, similar to and probably imitative of the relations presumed to actually comprise kinship. When anthropologists have discussed the institutionalization of "going for sisters" (or brothers, or cousins) among urban blacks in the United States, for example, they have emphasized that such relationships can be "just as real" as blood ties to the persons involved (Kennedy 1980; Liebow 1967; Schneider and Smith 1978; Stack 1974). While framed as a defense of participants' perspectives, this type of argument implicitly takes blood relations as its point of departure. Insofar as analysis becomes circumscribed by the unvoiced question that asks how authentic these "fictive" relations are, it makes little difference that authenticity refers back to a privileged and apparently unified symbolic system rather than an empirically observable universe.

Theoretically I have adopted a very different approach by treating gay kinship ideologies as historical *transformations* rather than derivatives of other sorts of kinship relations. Some might contend that these emergent ideologies represent variations modeled on a more generalized "American kinship" to the extent that they utilize familiar symbols such as blood and love, but this terminology of modeling would prove misleading.[1] As Rayna Rapp has convincingly argued,

> When we assume male-headed, nuclear families to be central units of kinship, and all alternative patterns to be extensions or exceptions, we accept an aspect of cultural hegemony instead of studying it. In the process, we miss the contested domain in which

symbolic innovation may occur. Even continuity may be the result of innovation (1987:129).

Gay families do not occupy a subsidiary domain that passively reflects or imitates the primary tenets of a coherent "American kinship system." The historical construction of an ideological contrast between chosen (gay) families and blood (straight) family has not left biologistic and procreative conceptions of kinship untouched. But if coming out has supplied gay families with a specific content (the organizing principle of choice) by exposing the selective aspects of blood relations, it remains to be shown how choice became allied with kinship and gay identity to produce a discourse on families we choose.

BUILDING GAY FAMILIES

The sign at the 1987 Gay and Lesbian March on Washington read: "Love makes a family—nothing more, nothing less." From the stage, speakers arguing for domestic partner benefits and gay people's right to parent repeatedly invoked love as both the necessary *and the sufficient* criterion for defining kinship. Grounding kinship in love deemphasized distinctions between erotic and nonerotic relations while bringing friends, lovers, and children together under a single concept. As such, love offered a symbol well suited to carry the nuances of identity and unity so central to kinship in the United States, yet circumvent the procreative assumption embedded in symbols like heterosexual intercourse and blood ties.

It has become almost a truism that "family" can mean very different things when complicated (as it always is) by class, race, ethnicity, and gender (Flax 1982; Thorne with Yalom 1982). In her studies of kinship among Japanese-Americans, Sylvia Yanagisako (1978, 1985) has demonstrated how the unit used to calculate relatedness ("families" or "persons") may change, and additional meanings adhere to symbols like love, based on variable definitions of context that invoke racial or cultural identities. Determining who is a relative in a context that an individual perceives as "Japanese" may draw on different meanings and categories than determining relationship in a context defined as "American."

In speaking broadly of "gay families," my objective is not to focus on that most impoverished level of analysis, the least common denominator, or to describe symbolic contrasts in pristine seclusion from social relations. Neither do I mean to imply an absence of differences among lesbians and gay men, or that gay families are constructed in isolation from identities of gender, race, or class. Rather, I have situated chosen families in the specific context of an ideological opposition between families defined as straight and gay—families identified with biology and choice, respectively. On the one hand, this highly generalized opposition oversimplifies the complexities of kinship organization by ignoring other identities while presenting its own categories as timeless and fundamental. On the other hand, the same discourse complicates understandings of kinship in the United States by pairing categories previously believed to be at variance ("gay" and "family").

The families I saw gay men and lesbians creating in the Bay Area tended to have extremely fluid boundaries, not unlike kinship organization among sectors of the African-American, American Indian, and white working class. David Schneider and Raymond Smith (1978:42) have characterized this type of organization as one that can "create kinship ties out of relationships which are originally ties of friendship." Listen for a moment to Toni Williams' account of the people she called kin:

> In my family, all of us kids are godparents to each others' kids, okay? So we're very connected that way. But when I go to have a kid, I'm not gonna have my sisters as godparents. I'm gonna have people that are around me, that are gay. That are straight. I don't have that many straight friends, but certainly I would integrate them in my life. They would help me. They would babysit my child, or . . . like my kitty, I'm not calling up my family and saying, "Hey, Mom, can you watch my cat?" No, I call on my inner family—my community, or whatever—to help me with my life.
>
> So there's definitely a family. And you're building it; it keeps getting bigger and bigger. Next thing you know, you have hundreds of people as your family. Me personally, I might not have a hundred, because I'm more of a loner. I don't have a lot of friends, nor do I *want* that many friends, either. But I see [my lover] as having many, many family members involved in what's going on.

What Toni portrayed was an ego-centered calculus of relations that pictured family members as a cluster surrounding a single individual, rather than taking couples or groups as units of affiliation. This meant that even the most nuclear of couples would construct theoretically distinguishable families, although an area of overlapping membership generally developed. At the same time, chosen families were not restricted to person-to-person ties. Individuals occasionally added entire groups with preexisting, multiplex connections among members. In one such case, a woman reported incorporating a "circle" of her new lover's gay family into her own kinship universe.

In the Bay Area, families we choose resembled networks in the sense that they could cross household lines, and both were based on ties that radiated outward from individuals like spokes on a wheel. However, gay families differed from networks to the extent that they quite consciously incorporated symbolic demonstrations of love, shared history, material or emotional assistance, and other signs of enduring solidarity. Although many gay families included friends, not just any friend would do.[2]

Fluid boundaries and varied membership meant no neatly replicable units, no defined cycles of expansion and contraction, no patterns of dispersal. What might have represented a nightmare to an anthropologist in search of mappable family structures appeared to most participants in a highly positive light as the product of unfettered creativity. The subjective agency implicit in gay kinship surfaced in the very labels developed to describe it: "families *we* choose," "families *we* create." In the language of significant others, significance rested in the eye of the beholder. Participants tended to depict their chosen families as thoroughly individualistic affairs, insofar as each and every ego was left to be the chooser. Paradoxically, the very notion of idiosyncratic choice—originally conceived in opposition to biogenetic givens—lent structural coherence to what people presented as unique renditions of family.

The variety in the composition of families we choose was readily apparent. At the MCC service described in chapter 2, when the time came for communion, the pastor invited congregants to bring along family members. In groups and in couples, with heads bowed and arms linked, people walking to the front of the church displayed ties of kinship and friendship for all to see. On a different occasion, I joined several people preparing for a birthday party in someone's home. When I asked what, if anything, separated those who came early to help decorate from those who arrived after the time officially set for festivities to begin, the host explained that the helpers were family, closer to her than most of the other guests.

Obituaries provide a relatively overlooked, if somber, source of information about notions of kinship. Death notices in the *Bay Area Reporter* (a weekly newspaper distributed in bars and other gay establishments) were sometimes written by lovers, and included references to friends, former lovers, blood or adoptive relatives (usually denominated as "father," "sister," etc.), "community members" present at a death or assisting during an illness, and occasionally coworkers. While I was conducting fieldwork, the *San Francisco Chronicle*, a major citywide daily, instituted a policy of refusing to list gay lovers as survivors, citing complaints from relatives who could lay claim to genealogical or adoptive ties to the deceased. Although the *Chronicle*'s decision denied recognition to gay families, it also testified to the growing impact of a discourse that refused to cede kinship to relations organized through procreation.

By opening the door to the creation of families different in kind and composition, choice assigned kinship to the realm of free will and inclination. In the tradition of Thoreau's *Walden*, each gay man and lesbian became responsible for the exemplary act of creating an ideal environment (cf. Couser 1979). People often presented gay families as a foray into uncharted territory, where the lack of cultural guideposts to mark the journey engendered fear and exhilaration.[3] Indeed, there was a utopian cast to the way many lesbians and gay men talked about the families they were fashioning. Jennifer Bauman maintained that as a gay person, "you're already on the edge, so you've got more room to be whatever you want to be. And to create. There's more space on the edge." What to do with all that "space"? "I create my own traditions," she replied.

"Choice" is an individualistic and, if you will, bourgeois notion that focuses on the subjective power of an "I" to formulate relationships to people and things, untrammeled by worldly constraints. Yet as Karl Marx (1963:15) pointed out in an often quoted passage from *The 18th Brumaire*, "Men [sic] make their own history, but they do not make it just as they please; they do not make it under circumstances chosen by themselves, but under circumstances directly encountered, given and transmitted from the past." Only after coming out to blood relatives emerged as a historical possibility could the element of selection in kinship become isolated in gay experience and subsequently elevated to a constitutive feature of gay families.

Despite the ideological characterization of gay families as freely chosen, in practice the particular choices made yielded families that were far from randomly selected, much less demographically representative. When I asked people who said they had gay families to list the individuals they included under that rubric, their lists were primarily, though not exclusively, composed of other lesbians and gay men. Not surprisingly, the majority of people listed tended to come from the same gender, class, race, and age cohort as the respondent.

Both men and women consistently counted lovers as family, often placing their partners at the head of a list of relatives. A few believed a lover, or a lover plus children, would be essential in order to have gay family, but the vast majority felt that all gay men and lesbians, including those who are single, can create families of their own. The partner of someone already considered family might or might not be included as kin. "Yeah, they're part of the family, but they're like in-laws," laughed one man. "You know, you love them, and yet there isn't that same closeness."

Former lovers presented a particularly interesting case. Their inclusion in families we choose was far from automatic, but most people hoped to stay connected to ex-lovers as friends and family (cf. Becker 1988; Clunis and Green 1988).[4] When former lovers remained estranged, the surprise voiced by friends underscored the power of this ideal. "It's been ten years since you two broke up!" one man exclaimed to another. "Hasn't he gotten over it yet?" Of course, when a breakup involved hard feelings or a property dispute, such continuity was not always realizable. After an initial period of separation, many ex-lovers did in fact reestablish contact, while others continued to strive for this type of reintegration. As Diane Kunin put it, "After you break up, a lot of people sort of become as if they were parents and sisters, and relate to your new lover as if *they* were the in-law." I also learned of several men who had renewed ties after a former lover developed AIDS or ARC (AIDS-Related Complex). This emphasis on making a transition from lover to friend while remaining within the bounds of gay families contrasted with heterosexual partners in the Bay Area, for whom separation or divorce often meant permanent rupture of a kinship tie.

Jo-Ann Krestan and Claudia Bepko (1980:285) have criticized lesbians' efforts to maintain relationships with former lovers as "triangling" (a no-no in therapeutic circles). They argue that such relationships "tend to be intrusive and involve inappropriate claims." But notions of appropriateness are culturally constituted and contested. What a person expects from an "ex" may not be what they expect from a friend who is also family. In the context of gay kinship, former lovers can be both.

A lover's biological or adoptive relatives might or might not be classified as kin, contingent upon their "rejecting" or "accepting" attitudes. Gina Pellegrini, for example, found refuge at a lover's house after her parents kicked her out of her own home as an adolescent. She was out to her lover's mother before her own parents, and still considered this woman family. Jorge Quintana claimed that his mother adored his ex-lover and vice versa, although Jorge had broken up with this man many years earlier. After years of listening to her father attack homosexuality, remembered Roberta Osabe, "My girlfriend Debi and my father shot pool together. And she whipped his ass! . . . That was his way, I think, of trying to make amends." Jerry Freitag and his partner Kurt had made a point of introducing their parents to one another. "My mother and his mother talk on the phone every once in a while and write letters and stuff. Like my grandmother just died. Kurt's mother was one of the first people to call my mom." For Charlyne Harris, however, calling her ex-lover's mother "family" would have been out of the question. "Her mother didn't like me. Number one, she didn't want her to be *in* a lesbian relationship; number two, she knew that I was black. So I didn't have a lot of good things to say about her mother. . . . Pam told me, 'She can't even say your name!' "

In addition to friendships and relationships with lovers or ex-lovers, chosen family might also embrace ties to children or people who shared a residence.[5] *Gay Community News* published a series of letters from gay male prisoners who had united to form "the Del-Ray Family" (only to be separated by the warden). Back in San Francisco, Rose Ellis told me about the apartment she had shared with several friends. One woman in particular, she said, was "like a big sister to me." When this woman died of cancer, the household split up, and "that kind of broke the family thing." In other circumstances, however, hardship drew people together across household lines. Groups organized to assist individuals who were chronically or terminally ill often incorporated love and persisted through time, characteristics some participants took as signs of kinship. Occasionally a person could catch a glimpse of potential family relationships in the making. When I met Harold Sanders he was making plans to live with someone to prepare for the possibility that he might require physical assistance as he moved into his seventies. Harold explained that he would rather choose that person in advance than be forced to settle for "just anyone" in an emergency.

The relative absence of institutionalization or rituals associated with these emergent gay families sometimes raised problems of definition and mutuality: I may count you as a member of my family, but do you number me in yours? In this context offers of assistance, commitment to "working through" conflicts, and a common history measured by months or years, all became confirming signs of kinship. By symbolically testifying to the presence of intangibles such as solidarity and love, these demonstrations operated to persuade and to concretize, to move a relationship toward reciprocity while seeking recognition for a kin tie.

Like their heterosexual counterparts, most gay men and lesbians insisted that family members are people who are "there for you," people you can count on emotionally and materially. "They take care of me," said one man, "I take care of them." According to Rayna Rapp (1982) the "middle class" in the United States tends to share affective support but not material resources within friendships. In the Bay Area, however, lesbians and gay men from all classes and class backgrounds, regularly rendered both sorts of assistance to one another. Many considered this an important way of demarcating friend from family. Diane Kunin, a writer, described family as people who will care for you when you're sick, get you out of jail, help you fix a flat tire, or drive you to the airport. Edith Motzko, who worked as a carpenter, said of a woman she had known ten years, "There's nothing in the world that [she] would ask of me that I wouldn't do for her." Louise Romero joked that a gay friend "only calls me when he wants something: he wants to borrow the truck 'cause he's moving. So I guess that's family!"

Overall, the interface between property relations and kinship relations among lesbians and gay men who called one another family seemed consistent with such relations elsewhere in the society, with the exception of a somewhat greater expectation for financial independence and self-sufficiency on the part of each member of a couple. Individuals distributed their own earnings and resources; where pooling occurred, it usually involved an agreement with a lover or a limited common fund with housemates. Some households divided bills evenly, while others negotiated splits proportionate to income. A person might support a lover for a period of time, but this was not the rule for either men or women. Putting a partner through school or taking time off from wage work for childrearing represented the type of short-term arrangements most commonly associated with substantial financial support.

Across household lines, material aid was less likely to take the form of direct monetary contributions, unless a dependent child was involved. Services exchanged between members of different households who considered themselves kin included everything from walking a dog to preparing meals, running errands, and fixing cars. Lending tools, supplies, videotapes, clothes, books, and almost anything else imaginable was commonplace in some relationships. Many people had extended loans to gay or straight kin at some time. Some had given money to relatives confronted with the high cost of medical care in the United States, and a few from working-class backgrounds reported contributing to the support of biological or adoptive relatives (either their own or a lover's).

Another frequently cited criterion for separating "just plain" friends from friends who were also family was a shared past. In this case, the years a relationship had persisted could become a measure of closeness, reflecting the presumption that common experiences would lead to common understandings. Jenny Chin explained it this way:

> I have, not blood family, but other kind of family. And I think it really takes a lot to get to that point. Like years. Like five years, ten years, or whatever. I think that we're gonna have to do that to survive. That's just a fact of life. Because the whole fact of being gay, you're estranged from your own family. At a certain level, pretty basic level. Unless you're lucky. There are some exceptions.
>
> So to survive, you have to have support networks and all that kind of stuff. And if you're settled enough, I think you do get into a . . . those people become family. If you kind of settle in

together. And your work, and your lives, and your house, and your kids or whatever become very intertwined.

While people sometimes depicted the creation of ties to chosen kin as a search for relationships that could carry the burden of family, there are many conceivable ways to move furniture, solicit advice, reminisce, share affection, or find babysitters for your children. All can be accomplished by calling on relationships understood to be something other than family, or by purchasing services if a person has the necessary funds. But allied to the emphasis on survival in Jenny's account was the notion of a cooperative history that emerged as she bent her litany of years to the task of establishing rather than assuming a solidarity that endures.

Relationships that had weathered conflict, like relationships sustained over miles but especially over time, also testified to attachment. Allusions to disagreements, quarrels, and annoyance were often accompanied by laughter. Charlyne Harris named five lesbians she counted as kin "because if they don't see me within a certain amount of time [they check up on me], and they're always in my business! Sometimes they get mad, too. They're like sisters. I know they care a lot." Another woman chuckled, "I never see these family, so you can tell they're family!" Still others mentioned, as a sign of kinship, hearing from people only when they wanted something. Through reversal and inversion, an ironic humor underscored meanings of intimacy and solidarity carried by the notion of family in the United States (cf. Pratt 1977).

In descriptions of gay families, sentiment and emotion often appeared alongside material aid, conflict resolution, and the narrative encapsulation of a shared past. "Why do you call certain people family?" I asked Frank Maldonado. "Well," he responded,

Some of my friends I've known for fifteen years. You get attached. You stay in one place long enough, you go through seasons and years together, it's like they're part of you, you're part of them. You have fights, you get over them. . . . It's just unconditional love coming through to people that you didn't grow up with.

Though imaged here as the sole defining feature of kinship, love represents as much the product as the symbolic foundation of gay families. Closely associated with the experience of love were the practices through which people established and confirmed mutual, enduring solidarity.

SUBSTITUTE FOR BIOLOGICAL FAMILY?

Far from viewing families we choose as imitations or derivatives of family ties created elsewhere in their society, many lesbians and gay men alluded to the difficulty and excitement of constructing kinship in the *absence* of what they called "models." Others, however, echoed the viewpoint—popular in this society at large—that chosen families offer substitutes for blood ties lost through outright rejection or the distance introduced into relationships by remaining in the closet.[6] "There will always be an empty place where the blood family should be," one man told me. "But Tim and I fill for each other some of the emptiness of blood family that aren't there." In Louise Romero's opinion,

> A lot of lesbians . . . I think they're just looking for stuff— maybe the same stuff I am. Like my family ties, before coming out, there was a lot of closeness. I could share stuff with my sisters. You used to talk all your deep dark secrets. You can't any more 'cause they think you're weird. Which is true in my case— they really do. . . . I think a lot of women look for that, and you need that.

This theory has a certain appeal, not only because it speaks to the strong impact of coming out on lesbian and gay notions of kinship, but also because it is consistent with the elaboration of chosen families in conceptual opposition to biological family. On a practical level, most of the services that chosen kin provide for one another might otherwise be performed by relatives calculated according to blood, adoption, or marriage.

Although gay families are families a person creates in adult life, this theory portrays them primarily as *replacements* for, rather than chronological successors to, the families in which individuals came to adulthood. If chosen families simply represent some form of compensation for rejection by heterosexual relatives, however, gay families should logically focus on the establishment of intergenerational relationships. (Remember that the loss of parents, as opposed to other categories of relatives, was the main concern in deciding whether or not to reveal a gay or lesbian identity to straight family.) But when lesbians and gay men in the Bay Area applied kinship terminology to their chosen families, they usually placed themselves in the relationship of sisters and brothers to one another, regardless of their respective ages. In cases where gay families included children, adults who were chosen kin but not coparents to a child sometimes characterized themselves as aunts or uncles.

As with any generalization, this one admits exceptions. Margie Jamison, active in organizing a Christian ministry to lesbians and gay men, described her work with PWAs (persons with AIDS) while tears streamed down her face. "When I have held them in my arms and they were dying, it's like my sons. Like my sons." In this case the intergenerational kinship terminology invoked Margie's pastoral role as well as her experience raising two sons from a previous heterosexual marriage. However, the characterization of most ties to chosen kin as peer relationships brings families we choose closer to so-called "fictive kin" relations found elsewhere in the United States than to even a moderately faithful reconstruction of the families in which lesbian- and gay-identified individuals grew up.

Equally significant, the minority of gay people who had been disowned were not the only ones who participated in the elaboration of gay kinship. Many who classified relations with their biological or adoptive relatives as cordial to excellent employed the opposition between gay and straight family. Among those whose relations with their straight families had gradually improved over the years, ties to chosen kin generally had not diminished in importance. If laying claim to a gay family in no way depends upon a break with one's family of origin, the theory of chosen family as a surrogate for kinship lost dissolves. A satisfactory explanation for the historical emergence of gay families requires an understanding of the changing relation of friendship to sexual identity among the large numbers of gay people who flocked to urban areas after the Second World War.

FRIENDS AND LOVERS

"That's the way one builds a good life: a set of friends." At 64, Harold Sanders had no hesitation about indulging his passion for aphorisms, the turn of phrase stretched backward to gather in experiences of a lifetime. His statement reflected a conviction very widely shared by lesbians and gay men of all ages. People from diverse backgrounds depicted themselves as the beneficiaries of better friendships than heterosexuals, or made a case for the greater significance and respect they believed gay people accord to friendship.[7] Most likely such comments reflected a mixture of observation and self-congratulation, but they also drew attention to the connection many lesbians and gay men made between friendship and sexual identity (as well as race or ethnicity). The same individuals tended to portray heterosexuals as people who place family and friends in an exclusive, even antagonistic, relationship. As a child growing up in a Chinese-American family, said Jenny Chin,

> I had a lot drilled into me about your friends are just your friends. *Just* friends. Very minimalizing and discounting [of] friendships. Because family was supposed to be all-important. Everything was done to preserve the family unit. Even if people were killing each other; even if people had twenty-year-old grudges and hadn't spoken.

In contrast, discussions of gay families pictured kinship as an *extension* of friendship, rather than viewing the two as competitors or assimilating friendships to biogenetic relationships regarded as somehow more fundamental. It was not unusual for a gay man or lesbian to speak of another as family in one breath and friend in the next. Yet the solidarity implicit in such statements has not always been a taken-for-granted feature of gay lives. According to John D'Emilio (1983b), recognition of the possibility of establishing nonerotic ties among homosexuals constituted a key historical development that paved the way for the emergence of lesbian and gay "community"—and, I might add, for the later appearance of the ideological opposition between biological family and families we choose.

When Harold Sanders was coming out in the 1930s, particularly in the white and relatively wealthy circles where he traveled, same-sex ties were experiencing a historical devaluation that coincided with a new affirmation of eroticism in relations between women and men embodied in the ideal of companionate marriage. Strong bonds between persons of the same sex became something best left behind with childhood (Pleck and Pleck 1980). By 1982 Lillian Rubin found that two-thirds of the single men in her sample of 200 could not name a best friend. While the disparagement of same-sex ties may have had a greater impact on men than women, all same-sex relationships became subjected to a higher degree of scrutiny. Today many heterosexuals in the United States are quick to judge certain friendships as "too intense," taking intensity as a sign of homosexuality.[8] According to Lourdes Alcantara, who was born in Peru during the 1950s, such associations are no longer confined to North America.

> I read an article in the newspaper, and they present two women hugging like friends in the street. Latin friends, right? And I was in love with this woman. We were lovers. And I was in her house. So I brought the Sunday newspaper to her house, and I took that page out, so her mother didn't see that. And then we were so hot, reading that. But the distortion! They put us like sick people. So to be a lesbian, the description was terrible! Even my girlfriend got upset. She said, "We better be friends, just friends, and get married." And we were eleven years old, nine years old! God! *Qué* terrible! Can you believe that?

In the United States during the twentieth century, sibling ties and friendship have offered some of the few cultural categories available for making sense of powerful feelings toward a person of the same sex. During high school, Peter Ouillette had what he later identified as a "crush" on another boy. "Absolutely under no circumstances would I think about sex," he said. "It was friendship. But *real close* friendship, that's the way I thought of it. Almost like brothers." Philip Korte remembered thinking, "Wouldn't it be nice to have a big brother. Or wouldn't it be nice to just have a best friend that I could be affectionate with and spend a lot of time with, companionship, those kinds of things. Now I recognize that as gay. But, at the time, what I knew of gay, that didn't fit at all." What did not seem to fit were his fantasies of love and caring for another man, since homosexuality then appeared to him as a matter of sex and sex alone.

Given this alliance between the language of kinship and the language of friendship, which Jonathan Katz (1976) dates to the nineteenth century, one might expect to uncover a direct link between the early interchangeability of these terms and contemporary discourse on gay families. However, historical evidence and day-to-day observation suggest otherwise. By mid-century coming out as a lesbian or gay man entailed learning to discriminate between feelings of erotic and nonerotic love, drawing meaningful contrasts between sexual attraction and friendship. A person could then theoretically sort relationships into two groups: "just friends" (not sexually involved) and "more than friends" (lovers). One day while sitting in a coffeeshop, for example, I overheard a woman in the next booth tell the woman sitting across from her that she was "only" interested in a friendship, since she already had a lover. Coming-out narratives invoke this distinction when they establish a double time frame, the "before" and "after" of coming out, effectively reinterpreting relationships previously described with the terminology of blood ties as having been "really" erotic all along.

The years following World War II—a watershed period for many groups in the United States—witnessed an unprecedented elaboration of nonerotic solidarities among homosexuals (Bérubé 1989; D'Emilio 1983a, 1983b, 1989b). During the 1950s and 1960s, gay men adapted kinship terminology to the task of distinguishing sexual from nonsexual relationships.[9] At that time the rhetoric of brothers, sisters, and friends applied primarily to nonerotic relationships. In the film version of *The Boys in the Band*, one character quips, "If they're not lovers, they're sisters." This camp usage of "sister" among gay men coexisted with the institutionalization of mentor relationships in which older men introduced younger men to "the life." Normatively, mentor relationships were intergenerational and emphatically nonsexual. Bob Korkowski, who flouted convention by having sex with his mentor, described the experience as "weird, because a mentor is kind of like a father. [It was] like sleeping with your father." This reservation of kinship terminology for nonsexual relations represents a very different usage from its subsequent deployment to construct gay families that could include both lovers and friends.

The contrast between the sexual and the nonsexual was drawn only to be blurred in later years after the possibility of nonerotic ties among gay people became firmly established. By the 1970s both gay men and lesbians had begun to picture friends and lovers as two ends of a single continuum rather than as oppositional categories. "We women been waiting all our lives for our sisters to be our lovers," announced the lyrics of the song *Gay and Proud* (Lempke 1977). The contribution of lesbian-feminism toward codifying this notion of a continuum is evident in Adrienne Rich's (1980) work on "compulsory heterosexuality." Carroll Smith-Rosenberg's (1975) classic article on relations between women in the nineteenth-century United States was also widely read in women's studies classes and cited to buttress the contention that sexual and sisterly relations were semantically separable but overlapping in practice—with little regard for efforts to distinguish precisely these relationships during the intervening decades.

The realignment that linked erotic to noneroteric relations through the device of a continuum was not confined to political activists. As San Francisco moved into the 1980s, "friend" seemed to be overtaking "roommate" in popularity as a euphemistic reference to a lover in situations where lesbians and gay men elected not to reveal their sexual identities. Victoria Vetere's 1982 study of lesbian interpretations of the concepts "lover" and "friend," though based on a small sample, found that most lesbians were uncomfortable with any suggestion of a dichotomy between the two terms. A similar continuity was implicit in coming-out stories narrated by women who had first claimed a lesbian identity during the 1970s. One said coming out was epitomized for her by the realization that "oh, wow, then I get to keep all my girlfriends!" Elaine Scavone explained with a laugh, "All of a sudden I felt I could be myself. I could be the way I really want to be with women: I could touch them, I could make friends, I could make my girlfriends and I could go home and kiss them." Although women were sometimes said to be more likely to come out by falling in love with a friend and men through an encounter instrumentally focused on sex, both men and women featured early attractions to friends in their coming-out stories.

The category of mentor, which epitomized one type of nonsexual relationship between gay men, appeared to be losing rather than gaining currency during the same period. In the few cases when the term came up in casual conversation during my fieldwork, its meaning seemed to be changing. One man in his early thirties described himself as a mentor to his *lover*, based on his claim to have been out longer and to know more about what he called "the gay world." Such a statement would have been a *non sequitur* not so many years ago.

Given that any continuum is defined by its poles, these changes did not represent a complete collapse of the categories "lover" and "friend" into one another. The phrases "just friends" and "more than friends" remained in common usage to indicate whether two people had incorporated sex into their relationship. A certain unidirectionality also characterized the enterprise of melding sex and friendship. While a lover ideally should become a friend, many believed that sex could ruin a preexisting friendship. People who were single seemed as wont as ever to invoke the old gay adage that friends last, while lovers are simply "passing through."

In a 1956 study (reprinted in 1967) Maurice Leznoff and William Westley found that most gay men looked to friends, not lovers, for security in old age. Yet the dictum that friends rather than lovers endure took on a different cast for a later generation that believed lovers should not only double as friends, but continue as friends and kin following a breakup. New contexts can engender novel interpretations of received wisdom.

In retrospect, this shift from contrast to continuum laid the ground for the rise of a family-centered discourse that bridged the erotic and the nonerotic, bringing lovers together with friends under a single construct. But the historical development of friendship ties among persons whose shared "sexual" identity was initially defined solely through their sexuality turned out to be merely an introductory episode in a more lengthy tale of community formation.

FROM FRIENDSHIP TO COMMUNITY

Among lesbians and gay men the term "community" (like coming out) has become as multifaceted in meaning as it is ubiquitous. In context, community can refer to the historical appearance of gay institutions, the totality of self-defined lesbians and gay men, or unity and harmony predicated upon a common sexual identity. Older gay people generally considered the term an anachronism when applied to the period before the late 1960s, since "community" came into popular usage only with the rise of a gay movement.[10]

Often contrasted with "isolation," community subsumed one of the earlier senses of coming out: making a public debut at a gay bar. The area of overlap involved locating other gay people, a project that can remain surprisingly difficult in an era when homosexuality makes headline news. Toni Williams, who had grown up in a large metropolitan area and begun identifying as a lesbian only a few years before I interviewed her, insisted, "I didn't think that there was *nobody* that was going to be like me. But I didn't know *where* to search for that person. I didn't think that there was a community."

Finding community, as one man very eloquently put it, meant

discovering "that your story isn't the only one in the world." Such a discovery need not entail meeting other gay people, but rather becoming convinced of their existence. Sean O'Brien, originally from New York City, used to listen to a weekly gay radio show, "a voice coming through a box once a week," which he said helped him "understand myself as part of a community, even though I was not connected with that community." During the 1970s the concept of community came to embody practical wisdom emerging from the bars, friendship networks, and a spate of new gay organizations: the knowledge that lesbians and gay men, joining together on the basis of a sexual identity, could create enduring social ties. In the process, sexuality was reconstituted as a ground of common experience rather than a quintessentially personal domain.

From its inception, activists pressed the community concept into the service of an identity politics that cast gays in the part of an ethnic minority and a subculture.[11] Lesbians and gay men represent a constant 10 percent of the population, they contended, a veritable multitude prepared to claim its own distinct history, culture, and institutions. The basis for these arguments was, of course, laid earlier with the recognition that homosexuals could unite through bonds of friendship as well as sex, and elaborated through analogies with identity-based movements organized along racial lines.[12] Many social scientists of the period subscribed to a similar paradigm in their studies of "the gay world."[13] Whether describing an aggregate of persons in ongoing interaction (Evelyn Hooker) or a "continuing collectivity" of individuals with common interests and activities (William Simon and John Gagnon), they tended to treat homosexuals as a fairly homogeneous group with concrete, if not readily ascertainable, boundaries. More recently Stephen Murray (1979) has used sociological criteria to argue for the validity of applying the community concept to gay men in urban areas of the U.S. and Canada, dubbing them a "quasi-ethnic community."[14]

Deborah Wolf's (1979) ethnography of lesbians (actually lesbian-feminists) in the Bay Area falls prey to many of the same traps that have ensnared other investigators who treat lesbians and/or gay men as members of an integrated subculture. Most studies that set out to explore a "gay world" or "gay lifestyle" not only situate their subjects in a historical vacuum, but assume an amazingly uncomplicated relationship between claiming an identity and feeling a sense of belonging or community. With their presumptions of harmonious solidarity and their reduction of varied experience to a single worldview, such approaches have proven far from satisfactory.

Yet the shortcomings of previous research offer no reason to reject the community concept altogether, as Kenneth Read (1980) does in his study of patrons in a gay bar on the West Coast. It is important to understand how gay men and lesbians came to use a category that over time has served as everything from a rallying cry for political unity, to a demographic indicator, to a symbol for a small sector of wealthy white men set apart from the majority of people who call themselves lesbian or gay. Viewed in cultural and historical context, the so-called minority model appears as part of a series of historical struggles to define and dispute the boundaries of communities based on sexual identity, struggles that in turn paved the way for a discourse on gay families. Gay community can best be understood not as a unified subculture, but rather as a category implicated in the ways lesbians and gay men have developed collective identities, organized urban space, and conceptualized their significant relationships.

My interpretation of community departs in several key respects from the long tradition of community studies in the United States (see Hillery 1955). Conrad Arensberg (1954), for example, treats community primarily as a setting in which to conduct sociology, whereas gay communities are only roughly defined spatially and rest on variable interpretations of identity. In the hands of W. Lloyd Warner (1963), community becomes a microcosm of society at large, yet lesbians and gay men have contested and transformed hegemonic understandings of kinship and sexuality. My approach perhaps comes closest to Robert Lynd's and Helen Lynd's (1937) depiction of community as a vantage point from which to view historical events (in their case, the Great Depression), but again I am not concerned with a bounded entity or with community as locale. To comprehend the historical ascendance of a family-centered discourse among lesbians and gay men, my analysis focuses on social movements, and on the meanings of togetherness and identity that have shaped community as a cultural category defined in opposition to equally cultural notions of individualism and selfhood (Varenne 1977).

Although lesbian and gay communities cannot be reduced to a territorial definition, this has not prevented San Francisco from becoming a geographical symbol of homosexuality, renowned here and abroad as the "gay capital" of the United States. With the gay movement came the consolidation of "gay ghettos," neighborhoods featuring a variety of gay-owned businesses and residential concentrations' of gay men (Castells 1983). "At some points I have thought, 'Oh, my life is too gay.' I work in a gay environment, I live in a gay neighborhood, most of my friends are gay," remarked Stephen Richter, who rented an apartment in the Castro district. "But I don't know, you go out in the straight world and you can't wait to get home!" Ronnie Walker agreed: "For all the dishing that people do about Castro Street, whenever I go away to middle America, I'm always glad to kneel down and kiss the earth when I get to Castro Street." Others who lived in outlying areas traveled to gay neighborhoods for the express purpose of "feeling the community." Neighborhood had become another marker of the contrast between gay and straight, signifier of belonging, "home," and things held in common.

During the 1980s gay areas of San Francisco did not escape the restructuring of the urban landscape taking place in cities across the United States.[15] On Castro and Polk Streets, many small gay businesses gave way to banks, chain stores, and franchises. Residents fought extension of the downtown financial district into the South of Market region. Even under these economic pressures, however, gay neighborhoods retained enough of their character to contribute materially to the formation of gay identity by offering a place to meet and forge ties to other gay people.

Because gay neighborhoods in San Francisco have been formed and populated principally by men, many lesbians looked to the Bay Area at large as a place to make such connections. John D'Emilio (1989b) has pointed out the link between male control of public space and the greater public visibility of gay male (as opposed to lesbian) institutions in the United States. Economic factors are also involved, since rental or ownership in the Bay Area can be prohibitive, and women in general receive lower incomes than men. By the mid-1980s, however, lesbian institutions and residential concentrations had begun to appear in the less expensive Mission and Bernal Heights districts.

"In terms of meeting people," said Sharon Vitrano,

I feel a bit controlled by [being a lesbian], in that I'd like to at least have the option of living in a small town. One of the reasons that I came out here was that I felt I could meet lesbians in a context that was "normal." Where I could go about my business and meet people that way. I don't like having to hang out with a group of people just because they're gay.

Sharon's juxtaposition of small towns with life in the metropolis echoed the folk wisdom that gay men and lesbians are better off relocating in a big city where they can find others "like" themselves. Almost paradoxically, many people described the urban community they had hoped to discover in terms that incorporated mythical notions of the rural "America" of a bygone era. Expectations of homogeneity based on a common sexual identification lent credence to bids for political power, while depictions of lesbian and gay community as a club or secret society composed of "people who know people" invoked the face-to-face relationships supposed to typify small-town life.

Nonterritorial understandings of community that rest on a sense of belonging with one's "own kind" have numerous antecedents in the United States; those most relevant to a gay context include such unlikely compatriots as religion and the tavern. Long before the first gay activists portrayed lesbians and gay men as sisters and brothers, the Puritans elaborated a notion of brotherhood based on the leveling effect of original sin (Bercovitch 1978; Burke 1941). A concept of "beloved community" ushered in the Civil Rights struggle so instrumental to the emergence of later social movements (Evans 1979). On the secular side, community has been symbolically linked to bars, saloons, and neighborhood in the United States since the massive urban immigrations of the late nineteenth century (Kingsdale 1980). During that period, the saloon became a locus for the formation of same-sex (in this case male) solidarity and a proxy for small-town paradise lost. Although lesbians and gay men are now as likely to "find community" through a softball team, a coming-out support group, or the Gay Pride Parade as through a bar, bars remain a central symbol of identity, and almost everyone has a story about a first visit to a gay club (see Achilles 1967).

Among political activists and the bar crowd alike, the notion of community voiced during the 1970s resembled nothing so much as a Jeffersonian version of Victor Turner's (1969) *communitas:* an alternative, nonhierarchical, and undifferentiated experience of harmony and mutuality.[16] Founded on the premise of a shared sexual identity, gay community remained, like friendship, an egalitarian and fundamentally nonerotic concept.

In extending homosexuality beyond the sexual, the notion of identity-based community opened new possibilities for using kinship terminology to imagine lesbians and gay men as members of a unified totality.[17] Identity provided the linking concept that lent power to analogies between gay and consanguineal relations. Wasn't this what families in the United States were all about: identity and likeness mediated by the symbolism of blood ties?

Yet the application of kinship terminology to gay community differed from the subsequent discourse on gay families in that it described *all* lesbians and gay men as kin: no "choice" determined familial relationships. To claim a lesbian or gay identity was sufficient to claim kinship to any and every other gay person. Some people hoped community would replace alienated biological ties (Altman 1979), appealing not to chosen families but to the collectivity: "If I could gain acceptance in the community of lesbians, I would have, I hoped, the loving family I missed" (Larkin 1976:84).[18] In gay bars across the nation, this was the era of circle dances to the popular music hit, *We Are Family* (Rodgers and Edwards 1979).

While the use of kinship terminology to indicate community membership has fallen into disfavor as the politics of identity have given way to the politics of difference, people still employed it from time to time as a way of hinting at sexual identity. "Don't worry, he's one of the brethren," explained a man I was meeting for lunch when his housemate walked into the room. On another occasion, a woman told me to expect a relatively smooth job interview because the person I would be seeing was "a sister." Marta Rosales, who worked at a hospital, reported one of the nurses asking if a new staff member was "family," and another woman remembered the back door of an East Bay bar being fondly termed the "family entrance." In 1985 a blood drive for persons with AIDS incorporated a unique play on biogenetic notions of kinship and the materialization of identity as shared substance. Leaflets bearing the headline "Our Boys Need Blood" called on lesbians as "blood sisters" to help "our brothers" in a time of need. By all accounts the drive was a great success, and soon became a model for similar events (with similarly styled publicity) across the country.

Tales of "coming home" into community are structured much like the scenes in Victorian novels that depict the recognition of concealed kinship. As metaphor, "home" merges the meanings of coming out and living in a place with a large lesbian and gay population (cf. Dank 1971:189).

> [Coming out] was like coming home. I can't explain it. It felt so right. It really felt so right. It was like, you know, keeping your eyes shut and looking around a floor full of shoes and when you put your foot into your shoe you know it fits. You don't have to see it, you just know it.

Portrayals of fitting and belonging became a conventional element in coming-out stories with reference to which individuals either equated or distinguished their experiences.

> I've heard of people's experience, like moving from different parts of the country, moving here, and just like going into a women's bar and feeling, oh, wonderful. They've finally found their home, or something like that. The experience that I wanted, but I just haven't had. . . . I don't feel like I've come home or anything or that I belong here.

Identity and community, so often taken to define the limits of lesbian and gay experience, have become polarized in ways that presuppose culturally specific values of individualism. In the United States, tensions between notions of personhood and collectivity date back to Tocqueville's warnings about a tyranny of the majority. The paradigm that casts lesbians and gay men in the part of a minority (or subculture) interposes community between "the individual" and "society." In this context, it becomes relatively easy to move from a view of community as a comfortable home or unified interest group to a picture of community as a mini-enforcer, mediator of all the conformity and oppression attributed to Society with a capital "S."

By the late 1970s, signs of disenchantment with the unity implicit in the concept of community began to appear: a popular critique of the look-alike styles of "Castro clones"; a resurgence of butch/fem relations among lesbians that flew in the face of feminist prescriptions for androgyny; and a heated debate about sadomasochism (s/m), pedophilia, and other marginalized sexualities. Though some dissenters insisted upon their right to be included in the larger collectivity of lesbians and gay men, others did not experience themselves as community members, much less as agents in community formation. "I was just me, in a gay world," explained Kevin Jones.

During the same period, lesbians and gays of color critiqued the simplistic assumption that mutual understanding would flow from a shared identity. Along with Jewish lesbians and gay men, they drew attention to the racism and anti-Semitism pervading gay communities, and exposed the illusory character of any quest for an encompassing commonality in the face of the crosscutting allegiances produced by an identity politics. Predictably, this recognition of differences, while important and overdue, tended to undermine meanings of harmony and equality carried by "community." Accompanying the positive explorations of what it meant to be black and gay or lesbian and Latina was widespread disillusionment with the failure to attain the unity implicit in the ideal of *communitas*.

DELIBERATING DIFFERENCE

By the 1980s the rhetoric of brotherhood and sisterhood had begun to seem dated and trite. Sherry McCoy and Maureen Hicks (1979:66), attempting to grapple with "disappointment" and "unrealistic demands" among lesbian-feminists, wrote, "The concept of 'sisterhood' at times seemed to evaporate as we watched." [19] This newfound reluctance to apply kinship terminology to all other lesbians and gay men extended well beyond activist circles. Many gay men and lesbians began to doubt the existence of "the" community or any single gay "lifestyle." Some abandoned the notion of identity-based communities altogether, attempting to escape social categorization by adopting extreme forms of individualism. "I am who I am," they explained. Others associated community strictly with wealthy white men, who were neither representative of nor identical with the totality of gay people. Along with a recognition of the relative privilege of this sector came the refusal to allow this part to stand for the whole. Seemingly unable to comprehend the inequalities that structure identity-based difference in the United States (white being privileged over Native-American, men over women, and so on), the concept of community lost credibility.

The most popular alternative was to divest community of its egalitarian associations by using it as a proxy for "population." Dissemination of Alfred Kinsey's (1948, 1953) data on the incidence of homosexual sex in the United States had opened the way for picturing an essential 10 percent who make up the imagined universe ("community") of gay men and lesbians. One indication of the extent of this muddle in the model of community is that, by the time of my fieldwork, most people qualified the term by adding a phrase such as "whatever that means."

The practice of identity politics in the United States has rested upon the cultural configuration of race, ethnicity, class, gender, and sexual identity as categories for organizing subjective experience (Epstein 1987; Omi and Winant 1983). What motivated the transition from "speaking sameness" to a division of community into ever-narrower circumscriptions of identity?[20] In the first place, perceptions of fragmentation represent a view from the top. Attempts to understand the integration of sexuality with other aspects of identity were not experienced as "splits" by those who had never felt included in community from the start. Paradoxically, however, the very process of building gay community contributed to the emergence and timing of this discourse on difference.

John D'Emilio (1989b) has argued that the political tactic of coming out to others as a means of establishing gay unity had the contradictory effect of making differences *among* lesbians and gay men more apparent. The distance is considerable from the Chicago of the late 1960s, where Esther Newton (1979) found little social differentiation among gay men and no gay economy to speak of, to the San Francisco of the 1980s, where gay institutions had multiplied and residents were heirs to a social movement for gay pride and liberation. In the Bay Area the sheer size of the relatively "out" gay and lesbian population permitted the recognition and replication of differences found in the society at large.

During the 1980s, categories of identity remained integral to the process of making and breaking social ties among lesbians and gay men. Most gay bars and social or political organizations in San Francisco were segregated by gender. Some of the community institutions that lesbians associated with gay men maintained a nominal lesbian presence. A gay theater, for example, included scripts with lesbian characters in its annual repertoire, and the number of women in attendance grew from two or three to a third of the audience when lesbian plays were performed. Yet the most visible gay institutions, businesses, and public rituals (such as Halloween on Castro Street) remained male-owned and male-organized. Even the exceptions seemed to prove the rule. After a crafts fair in the gay South of Market area, the *Bay Area Reporter* published a picture of two women kissing, over the caption, "It wasn't all men at the Folsom Street Fair either."

When gay groups in southern California suggested adding a lambda to the rainbow flag supposed to represent all gay people, lesbians denounced the addition as a noninclusive male symbol. At a benefit for the Gay Games sponsored by the Sisters of Perpetual Indulgence (a group of gay men in nun drag), lesbians cheered the women's softball game and martial arts demonstration, but some voiced impatience with "all the boys parading around in their outfits." Disagreements periodically erupted concerning the proportion of men's to women's coverage in newspapers that attempted to serve "the community" as a whole. It was not uncommon for lesbians and gay men to stereotype one another, building on constructions of identity and difference in the wider culture. Jenny Chin, herself Chinese-American, combined notions of gender, sexuality, and racial identity with the image of the Castro clone to portray difference and position herself outside "gay community":

> I would read the *Bay Guardian*, and they'd say "gay rap." And I would take all these buses crosstown, through all these parts of town I'd never been at night, and transfer, and wait on bus corners, and go to this huge room that had like 300 gay men. . . . These men were very much talking from their hearts, and they were really needing the support, but it's hard for me to identify with all these tall white guys with moustaches talking about how they're being judged because they're not coming well enough, or something like that.

Joan Nestle (in Gottlieb 1986) has condemned the essentialism implicit in generalizations that assert "lesbians do this, gay men do that." When it comes to something like public sex, Nestle points out, some do and some don't. Like other differences, divisions between lesbians and gay men are not absolute, but socially, historically, and interpretively constructed. After a women's musical troupe was asked to play for a gay male swimsuit contest, group members voiced positions ranging from "support our gay brothers," to "porn is porn," to "who cares, let's take the money!" Several lesbians cited their work with AIDS organizations as an experience that had helped them "feel connected" to gay men. Social contexts defined as heterosexual also fostered expectations of solidarity based on sexual identity. At one of our Thursday evening family dinners, Liz told with dismay the story of fighting with a male coworker at a holiday party given by her employer. "There we were," she explained, "the only two gay people in the place, having it out with each other."

Class differences traced out lines of division within as well as between the men's and women's "communities." Many lesbians attributed the visibility of gay male institutions to the fact that men in general have greater access to money than women. Gay vacation spots at the nearby Russian River proved too expensive for many lesbians (as well as working-class and unemployed gay men), who tended to stay at campgrounds rather than resorts if they visited the area. Popular categories opposed "bikers" to "professionals" and "bar gays" (presumably working-class) to "politicals" (stereotyped as "middle class"). People described making painful choices regarding employment, based on their perceptions of how out a person could be in a particular type of job. David Lowry, for example, had dropped out of an MBA program to become a waiter after he experienced pressure from corporate employers to be more "discreet" about his sexual identity.

Individuals who had purposefully sought employment in gay businesses reported their surprise at finding the gay employer-employee relationship as marked by conflict and difference as any other (cf. Weston and Rofel 1985). In a dispute between the lesbian owner of an apartment building and one of her lesbian tenants, both sides seemed perplexed to discover that their shared sexual identity could not resolve the issue at hand. The hegemony of a managerial and entrepreneurial class within "the community" was also evident in the relative absence of gay owned and operated discount stores. While merchants encouraged people to "buy gay" and pointed with pride to the proliferation of shops that had made it theoretically possible to live without ever leaving the Castro, only a very small segment of lesbians and gay men could have afforded to do so, even if they were so inclined.

Anyone who visits a variety of lesbian and gay households in the Bay Area will come away with an impression of generational depth. Gay organizations and establishments, however, tended to serve a relatively narrow middle age range. Bowling, for instance, is a sport that many people in the United States pursue into their older years.

But gay league nights at bowling alleys across the city found the lanes filled with teams predominantly composed of men in their twenties and thirties. Young lesbians and gay men came to San Francisco expecting to find acceptance and gay mecca but instead experienced trouble getting into bars and often ended up feeling peripheral to "the community" (cf. Hefner and Austin 1978; Heron 1983). Gina Pellegrini had initially gained entrance to one bar with a fake ID, only to encounter hostility from one of the older "regulars":

> I just felt like we all should have been the same no matter [what] —age or not. And she was discriminating against her own quote "kind" unquote. That was very strange to me. I didn't realize that a fifteen-year-old could be pretty damn much of a pain in the ass when you want to relax and talk to your friends and have a drink.

For their part, older people mentioned ageist door policies at bars, and complained about feeling "other" when surrounded by younger faces at community events.

Racially discriminatory treatment at gay organizations, white beauty standards, ethnic divisions in the crowds at different bars, and racist door policies were other frequently cited reasons for questioning the community concept. Kevin Jones, an African-American man, said that when he first came to San Francisco,

> I thought that if I was white, it would be a lot different then. Because it seemed like it was hard for me to talk to people in bars. But it didn't seem like other people were having a hard time talking to each other. It almost seemed like they *knew* each other. And if they didn't know each other, they were gonna go up and talk to each other and meet. But I'd go to the bars, and I could sit there and watch pool, and nobody would ever talk to me. And I couldn't understand that. And I thought, "If I was white, I bet you I would know a lot more of these people."

Something more is involved here than racial identity as a ground for difference and discrimination, or ethnicity as an obstacle to the easy interaction implicit in notions of community. Most people of color claimed membership in communities defined in terms of racial identity, attachments that predated coming out as a lesbian or gay man. Simon Suh, for example, believed that his own coming out was complicated by thinking of gays as "very outside of my own [Korean-American] community." Metaphors like "home" served as well for describing race and ethnicity as sexual identity. Because his best friend was also Latino, Rafael Ortiz explained, "it makes it more like home." This is not to deny divisions of class, language, age, national origin, gender, and so forth that cut across communities organized through categories of race or ethnicity. It is simply to note that many, if not most, lesbians and gay men of color did not experience coming out in terms of any one-to-one correspondence of identity to community.[21]

Whites without a strong ethnic identification often described coming out as a transition from no community *into* community, whereas people of color were more likely to focus on conflicts *between* different identities instead of expressing a sense of relief and arrival. Implicit in the coming-out narratives of many white people was the belief that whites lack community, culture, and a developed sense of racial identity. As Scott McFarland, a white man, remarked when we were discussing the subject of gay pride day, "There were no other parades that I could march in."

Division of the master trope of community into multiple communi*ties* has forced individuals to make difficult choices between mutually exclusive alternatives, like living in an Asian-American or a gay neighborhood, or working for a gay or an African-American newspaper. Some political activists have endeavored to fabricate a solidarity capable of spanning "the community" without denying differences that divide its members. The general trend, however, has involved building coalitions composed of autonomous groups that invoke more specialized combinations of identities (cf. Reagon 1983).

To avoid prioritizing identities, a person could integrate them—seeking out other gay American Indians, joining a group for lesbians over 40, or hanging out in a bar for gays of color—but this solution is limited in the number of identities and settings it can encompass. A person could move back and forth among communities as an "out" lesbian or gay man, giving up the hope of having all identities accepted in any one context. He or she could pass for heterosexual in situations defined by race or ethnicity, like Kenny Nash, who had decided to remain closeted to other African-Americans. "I didn't want people to think that I'd left the [black] community," he explained, "so that therefore I had no right to speak about things that were of concern to me." Or that person could turn toward a radical individualism which focused on issues of style and railed against conformity, whether it be as a "lesbian for lipstick" or a gay man who objected to uniforms of jeans, keys, and sculptured muscles.

For some, sexual identity had become a minimal defining feature, all "we" have in common. Scott McFarland told the story of getting on the wrong bus when he first arrived in the city during the 1970s, and finding himself on Castro Street:

> It just devastated me. [I thought], this is *it*! This is the dream of all these people like me moving to somewhere [gay]. . . . Everybody was dressed in these incredibly macho fashions. . . . These weigh-a-ton shoes. Jeans. The first five years I lived in San Francisco, I refused to wear blue jeans. . . . It took me years to recover from finding out that gay people weren't like me much at all!

"I knew that I didn't fit into the Castro any more than I fit into my family," another man insisted. Whether that sense of difference was based on categorical understandings of self (mediated by race, age, class, gender) or on tensions between the individual and the social, the result has been a generalized rejection of the unity and above all the sameness implicit in the concept of gay community.

In contrast, the family-centered discourse emerging during this period did not assume identity (in the sense of sameness) based upon sexuality alone. Lesbians and gay men who claimed membership in multiple communities but felt at home in none joined with those who had strategically repositioned themselves outside community in transferring the language of kinship from collective to interpersonal relations. While familial ideologies assumed new prominence in the United States at large during the 1980s, among gay men and lesbians the historical legacy of community-building and subsequent struggles to comprehend relations of difference mediated a shift in focus from friendship to kinship. Meanwhile the possibility of being rejected by blood relatives for a lesbian or gay identity shaped the specific meanings carried by "family" in gay contexts, undermining the permanence culturally attributed to blood ties while highlighting categories of choice and love.

Defined in opposition to biological family, the concept of families we choose proved attractive in part because it reintroduced agency and a subjective sense of making culture into lesbian and gay social organization. The institutionalized gay community of the 1970s, with its shops and bars and associations, by the 1980s could appear as something prefabricated, an entity over and above individuals into which they might or might not fit. Most understood gay families to be customized, individual creations that need not deny conflict or difference. Family also supplied the face-to-face relationships and concrete knowledge of persons promised by the romantic imagery of small-town community (Mannheim 1952). As a successor to nonerotic ties elaborated in terms of community or friendship, chosen families introduced something rather novel into kinship relations in the United States by grouping friends together with lovers and children within a single cultural domain.

SIX | LOVERS THROUGH THE LOOKING GLASS

> But the picture? What was he to say of that? It held the
> secret of his life, and told his story. It had taught him to
> love his own beauty. Would it teach him to loathe his own
> soul? —OSCAR WILDE, *The Picture of Dorian Gray*

What to make of the relationships that lesbians and
gay men label lovers and claim as kin, erotic ties that bear no intrinsic
connection to procreative sexuality or gendered difference?[1] In the
United States, where procreation occupies the cultural imagination in
its guise as the outcome of differences between women and men, both
gender and kinship studies "begin by taking 'difference' for granted
and treating it as a presocial fact" (Yanagisako and Collier 1987:29).
When David Schneider (1977:66) discusses the distinction between
erotic and nonerotic love in the United States, for example, he treats
erotic love as "the union of opposites, the other the unity which
identities have."

Viewed against the backdrop of accounts that ground erotic relations in the symbolism of genital and gendered difference, lesbian or
gay lovers appear "the same" and therefore incomplete. Looking-glass
imagery casts gay couples in the one-dimensional relations of a likeness defined by its opposition to the differences of anatomy and
gender understood to configure heterosexual marriage, sexuality, and
procreation. To the extent that heterosexuals view lesbian or gay
lovers as two like halves that cannot be reconciled to make a whole,
gay relationships seem to yield a cultural unit deficient in meaning
(which, as any good structuralist knows, must be generated through
contrast). Representations that draw on mirror imagery reduce this
apparent similarity of gay or lesbian partners to mere replication of
the self, a narcissistic relation that creates no greater totality and
brings little new into the world.

How can lesbian and gay relationships gain legitimacy as bonds of kinship, shaped within a discourse on families we choose, if they lack this more basic recognition as authentically social ties? More than a bias toward procreative sexuality contributes to the devaluation of gay relationships. In a society that symbolically links procreation to heterosexual intercourse and gendered difference, depicting gay couples exclusively in terms of a gender identity shared by both partners tends to make "same-same" relationships appear problematic, unworkable, meaningless, even "unnatural." Not only one's lover, but features of the cultural construction of heterosexuality, implicitly return to the gay or lesbian self as reflection.

In scholarly analysis of gay relationships as well as in the perceptions of most lesbians and gay men, a focus on gendered continuity has replaced the interpretation that prevailed earlier in the century of homosexuality as a transgender identification. Rather than perpetuating stereotypes of gay men who are universally effeminate and lesbians who "really" want to be men, contemporary wisdom has it that lesbians are more like heterosexual women than like gay men. Correspondingly, gay men are supposed to have more in common with straight men than with lesbians (Bell and Weinberg 1978; Simon and Gagnon 1967a, 1967b). Typical of this line of reasoning is Denise Cronin's (1975:277) assertion that "lesbians are women first and homosexuals second." From personal narratives and sociological studies to psychoanalytic and literary accounts, too often each member of a gay or lesbian couple appears as the mirror image of the other, based upon a presumption of the overwhelming saliency of gender identity within the relationship. After studying San Francisco's Castro neighborhood, Frances FitzGerald (1986:57) concluded, "Liberated gay women . . . turned out to be archetypally women, and gay men in the Castro archetypally men—as if somehow their genders had been squared by isolation from the other sex." Associated with this shift in scholarly representation was the de facto separation of most lesbian and gay male institutions during the 1970s-1980s.

THE LOOKING-GLASS OTHER

In the United States, mirror imagery clearly does not confine itself to the context of lesbian and gay relationships. From at least the time that the Puritans saw themselves reflected in the "wilderness" of a new land, likening their surroundings to the biblical Garden of Eden and seeking in them a "mirror of prophecy," mirrors have signified a source of self-knowledge, identity, and revelation (Bercovitch 1978). The metaphorical act of holding up a mirror to something invokes a certain naive realism, a referential theory of a world "out there" believed consistent and amenable to representation.

In coming-out narratives, seeking one's own reflection often symbolizes an effort to affirm a coherent self in a situation that promises (or threatens) to transform identity. After his first night at a gay bar, as Al Collins told the story, "The next day at work I remember I went into the restroom and I looked at myself in the mirror—it was so funny—and I told myself, 'Okay, you're gay, but you're not weird!' " In another anecdote, a man described a mirror window that dominated the outside door to a gay bar, preventing passers-by from seeing in but permitting the narrator to pass through and encounter revelations about "gay life" on the other side. By evoking the popular notion of traveling through the looking glass to other realms, the mirror can serve not only to establish coherence of identity but also to signify an escape from isolation on an extended journey to gayness. Coming out presents one context in which the paradox of seeing ourselves in the act of gazing upon another presents a welcome alternative to the conventionalized terror of remaining imprisoned in the belief of being "the only one."

The sociological conception of a looking-glass self who gains personal awareness in the process of being evaluated by others experiences a sort of turnabout in depictions of gay relationships, within which knowledge of a partner is often supposed to be mediated by knowledge of the self. In his widely read advice manual *Loving Someone Gay*, Don Clark (1977:51) contends, "A Gay person often starts the love-search being attracted to people who are opposite or shadows of the self, as if seeking some sort of integration or completion. This phenomenon may have to do with anti-Gay training that taught you to devalue yourself." His recommendation is to value likeness, taking oneself as the point of departure and comparison. Writing in the gay press, Ken Popert (1982:73) utilized the language of the looking glass when he described "the realization that, in turning away from unknown gay men, I was turning away from myself." Such constructions of gay relationships as relationships of identity implicitly cede the territory of difference and opposition to heterosexual couples. My same-sex partner becomes a reflection of myself, based upon an inferred likeness that in turn depends upon gendered differences defined in the culture at large. "We're both women," Rose Ellis insisted, speaking of a lover, "so we *understand* each other, so to speak." The contrast between sameness and difference then joins the distinction between biological family and families we choose in patrolling the border that separates gay from straight identity.

Given the widespread influence of imagery that emphasizes gendered continuities between gay partners, it should not be surprising to find that lesbians and gay men in the Bay Area tended to depict one another as approaching relationships from different directions—women from the side of love and men from the side of sex. When they spoke in generalities, most agreed on the terms of the cultural equation: love + sex = a relationship. To call a relationship "committed" signaled for both men and women not only a mutual intention for it to endure, but often a claim to kinship as well. This ideal combination of emotional with physical unity made gay couples "about" love and friendship as well as sex, in a manner consistent with twentieth-century ideologies of companionate marriage. But in their coming-out stories, men frequently highlighted the shock of realizing that it could be possible for two men to love, dance, kiss erotically, become jealous, or have ongoing relationships rather than a string of sexual encounters. Women, in contrast, were more likely to report originally finding it easy to imagine love between women without recognizing the option of adding an erotic component (cf. Peplau et al. 1978:8). When I asked interview participants if they were currently involved in a relationship, a few were uncertain how to answer. Of those who hesitated, the women wondered whether they should count primary emotional bonds as relationships in the absence of sexual involvement, while the men wondered whether to include routinized sexual relationships that lacked emotional depth and commitment.

Identifying (gay) men with sex and (lesbian) women with love reinforces the appearance of an overwhelming continuity and similarity between partners who share a common gender identity. Significantly, interviews and everyday encounters also turned up plenty of exceptions to such gender-typed generalizations: men whose first same-sex involvement occurred with a best friend, women sexually active with multiple partners since childhood. In a humorous play on conventional understandings of gendered difference, Louise Romero portrayed herself being socialized into the proper way for a lesbian to go about meeting a partner.

> Coffee goes good. Usually coffee first date, and then they go to bed with you, but otherwise forget it. . . . My other friend, Stacey, that I lived with, she said, "Louise, you got to stop going to bed with somebody in one night. You can't just do that. You got to date for a few months, and *then* go to bed with them." I said, "Date?" She said, "That's the only way you get a steady girlfriend. You just can't rush into things." So I tried it once with this one woman. She came over for dinner. I fixed it real nice, I had the fireplace going and everything. And then I talked to her the next day and stuff. She goes, "Well, I didn't think you were interested." It was like she put it on *me*. She wanted to go to bed that night!

With the advent of AIDS, gay wit pointed out the ironic combination of a "new romanticism" and more cautious attitude toward sex among gay men with the "rediscovery" of sex by lesbians. During the 1980s the same gay publications that featured how-to articles on dating for gay men presented lesbians with tongue-in-cheek tips on cruising for a sexual partner. Strip shows, erotic magazines, more candid discussions of sexuality, and debates about controversial practices like s/m captured the attention of many lesbians in the Bay Area during this decade. Within the same time frame, according to a survey conducted by the San Francisco AIDS Foundation, gay men reported having less sex, safe or unsafe (Helquist 1985). Some concluded from such survey results that sex had become less important to gay men, yet what I observed was the development of new forms of camaraderie in the face of the epidemic, accompanied by a redefinition of what qualifies as sex. "Years ago," Harold Sanders maintained,

> the way men would treat each other in a sexual context, it would be very covert. Then there might be something like [gruff voice], "Do you want to suck my cock?" And you knew that what the other person wanted was the same kind of tenderness and sharing of affection that you wanted, but that you could not possibly exempt [yourself from] that definition of being a man.

In the early 1980s, gay men incorporated miniature teddy bears into the handkerchief color code developed to indicate preferences for various specialized sexual practices. Handkerchiefs of particular colors placed in particular pockets (right or left) coexisted with this novel symbol of the desire to hug or be hugged, to "share emotion." A similar move toward integrating love and caring with masculinity and toughness surfaced in the context of AIDS organizing. Pamphlets distributed by a major AIDS organization in San Francisco displayed the title "A Call to Arms" next to the graphic of a teddy bear, mixing metaphors of militarism (the battle with AIDS) and affection. In the 1986 Gay Pride Parade one man had handcuffed a teddy bear to the back of his motorcycle where a lover might ride, while another dressed in a full set of leathers carried a small bear attached to a picture of his lover and his lover's date of death.[2]

To a degree, then, the identification of sex and emotion with men and women, respectively, would seem to have blurred for gay men and lesbians during the 1980s. Yet this apparent integration of the two domains coincided with a sense of exploring unknown territories that members of the "opposite gender" would better understand. If a gay man wanted to know about dating and romance, the person to go to for information was a woman; if a lesbian wanted to try picking up someone in a bar, why not ask a gay male friend for advice? Ideologies of gendered contrast and continuity also persisted in the form of the common belief that gay men have difficulty maintaining relationships, whereas lesbian couples suffer from too much intimacy. Among interview participants, the longest same-sex relationships listed by lesbians had endured on average for more years than the longest same-sex relationships listed by gay men. However, based upon this limited sample, the gap appeared to narrow as the number of years together extended. Nearly equal numbers of men and women had partners at the time of the interview, while similar proportions of single women and men claimed they desired a committed relationship (see table 18 in the appendix).[3] Percentages notwithstanding, some gay men considered their relationships especially susceptible to dissolution because they believed men do not learn to "nurture." Many lesbians agreed that women are more empathetic and better prepared to keep the home fires burning, but asserted that they encountered a dilemma "opposite" to that facing gay men: difficulty setting limits to circumvent dependency within relationships. Put two women or two men together, they argued, and a magnification of the gendered traits attributed to each must surely result.

For every instance of a gay man or lesbian following the cultural logic of the looking glass, another portrayal contradicted or inverted its terms. When comparing themselves to straight men, many gay men described themselves as more sensitive or nurturing; in certain contexts, lesbians tended to present self-sufficiency, strength, and independence as characteristically lesbian traits. In the specific context of discourse on lovers, however, notions of gay relationships as relationships of likeness in which partners reflect back to one another their common gender identity shaped the way both lesbians and gay men configured eroticism and commitment.

Another correlate of the mirror metaphor, with its stress on sameness and the intensification of gender within gay relationships, is the application to couples of normative expectations that have long since been discredited in association with community. Roberta Osabe, like many of her peers, reported an initial anticipation of perfect harmony with her lover based on a shared gender identity.

When I realized that just because you were a lesbian doesn't mean your relationships with women are cut out—it doesn't mean you'll find happiness—that's when I *really* got depressed. 'Cause I thought it was gonna be just like la-la-la, you know— flowers (laughs). Happiness! I'd found the yellow brick road, and it was on the way to the Emerald City. [Then] I realized you still had a shitty job. You still had all your problems. People are still gonna leave you. You're still gonna be alone, basically. And that was a *big* disappointment.

To search for the man or woman in the mirror, the lover at the end of a journey to self-love and self-acceptance, is to fall under the spell of the oversimplified contrasts of likeness and difference implicit in the mirror metaphor. As Paulette Ducharme observed, "I do definitely think I have a preference for women's bodies over men's bodies. But also [a preference for] beings—there are beings in those bodies, and all women certainly aren't exactly the same." In addition to idiosyncratic differences such as squeezing toothpaste from different parts of the tube, differences of class, age, race, ethnicity, and a host of other identities that crosscut gender are sufficient to put to rest the notion of a single unified woman's or man's standpoint. The assumption that gender identity will be the primary *subjective* identity for every lesbian or gay man, universally and without respect to context, remains just that: an assumption.

Consider the case of interracial couples. Far from presenting an inherently unproblematic situation of sameness and identification between partners, the interracial aspect of a relationship can become a point of saliency that overwhelms any sense of likeness. For Leroy Campbell, a particular sort of difference, rooted in racist interpretations of the meaning of skin color and leading to painful reversals of situational expectations, became the overriding issue when he talked about trying to meet other men through the bars.

> See, I don't know if you can imagine what it's like seeing somebody walking towards you, or being in a bar and looking at someone, and feeling attracted to them, when there's a possibility that if you walk up to them and talk to them, that they're gonna say, 'I don't like black people.' So you have this perception of being attracted to this person who might *hate* you.

When issues of race and racism came up in her three-year relationship with a white woman, explained Eriko Yoshikawa, who was Japanese, "it always makes us feel how different we are, and it creates a certain kind of distance." On another occasion, Eriko's lover cautioned, "We're careful not to attribute all differences between us to the most obvious difference between us."

Some lesbians and gay men have extended mirror imagery to race and ethnicity with the argument that getting involved with someone of another race means "not really facing yourself," or through their expectation that relationships with someone of the same ethnic identification would prove intrinsically easier to negotiate. Yet likeness no more automatically follows from a common racial identity than from a shared gender identity. The challenge is to understand how, why, and in what contexts individuals abstract gender from a range of potential identities, elevating gender identity into *the* axis for defining sameness.

Some of the same individuals who emphasized gendered continuity when discussing their current lovers highlighted divergent racial identities, class backgrounds, or ages to explain recent breakups and describe past relationships. Because people in the United States conventionally attribute separation and divorce to "irreconcilable differences," here context becomes significant in determining whether the language of the looking glass will come into play. That individuals enjoy considerable interpretive leeway in this regard, however, is evident from a comment made by Kenny Nash as a black gay man: "It became more a matter of being gay [than being black] if a man I was with was white. . . . It was like, 'If you react badly because I'm with this man, it's not because he's white, it's because he's a man.' "

Refracting relationships through looking-glass imagery leads discussion toward the catch-all terms of sameness and difference, too often omitting the crucial questions: in what *way* the same, and in what *respect* different (Scott 1988)? Lost in a partner's reflection of the mirrored self are distinctive constructions of likeness and contrast, constructions that have varied through time as well as from couple to couple and between gay men and lesbians. The diversity of gendered relations associated with androgyny, "Castro clones," butch/fem among lesbians, the eclipse of elements of the campy style of 1950s queens by a "new masculinity" shared between gay male partners, and the eroticization of symbolic contrasts among gay men elaborated through class imagery, invalidate any attempt to confine lesbian and gay couples within the terms of an abstract gender symmetry.

POWER "DIFFERENTIALS," RELATIONSHIP "ROLES"

From the 1940s through the 1960s, the prevalence of butch/fem among lesbians (particularly those active in the nascent "communities" of the bars) coincided with very differently gendered constructions of erotic relationships among gay men. Well before the rise of a gay movement, Evelyn Hooker (1965) concluded that "pairs with well-defined differentiation" constituted a minority among gay men, and that most gay male couples could not accurately be sorted into active and passive or masculine and feminine partners. In the 1970s lesbian-feminism and gay liberation came along with their prescriptions for androgyny, a vaguely defined state that either entailed the elimination of gender itself or imaged all human beings as composed of two gendered halves. Because society accentuated the half that corresponded to a person's gender identity, the objective was to develop the neglected feminine or masculine side, bringing the self into balance and realizing its "full potential." Not everyone subscribed to such ideologies, and by the late 1970s or early 1980s androgyny had fallen into disfavor. On the

West Coast many gay men moved away from the look-alike styles of gay liberation militants and Castro clones, while lesbians discarded flannel shirts and "khaki drag" in favor of a more varied array of fashion statements. The gendered complementarity that accompanied the revival of butch/fem during the 1980s among a minority of lesbians found no parallel among gay men, though some gay men incorporated other types of symbolic contrasts into their allegedly "same-same" relationships.

In this section I want to examine not the changing and much-debated meanings carried by concepts like androgyny and contrasts like butch/fem, but rather the possibilities for creating differently gendered relations within lesbian and gay couples. The androgynous interlude of the 1970s had distinct implications for gay men and lesbians. During that period younger lesbian-feminists defined androgyny in opposition to "roles" (their preferred term for butch/fem), juxtaposing androgyny's prescription for a certain kind of sameness to a lesbian heritage of complementary differentiation. In contrast, many gay men continued to idealize gendered similarities between partners, although the specifics of the types of similarities considered desirable changed over the years.

Although most of the gay men I met readily applied the categories "queen" and "butch" to situate other gay men along a gendered continuum, the majority agreed that *within* an erotic relationship they were inclined to seek congruence rather than complementarity, with a preference for the butch end of the spectrum. According to Harold Sanders, who had observed several decades of gay relationships:

> Most of the men I know are fairly similar. I mentioned one [gay male] couple [into "roles"]—the reason I did was because they're *unusual*. With most of the people I know, it's a matched set. They're two of a kind, apparently. On the surface. . . . In fact, that may be one way I sort of recognize gay men. They seem to be very similar-looking guys. It's an affinity deal.

The relatively small number of men I met who enjoyed doing drag felt it was pointless to wear drag when looking for sex or a date.[4] In David Lowry's words, "If I'm dressed like this, it's gonna be nearly impossible for me to pick anyone up. So it's not about that. Yet it's about being gay." A few men described making a concerted effort to appear less "queeny" and more masculine in order to find a lover. The gendered correspondence sought need not be one of butch-to-butch and muscle-to-muscle. Idealized lovers might also share a desire for "softness" or "sensitivity" in body and temperament, again referring back to gendered similarities in presentation or sense of self.

This much said, there remained a number of ways in which some gay men cast partners in relations of complementarity. Choosing an outfit for a Saturday night out could involve the purposeful construction of class contrasts: one man might don a tweed jacket for that yuppie look in the hope of attracting another in work boots and jeans. The self-identification of a minority of gay men as "top man" or "bottom man" within a relationship also testified to the incapacity of looking-glass language to grasp the complexities of phenomena that pass for affinity, or alternatively, for gendered differentiation. Among both gay men and lesbians who practiced sadomasochism, the categories top and bottom occurred in the context of activities that "played with power" by elaborating symbolic contrasts organized through race and class imagery, a human/animal divide, and so on.

That mirrors can reflect inversion as well as likeness is recognized by anyone who has ever learned to tie a tie with the aid of a looking glass. Carolyn Fisher, an American Indian who described herself as "not very political," told me that in a lover she preferred "dark-complected people, Latin people. And just casual. Not real feminine, not real butch. Somewhat like me." But other lesbians and gay men described the type of partner they generally found attractive as the "opposite" of themselves. Brook Luzio, who identified as neither butch nor fem, mixed ideologies of gendered continuity and gendered complementarity without sensing any contradiction. She contended that relationships between women are more conducive to trust and intimacy "because we're more alike physically. There's more affinity." Yet she found herself drawn to women with dark hair and dark skin, very different in appearance from her own light features and blond hair. Of course, the kind of person an individual finds attractive may not correspond to the kind of person she or he chooses for a lover. But the symbolism of opposition that sometimes surfaced in discussions of "types" and eroticism has its own significance, revealing contrasts as well as continuities that people use to make sense of relationships.

The dark/fair contrast has a long history in depictions of lesbian couples, epitomized by the blond (fem) and brunette (butch) figures that grace the covers of lesbian pulp novels from the 1950s. Although the majority of lesbians in the Bay Area did not identify as fem or butch, most acknowledged the contrast, at least implicitly. Even lesbians who vociferously rejected these identities as confining "roles" knew the categories, and most occasionally used them to describe aspects of themselves or to classify their peers. In the San Francisco of the 1980s lesbian interpretations of butch/fem ranged from condemnations that portrayed it as an oppressive imitation of the gendered differentiation found among heterosexual couples to its glorification as a unique creation of "lesbian culture" that should be more highly valued. At the same time, many lesbians had rejected androgyny, feeling that in practice women who called themselves androgynous had cultivated male attributes at the expense of female. The rhetoric of "fluidity" in gendered presentations of self offered an attractive alternative to some, while others embraced an individualistic variant of humanism: loving someone for the person she is, irrespective of gendered attributes.

Debate over what has been labeled a revival of butch/fem turned on issues of dependence and autonomy, asking whether structured difference necessarily leads to the creation of a power differential between partners. Lesbians on both sides of the debate and gay men of all political persuasions tended to value parity within relationships. Achieving consensus on what constituted an egalitarian relationship was another matter.

Chapter 5 explored how gay men and lesbians, like others in the United States, have invoked criteria of emotional and material assistance in the process of defining family. Family, they told me again and again, means having someone you can count on. But for many, confidence in their ability to secure support from kin concealed an everyday emphasis on self-sufficiency that became apparent in the way they qualified the contexts in which assistance would be acceptable. Family was supposed to give a person someone to turn to in an emergency or time of need—that is, in extenuating circumstances. However, not everyone preferred to handle everyday affairs entirely on their own, and even among those who valued self-sufficiency, some calculated it on an individual and some on a household or familial basis. Certain people linked their involvement in barter and labor exchanges to "survival issues" or to their identities as poor or working-class people. In other cases, however, lovers who operated as an interdependent unit by pooling money and other resources emphasized the ability of each to survive in the absence of the other. Paulette Ducharme proudly related an anecdote about meeting her lover's father, who tried to show his acceptance of their relationship by asking if she was "taking good care of his daughter." Paulette's response (and the punch line of the story) assured him that her lover "did a pretty good job taking care of herself."

Many people cited the lack of any prescribed division of labor between members of a couple as one index of an egalitarian relationship. Few thought that an equitable division of labor would require that both lovers possess identical skills, as the sameness of a mirror image would imply. In descriptions of their relationships, some allocation of chores characterized as "50/50" usually prevailed, which could mean either rotating the same tasks between partners or having individuals specialize in particular tasks based on skill or preference.[5] Among women as well as men, both partners generally expected to pursue paid employment. Only four interview participants were financially supporting or being supported by a lover, and each viewed this as a temporary situation. One immigrant, for example, was depending on her partner for monetary support until she could acquire the green card that would legally allow her to work for wages. Butch/fem identifications seldom coincided with divisions of labor in which only one partner worked outside the home. None of those providing or receiving financial support connected their situation to butch/fem, while the fem- and butch-identified women in the sample earned their own incomes.

The portrayal of lovers as a union of equals rather than a relation of subjugation has clear ties to romantic ideologies of heterosexual marriage. Yet some gay people—especially those with a feminist orientation—regarded equality as a distinguishing feature of relations within lesbian and gay couples. Following the logic of the looking glass, heterosexual relationships appeared to them to lack the structural foundation to foster equality in place of male dominance, since those relationships were grounded in gendered difference. Lesbians who rejected (or tolerated) butch/fem often viewed the contrast as inherently inegalitarian because they believed "roles" to be modeled on the unity of symbolic opposites (man and woman) characteristic of heterosexual alliances. Nevertheless, from the lack of correspondence between butch/fem identification and any particular division of labor within lesbian relationships, it is evident that an egalitarian ideal has the potential to assimilate competing ideologies of androgyny, affinity, humanism, and contrast or complementarity. What counts as a "50/50" allocation of tasks is open to endless interpretation. No direct line links difference in gendered constructions of self to differentials in power between partners.

Lesbians who identified as fem or butch often dismissed "roles" as a concept inadequate to their experience (cf. Nestle 1987). Even *had* butch/fem originated as straightforward imitation, the best-laid plans of mice and women would likely have failed to bring forth the exact "reproduction" of heterosexual relationships pictured by its detractors. To complicate matters, there is tremendous variety in the ways individuals construct power and difference—including a potentially flexible deployment of identities if they move between fem and butch —that mirror imagery cannot comprehend. In looking-glass reasoning, the meaning of any gendered difference in lesbian or gay relationships can be reduced to the opposition between male and female, with its (allegedly) attendant relations of inequality. Alternatively, a person can think the unthinkable in a two-gender system, treating butch/fem as a *transformation* of the male/female contrast—related, to be sure, but worthy of explication in its own right.

THE URGE TO MERGE

The extensive elaboration of mirror imagery in psychoanalytic theory and the complex history of relations between gay people and mental health professionals have coincided in recent years with the popularization of theories about lovers who "merge."[6] A lesbian couple who had entered couples therapy to "deal with a merging problem" explained merging as "losing ourselves in one another." Not only therapists but many gay men and lesbians in the Bay Area at large blamed merging for a variety of ills, including low-frequency sex, "overintimacy," and threats to individuality. By the late 1980s, taking steps to counter this tendency to merge was touted as a panacea to cure whatever ailed the committed couple.

Because the notion of two partners merging contravenes the cultural dictum that individuals may "become one" during sex but should maintain distinct selves in other domains, it is supposed to lead to dependence and loss of identity. The formula for recognizing merging makes its symptoms readily observable: when one does what the other does, the two are charged with fusion—the failure to lead separate lives, maintain separate friendships, and participate in separate activities.[7] In contrast, "healthy" relationships are supposed to allow persons to grow as individuals who highly value independence and self-sufficiency. Psychological theories that place a premium on the development of "strong ego boundaries" idealize this isolated self of an atomistic society.

At a small party I attended one evening, all the invited guests had arrived but Sophia Ghiselli. When Sophia finally showed up at the door, bringing along her lover as a matter of course, the guests (all lesbians) expressed surprise and disapproval. Only merging, they whispered, could explain such "strange" behavior. Why else would she arrive with a lover who had not received an invitation, never thinking to ask the host if her partner was welcome to attend? Allegations of identity "confusion" also surfaced in condemnations of "couple-ism." In the medium-sized city where she came out, Sharon Vitrano told me with annoyance, "You never really knew what people did [for work]. But boy, people's names were like, 'Jean-and-Jane.' That was somebody's name!"

Many considered a tendency to merge inherent in the likeness they attributed to lesbian and gay male relationships. One man voiced his concern with:

> the problem of merging and keeping separate identities in a gay relationship as opposed to keeping identities in a straight relationship. I think superficially it's obviously easier to keep an identity in a relationship where you've got people who are *that* much different than where there isn't that.

The psychosocial theories that inform the identification of merging as a problem trace gender development to early childhood experiences, including the effects of childrearing by female caretakers on children of different genders. Because women are raised by women, they experience difficulty differentiating themselves from others, while men have a harder time achieving intimacy (Chodorow 1978; Gilligan 1982). Following this logic, lesbian couples may appear as an extension of a chronologically prior mother-daughter relationship.[8] Heterosexual relationships, based on the union of "opposite genders," are believed to supply built-in controls because the difference between women and men (taken as a given) is supposed to "en-gender" the emotional distance promoted by well-defined ego boundaries.[9]

Jennifer Bauman, a lesbian and a sex therapist, invoked this ideology when she discussed contrasts between her heterosexual and lesbian clients.

> It was always the woman who has a glimmer for thirty seconds of how wonderful intimacy feels, how close it feels, and then the guy jumps up and wants a cup of coffee or wants to do this or wants to do that. . . . You put two women together who know what it is they're after, and it's hard to resist the wanting a constant peak experience. . . . You have a system of checks and balances the minute you put a man in there. Just about always, not always.

Some gay men as well as lesbians applied the merging metaphor to themselves and their partners, based not so much on psychosocial theories of gender development but on abstract depictions of gay relationships as "same-same" relationships. Nevertheless, there seemed to be a consensus among those who subscribed to merging theory that lesbians are more susceptible to fusion than gay men, due to lesbians' gender-specific socialization as women.

Critics of merging theory have tended to glorify merging as a positive phenomenon without disputing the validity of the concept. Jean Wyatt (1986:115) sees merging as a praiseworthy trait, noting that in twentieth-century novels by women authors, female characters do not resist "what is inchoate and amorphous in themselves, but welcome the chaos of a diffused self for its promise of change and celebrate the possibilities for renewal in the experience of merging." Similarly, Jennifer Bauman emphasized the potential for innovation in relationships without clearly demarcated boundaries.

> What if you have two women who don't have the stops on? I mean, it's very exciting, but we don't have a lot of models for how you do that. And it's very scary because you haven't the faintest idea of where you're going, 'cause nobody's gonna stop you. So you can create whatever it is you want to create.

For Jennifer, merging represented an opportunity for lesbian lovers to partake of the choice and free creativity that constitutes the organizing principle of gay families.

Lourdes Alcantara was among a handful of lesbians who questioned the exaltation of the bounded individual implicit in merging theory. "I always wanted to live on top of the mountain," she explained. "Just me and my lover. No people around at all. That's why it was so weird when I heard the . . . word 'merge.' To me, it doesn't exist." Perhaps it was more than coincidental that Lourdes, a woman born and raised in Latin America, articulated this critique. As metaphor, merging depends upon culturally specific constructions of an essentialized self that can be lost and alienated as well as discovered and loved.

In the United States many people believe that in the absence of distinctions between partners, the boundaries understood to demarcate self and order the social world would prove difficult to construct. They arrive at this cultural conclusion not only because they view social ties as fragile and susceptible to dissolution, but also because they believe larger social wholes must be fabricated from the building blocks of selves that are in turn defined through difference (cf. Varenne 1977). Chaos looms on both levels. Michelle Rosaldo has described very different notions of self among the Ilongot of the Philippines, who, assuming that people desire to be equivalent or "the same," would see in the individualism underlying the Western therapeutic attack on merging "a person born of conflict" (1983:137).

The project of tracking down the excesses of compounded gender in relations between partners rests upon an extremely atomistic notion of what a self should be. At the same time, merging privileges gender over other identities, assuming before it observes the likeness of lovers. While the application of mirror imagery to lesbian and gay couples may lend plausibility to theories like merging, it should be remembered that mirrors are equally capable of conveying distance from self—what James Fernandez (1986) calls the sense of "I am here and my body is there"—rather than blurring boundaries imagined to insulate self from the world.

NARCISSISM, KINSHIP, AND CLASS CONVICTIONS

If the diffusion of self remains an ever-present danger, self-absorption constitutes an equivalent (though antithetical) evil for many people in the United States. In the figure of Narcissus lies a precursor to the stereotype of "the homosexual" as a self-centered being, concerned more with his or her own pleasures and appearance than with anything a partner might have to offer (cf. Kleinberg 1980). The image of a lesbian or gay man staring fixedly into the mirror on the wall—or the mirror of a lover's face and body—reinforces popular perceptions of gays as people without social ties or family, a species set apart. In John Rechy's *City of Night*, for example, the protagonist is not a member of a couple or even gay-identified, but a male hustler proud of his autonomy: "There was still, too, the narcissistic obsession with myself—those racked interludes in the mirror—the desperate strange craving to be a world within myself. And I felt somehow, then, that only the mirror could really judge me for whatever I must be judged" (1963:120).

Condensed within this sort of imagery are the very ambiguities that make narcissism, like reproduction, such a handy epithet for defenders of heterosexist prejudices and purveyors of old psychiatric orthodoxies. Narcissus peers out from the looking glass with an encompassing gaze that melds notions of selfishness, isolation, decadence, irresponsibility, and social class.

In the United States mental health professionals long considered homosexuals the victims of "arrested development," doomed to a kind of perpetual adolescence because of their sexuality (Hoffman 1968; Schafer 1976). Previous to the 1970s the Freudian concept of narcissistic object-choice, which was widely applied to homosexuality, extended the mirror's range beyond the self to lovers and sex partners. A fair number of the lesbians and gay men I interviewed had encountered popular interpretations of this psychoanalytic perspective as obstacles along the path to coming out. Before she claimed a lesbian identity in her mid-twenties, Paulette Ducharme believed that being a lesbian would mean:

> You're a little girl; you don't want to grow up; you want to be pampered forever and ever and nurtured forever and ever; you never want to stop sucking your mother's breast; you're perverted; you're kind of sick; there's no way of telling what kind of terrible thing that you're capable of doing since you're capable of being a lesbian.

For Paulette at that time, having a woman lover would have represented a failure to break with her own gender at puberty by seeking "opposite gender" partners. In her white, working-class environment, the absence of such a break contravened prescriptions for an autonomy that should have grown with adulthood. Detachment from parents through the establishment of a family of her own, symbolically organized in terms of procreation, would have signified the maturity necessary to be taken seriously as an adult member of society.

Although the concept of homosexual narcissism and the medical model of homosexuality as disease have been discredited, mirrors remain an organizing metaphor in many theories of psychological development.[10] For Jacques Lacan (1977:2), it is during a mirror stage that the infant learns its first lessons in identification, "the transformation that takes place in the subject when he [sic] assumes an image." Here the looking glass takes its place in the gradual separation of the me from the not-me, for "the precursor of the mirror is the mother's face" (Winnicott 1971:111). Ideally this mirror stage should represent a way station along the path of distinguishing self from surroundings and from other selves.

The resonance between mirror imagery in depictions of gay couples and mirror imagery in psychoanalytic theory intimates that gay men and lesbians foster a confused relationship with their environment, having "failed" to progress from identification to differentiation. In her discussion of the consequences for women when menstruation is characterized as "failed" reproduction, Emily Martin (1987) has explored the power of metaphor to shape expectations and inform identity. After being refracted through the looking glass, a lesbian or gay relationship can appear as a mark of inadequacy and immaturity, a passive reflection of the parent or the self's own attributes.

While psychoanalysis hardly legislates attitudes from above, the popularization of the theory of homosexual narcissism reinforced preexisting perceptions that gay men and lesbians lack significant interpersonal and kinship ties, whether those ties have been lost through rejection by relatives or abdicated through a presumed "failure" to procreate. To the extent that a lover appears as a proxy for the image in the mirror, loved not for herself but for the reflected likeness of the viewer's own gender identity, the bond between lovers cannot qualify as a genuinely social tie. Significantly, this impression does not arise from observation of gay relationships, but remains an artifact of the mirror imagery used to analyze and describe gay couples.

The category of decadence overlaps with narcissism in characterizations of lesbians and gay men as promoters of a "gay lifestyle" diametrically opposed to "the simple life" periodically glorified in the

United States. As early as the Revolutionary War, Benjamin Rush linked luxury with effeminacy, while John Adams held "effeminate refinements" responsible for the fall of the Roman Empire (Shi 1985). More recently Christopher Lasch (1978) has recast the Narcissus myth in apocalyptic tones, warning of the eclipse of the old bourgeoisie by a culture of narcissism whose egocentricity and therapeutic sensibility threaten the social fabric of a "dying culture." From the witchhunts of Joseph McCarthy to the legislative initiatives of the New Right, conservatives have accused gay people of spearheading this invasion from within: because gays selfishly pursue nonprocreative relationships, they threaten civilization by promoting a society that declines to reproduce itself. Even gay liberation militants, like their "accommodationist predecessors" in the homophile organizations of the 1950s, stereotyped bar gays as decadent, frivolous, and cynical (D'Emilio 1983b).

Because gay and lesbian identity is organized primarily in terms of gender and sexuality rather than production or work, the most visible gay institutions have occupied the "personal" (read: ego-centered) sphere of leisure and consumption. Yet the heterogeneity of the interview sample for this study alone belies conjecture that gay people are predominantly white, male, wealthy, selfish, recreation-oriented, and above all single (cf. Goodman et al. 1983). The very differences among lesbians and gay men that led to the widespread disaffiliation from the concept of a unified "gay community" affirm the absence of any uniform "gay lifestyle." To claim a lesbian or gay identity is not necessarily to subscribe to a particular way of organizing one's time or interests.

Accusations that gay men willfully "spread" AIDS, a quintessential example of blaming the victim (or the survivor, as many persons with AIDS prefer to be called) could appear credible only in the context of generalized notions of homosexual narcissism and irresponsibility.[11] Ironically, gay men have assumed the greatest responsibility for providing social services to PWAs, developing and publicizing safer sex guidelines, and educating the public at large about AIDS. The leveling off of AIDS rates among gay men in San Francisco can be attributed to the efforts of gay men themselves, along with their lesbian and heterosexual allies working in AIDS organizing projects. Adding injury to insult are the practices of insurance companies accused of redlining neighborhoods with large concentrations of "single men," thus denying much-needed health coverage to gay men while perpetuating the stereotype of gay people as invariably single and therefore unattached.

People in the United States often view selfishness as an outgrowth of narcissistic self-absorption, but in the case of homosexuality allegations of selfishness also relate to beliefs about how lesbians and gay men are situated within class relations. Typical of the class stereotyping of gay people is this unsupported generalization from a *Boston Herald* editorial against passage of a gay rights bill: "Gays tend to be better off financially than the average American" (in Allen 1987). There is a certain inconsistency, however, in accusing gay people of being irresponsibly "promiscuous" and failing to sustain stable relationships (much less family), while simultaneously attacking them for an affluence predicated upon the combined power of two incomes. Such portraits of class allegiances are further complicated by the (often erroneous) perception of gay men as leaders in the gentrification of urban areas. In Terri Burnett's opinion, gentrification in the Bay Area had fueled "anger that the loss of [neighborhood and ethnic] community is based upon gay male community."

Attributions of wealth that ascribe class privilege to all gay people are linked not only to the reduction of sexual identity to sexuality, but also to presumptions that gay men and lesbians lack family ties. "Doubtless to many . . . people," Quentin Crisp (1968:130) observed of his native Britain, "an effeminate homosexual was simply someone who liked sex but could not face the burdens, responsibilities, and decisions that might crush him if he married a woman." In the United States the very notion of responsibility is closely tied to family and adulthood. Among the well-to-do in the nineteenth century, "gay" described the relatively carefree existence led by single white women (Cott 1977).

In the context of families, responsibility carries an implicitly social orientation: a person is responsible to someone or for someone. A few lesbians and gay men in the Bay Area subscribed to the ideology of family as a burden and responsibility that restricted "personal freedom." When Nils Norgaard talked about family, he used the word in a procreative sense:

If you get married, you sacrifice the rest of your life to raise a family—or a lot, if you get kids. And that's a very big responsibility. And a family is more than the wife and a kid. You usually have a couple of dogs, you have your own little life with your family. And I'm not sure if I want that, because if I don't get married, I will have all the time for myself. And I can go wherever I want. I can travel, and I can see the world. I can't do that with a family so much.

More common, however, were complaints about coworkers and acquaintances who assumed that a gay man or lesbian had no "immediate family" or financial dependents. If an individual was known to have a lover, acquaintances sometimes trivialized the relationship or dismissed it as an illegitimate derivative of the self. Even in the wake of national publicity about custody cases and the lesbian baby boom, many heterosexuals still do not recognize the potential for lesbians and gay men to become involved in childcare and coparenting arrangements, much less view them as persons capable of producing biological offspring. In a time and a culture that links sexual activity to identity, the nonprocreative character of sex between women or men casts gay men and lesbians as essentially nonprocreative beings. Since most people in the United States see discretionary income as an indicator of class privilege and a prerequisite for social mobility, the presumption that gay people do not contribute to the economic survival of others, including kin, lends a dubious credence to representations that systematically assign lesbians and gay men to a position of class dominance.

Not surprisingly, many of the gay men and lesbians I met had become adept at refuting accusations of gay selfishness and irresponsibility. Speakers from gay organizations who addressed high school classes, church groups, and other predominantly heterosexual audiences drew attention to the number of lesbian and gay parents and highlighted the contributions of gay people active in social service professions such as teaching or social work. Some people integrated notions of racial or ethnic identity into their rebuttals. Danny Carlson, himself Native American, told me he identified other lesbian and gay Indians by their selflessness. "Gay Indian people," he said, "are very creative. Very progressive. And when they do things, they think of the people, they don't think of themself." Placing the people's needs over one's own Danny considered part of "the Indian way."

Evidence abounds that lesbians and gay men, like others in this society, create, maintain, and fulfill responsibilities to social others. Yet depictions that locate gay and lesbian lovers within a relation of sameness reinforce popular perceptions that gay people enjoy class privilege because they lack dependents and kinship ties. At issue are the nuances of narcissism embedded in a mirror imagery that conflates the persons within lesbian and gay couples, turning relations symbolically constituted by love back in upon the self.

COUPLES VERSUS COMMUNITY

In her study of lesbians in a Midwestern town, Susan Krieger (1983) extended the looking-glass metaphor outward from the self past the lover to portray an entire community caught up in an ideology of sameness. Krieger had observed a relatively demographically homogeneous population at a time when feminist prescriptions for androgyny were at their peak. Moving between the categories of "the individual" and "the community," she recasts a debate from the sociology of the 1950s and 1960s on individuality versus conformity and equality versus excellence. For women who accepted the fundamental sameness of social ties among lesbians, community appeared to menace individuality, much as merging seems to threaten the autonomy of individuals within couples.[12]

Krieger's *The Mirror Dance* offers a fine descriptive account of the conflicts and dissatisfactions that can emerge from perceptions of likeness in lesbian relationships. From an analytic point of view, however, reworking this old debate in a lesbian or gay context has not proved particularly fruitful. To limit analysis to description of what these women felt or saw tends to perpetuate the very premise reflected in mirror imagery: that gender constitutes the unified and overriding ground of lesbian and gay relationships. Lost in this sea of sameness are subtleties such as the longstanding tension between gay couples and gay community.

Approximately half the participants in the interview sample described themselves as being in a relationship, a ratio that held equally for women and men. Many, though certainly not all, claimed they preferred having a partner over being single. Coming out, in particular, tended to launch individuals on a search for partners, suggesting relational aspects to claiming a gay or lesbian identity. The appearance of AIDS, too, had ushered in a renewed emphasis on relationships among gay men. Early in the AIDS epidemic, before the introduction of a concept of safer sex, many straight and gay commentators blamed the disease on "promiscuity" and encouraged gay men to "settle down" with monogamous partners. Drawing on cultural notions of adulthood, they celebrated the "new maturity" of gay relationships and congratulated "the community" for moving beyond adolescence. In the bars—"bars" operating as a trope for tricks, for sex without love or commitment—men began to joke, "Oh yes, I'm here because I want a *fulfilled* relationship tonight!"

Less affected by AIDS was the perception of any lover not one's own—that is, a lover in the generic sense—as someone who intervenes between the individual and community. In the 1970s lesbian-feminism counseled nonmonogamy as a way to avoid the exclusiveness believed to be inherent in coupled relationships.[13] Gay liberationists praised the leveling effect of regarding gay people as an "army of lovers" (Praunheim 1979). This sense of a partner as someone who competes with friends for a person's time and attention persisted into the 1980s (cf. Barnhart 1975). Some of the same men and women who complained that friends disappear from sight when they first become involved with a lover wryly predicted that couples active in "community" activities would not long survive.

A related grievance charged that although encouragement for breaking up was easy to come by, encouragement for staying together could be difficult to find. While I lived in San Francisco my lover and I became kin to a lesbian couple who numbered only singles in their gay families and wanted to add a couple to support their relationship. During the same period several people asked me to serve as a go-between to negotiate the return of material possessions from ex-lovers, and more than a few spent hours discussing a breakup. Breakups fell into the category of extenuating circumstances, a time when family and friends needed to "be there" for one another more than ever. In the context of representations that pitted couples against both friends and community, a person could experience ending an erotic relationship as a reintegration into larger social wholes.

When chosen families emerged during the 1980s, they bore the potential to mitigate this tension. Gay families grouped friends together with lovers and held forth the ideal of ongoing kinship with former partners in the years following a breakup. In the Bay Area, relationships with lovers did tend to be more symbolically marked by coresidence and rituals than other ties located within the diffuse boundaries of families we choose. But when gay men and lesbians spoke of chosen families, many pointed with pride to families that did not reduce to a couple. Applying the mirror metaphor indiscriminately to all forms of lesbian or gay relationships not only fails to comprehend the legacy of tension between couples and community, but completely misses this idealized shift from competition to continuity in the relationship of lovers to friends.

Controversy over gay weddings and other ritual celebrations of the tie to a lover has focused on the question of whether such ceremonies breach community solidarity and promote assimilation by appealing to a "straight model" for relationships (cf. Ettelbrick 1989; Stoddard 1989). In an interesting twist to theories of homosexual narcissism, some lesbian and gay critics have condemned participants in these ceremonies for self-centeredness. The irony of applying this label to a relationship rather than an individual becomes understandable only as the correlate of a mirror imagery that makes absorption in a "like" other the social equivalent of obsession with self. Advocates of such rituals have countered charges of assimilationism by emphasizing the originality of their ceremonies and the lack of "models" for lesbian and gay relationships. Utilizing the rhetoric of a distinctively gay kinship, a kinship of choice and creation, they usually placed great emphasis on planning and inventing their own ceremonies.

A year before I interviewed Lourdes Alcantara, she and her lover of five years had organized a ceremony to mark their commitment, complete with lesbian minister. The ritual, which brought friends together with biological kin, incorporated candles, flowers, and pictures of those unable to attend. Lourdes offered an elaborate rationale for the inclusion of each item used in the ritual.

> One candle was south, north, west, and east. East because Janet was from the east; south because I'm from the south; north, it's the orientation to lesbians to go ahead in the future . . . and west because we came to the west to make our home. . . . It was not a traditional marriage. *We* made it ourselves.

While it has become common for heterosexual couples in the United States to write their own marriage ceremonies, similar efforts by gay and lesbian couples can take on a different meaning in the context of gay kinship. The creative activity of composing the ceremony rhetorically ensconces a couple squarely within families we choose. By superseding depictions of couples as solidary units set off against other lesbians or gay men, discourse on gay families placed lovers in a new relationship to friends, not completely "like" and yet no longer opposed.

REFLECTIONS ON METAPHOR

With its allied categories of sameness and difference, mirror imagery orders relationships between lesbian and gay lovers along the axis of gender in such a way as to predispose findings of continuity between partners. To automatically position lovers in a relation of likeness is to overlook nuances such as the ideological tension between couples and community, or the way notions of class combine with procreative kinship ideologies to make allegations of homosexual narcissism appear plausible. Nothing in the mirror can distinguish the contrasts of butch/fem from the differentiation of lovers along lines of race, age, ability, ethnicity, or class. Trapped within the mirror's timeless reflection, the likeness embedded in certain interpretations of androgyny blends into the gendered imagery of 1970s Castro clones and the "new femininity" of lipstick lesbians.

To emphasize continuities between lovers is to assume that gender must invariably be the identity with the most subjective significance to each, when partners clearly do not always experience it as such. To equate difference with dependence or a power differential between partners likewise assumes gender to be *the* meaningful attribute that orders experience. Variations in context and in the cultural construction of identities ensure that likeness will not inevitably represent the same likeness, nor difference the same difference. To look no further than the mirror is to accede to an impoverishment of the language used to describe relationships.

Because the looking glass highlights specific issues such as merging and narcissism, these "problems" acquire credibility through the very use of the image. One larger effect of looking-glass imagery is to make relationships between lesbian or gay lovers appear inadequate, reducing lovers to mere derivatives of the self or to parodies of heterosexual relationships. In the process, not only the social significance of this tie but also its familial character become invisible to the heterosexual observer. As a metaphor intended to facilitate understanding, the mirror has proved too static, lacking the historical perspective and analytic power to comprehend nuanced meanings.[14] Instead, it paints lesbian and gay lovers with the broad strokes of identity, assuming a likeness grounded in the overriding saliency of gender and the unsubstantiated unity of male and female gender standpoints.

A lesson in the limits of metaphor can be learned from Michel Foucault's (1977) discussion of the Panopticon. Foucault used Jeremy Bentham's prison design to illustrate the historical development of disciplines (both scholarly and social) that take pleasure in subjugating with their all-encompassing gaze. Bentham's floor plan located guards in a central observatory, with cell wings radiating outward from this pivotal node. Missing from Foucault's discussion is any mention of the historical abandonment of the Panopticon by prison architects once captors realized that their subjects were capable of returning this gaze. Although guards in the Panopticon could monitor every aspect of prisoner behavior, prisoners could equally well follow every move the guards made. The same architectural design that promoted subjugation through surveillance also facilitated a number of escape attempts (Johnston 1973).

In similar fashion, the passive reflection of lesbian and gay couples trapped within the looking glass denies not only difference between partners, but agency and interaction. Directionality of the gaze is critical. Where does the gaze originate—from a member of the couple or an observer? How does an observer's sexual identity become implicated in descriptions of the couple? Remember, too, that each member of a couple looks out at a partner who may stand in many meaningful relations to the self. Each individual must draw out and interpret these meanings, actively taking up positions vis-à-vis the lover. In some situations, the gaze may shift from the lover to a category called "heterosexuals," emphasizing relations of contrast *or* continuity.

Likeness is not inherent in mirror imagery: reflections can also be construed as reversals of otherwise identical representations (Fernandez 1986). Historically, however, the mirror has been deployed to assert the "same-same" character of lesbian and gay couples, opposing these relationships to heterosexual ties that are symbolically grounded in procreation and gendered difference. The question then becomes: who is making this argument for sameness, and to what end? Intentionally or unintentionally, the magnification of gender through the prism of likeness has reinforced the exclusion of lesbians and gay men from kinship by portraying them as less than fully social beings. Unreflective recourse to the mirror metaphor cannot substitute for identification of its cultural presumptions and the politics embedded in its situational implementation. The rather unanthropological alternative is to echo an abstract symmetry of sameness and decontextualized assertion that does little justice to relations as multifaceted as those between lovers.

SEVEN

PARENTING IN THE AGE OF AIDS

> With a terrifying lucidity she had the vision of her corpse
> and she drew her hands over her body to go to the depths
> of this idea which, although so simple, had but just come
> to her—that she bore her skeleton in her, that it was not
> a result of death, a metamorphosis, a culmination, but a
> thing which one carries about always, an inseparable specter
> of the human form—and that the scaffolding of life is
> already the symbol of the tomb.
>
> —PIERRE LOUŸS, *Aphrodite*

During the 1980s Louise Rice (1988), a lesbian mother
of teenage sons, spoke at a fundraiser for *Choosing Children,* a film
about lesbian parents and their families. "In the course of my talk,"
she wrote, "I asked how many there were considering motherhood. I
remember my almost total disbelief as nearly every hand went up."
Beginning in the mid-1970s on the West Coast, the fantasies and
intentions of women like these gave way to the practice known as the
lesbian baby boom. In the Bay Area, the impact of this novel concern
reverberated throughout the lesbian population. The majority may
not have been directly involved in raising a child, but everyone seemed
to know another lesbian who was. Conferences and workshops
abounded on the topics of whether to have children, how to have
children, and what to do with them once you get them. Anthologies
of writings about lesbian and gay parenting appeared in the book-
stores.[1] Gay periodicals introduced columns that chronicled the ad-
ventures of new parents and offered advice on child rearing. Even the
progressive, politically oriented *Gay Community News* published a
page of birth pictures from a "lesbians having babies" support group.

Women between the ages of 30 and 45 seemed to predominate
among those bearing, adopting, coparenting, or otherwise incorporating children into their lives. Most of these women were members of
the relatively "out" cohort who came of age at the height of the
women's and gay movements. Yet approximately two-thirds of my
interview sample, including both men and women ranging in age from
19 to 63, claimed they would like to have children if conditions were

165

right and they could successfully overcome financial or legal obstacles. Several were raising children at the time of the interview, a few had children already grown, one had fought a bitter custody battle, and another had felt pressured to give up her child after coming out years ago. Many were actively investigating options such as adoption or alternative insemination.

In their coming-out narratives, interview participants sometimes described early expectations about what their lives would be like as adults. Storytellers were fairly evenly split between those who had anticipated having children or getting married, and those who claimed they had never entertained such thoughts. While it is impossible to judge how individuals would have reconfigured their stories in the absence of the current preoccupation with gay families, when they did report expectations of marriage or procreation, their retrospective accounts tended to highlight ties to children while minimizing any relation to a heterosexual partner.

> When I was little I used to think I would get married, but the married wasn't the big part, the big part was having kids. I always thought I was gonna have a *ton* of kids. I had all the kids' names picked out already. And I had close to fifteen names.

A man in his thirties laughingly told me that he had always counted on having children, "but not being married, no. I don't know how I expected them to appear!" Of those who had never married or had children before coming out, most found it much easier to imagine themselves as parents than as husband or wife in a straight relation‡ship.

Very often people felt that class relations, race, and ethnicity had influenced—sometimes in contradictory ways—their willingness to consider parenthood. Some cited lack of money and dead-end jobs as reasons to postpone childrearing, while others with low incomes and no prospects for upward mobility responded, "If not now, when?" With narratives of poverty, sterilization abuse, warfare, and holocaust, individuals linked their arguments to histories of oppression. Some from Native American, African-American, Jewish, and Latino(a) backgrounds welcomed the lesbian baby boom as the concrete refutation of allegations that gay relationships contribute to processes of racial and cultural genocide. Others felt that having "one or two strikes against you" (race or class oppression) was sufficient, without asking children to bear the added stigma of a gay or lesbian parent. Still others, less given to political analysis, viewed raising children as an opportunity to perpetuate racial and ethnic identities into the future.

For most, the combination of parenthood with a lesbian or gay identity posed no intrinsic moral dilemma. Convinced that they would make parents every bit as good as—if not superior to—heterosexuals, they countered stereotypes of homosexuals as child molesters with the observation that heterosexual men perpetrate the vast majority of child abuse in the U.S. (cf. Hollibaugh 1979). For those who expressed a serious wish to become parents, the primary problems associated with having children appeared to require strategic and technical solutions rather than extended ethical debate.

In actuality, of course, lesbian and gay parenting is nothing new. A large number of gay men and lesbians have children from previous marriages, or were single parents before coming out. Support groups for gay fathers and lesbian mothers have existed since the 1970s. One thing that *has* changed, however, is the conviction, often reported by older gays and lesbians, that a person should get married or at least renounce gay involvements if he or she wants children. Writing in the 1930s, Mary Casal (1975:137) anticipated the contemporary willingness to pursue parenting independent of marriage or an ongoing heterosexual relationship: "Had I been wise then as I am today and if the views of man had been different, I feel convinced that I might have had a child some time by a father chosen just for that occasion." Rather than maintaining a heterosexual facade or sacrificing gay relationships to raise children, more and more parents who identify as gay or lesbian have integrated their children into the gay families that are families we create. Those without children at the time they come out encounter a panoply of options, including foster care, surrogate parenthood, adoption, coparenting, alternative insemination, and "old-fashioned" (procreative, heterosexual) sex.

The popularization of alternative insemination among lesbians supplied the historical spark that set fire to this unprecedented interest in gay parenting. Although many gay men and lesbians share a desire for children, because gay men cannot physically bear babies, they confront additional obstacles to parenthood (McKinney 1987). My focus here will be on lesbian mothers as the fastest growing segment of gay parents, and on alternative insemination as the technique most closely associated with the lesbian baby boom.

Gay and lesbian involvement in childrearing must be viewed against the backdrop of growing numbers of single parents of all sexualities, coupled with the wave of pronatalism that swept the United States during the 1970s and 1980s. But the lesbian baby boom represents something more than a homosexual adjunct to this wider trend, insofar as it has developed and been meaningfully interpreted in the context of discourse on gay kinship. One result has been the subtle reincorporation of biology and procreation within gay families conceptualized as the products of unfettered creativity and choice.

THE LESBIAN MOTHER AS ICON

The characterization of lesbians as nonprocreative beings and the depiction of lesbian lovers as participants in "same-same" relationships renders the image of the lesbian mother shocking and disconcerting, a veritable *non sequitur* (Lewin 1981; Lewin and Lyons 1982). While I was attending a continuing education class on a spring afternoon during fieldwork, one of the students—herself a single, heterosexual mother—could not contain her surprise when the instructor's lover brought their young children to visit the class. "She just doesn't seem like the type," remarked my classmate, having previously speculated about the teacher's sexual identity.

Many lesbian parents described motherhood as a status that made their sexual identity invisible. In their experience, heterosexuals who saw a lesbian accompanied by a child generally assumed she was straight and perhaps married. Before the lesbian baby boom, gay activists often challenged this presupposition by calling attention to the numbers of lesbians and gay men with children from previous heterosexual involvements.[2] This information often surprised heterosexual audiences, but they were able to reconcile it with essentialist notions of homosexuality by treating these offspring as the product of earlier, "mistaken" interpretations of an intrinsically nonprocreative lesbian or gay identity.

If motherhood can render lesbian identity invisible, lesbian identity can also obscure parenthood. As the biological mother of three teenagers, Edith Motzko found it relatively easy to refute the popular notion that the term "lesbian mother" presents an oxymoron insofar as it joins a procreative identity (mother) to a sexual identity (lesbian) that is frequently represented as the antithesis of procreative sexuality. What Edith didn't count on was having to expose this sort of abstract thinking to her own father.

> When I told my father that I was gay . . . his comeback was that *society* didn't demand it, that *nature* demanded that as a female that I would produce the species. I said, "I did it three times. I quit. That's it!" (laughter) So he gave me a big hug and said, "Be happy."

Numerically, adopted children taken together with children from heterosexual alliances still account for the majority of lesbian and gay parents. During the 1980s, however, the children of alternative insemination began to overshadow these other kinds of dependents, assuming a symbolic significance for lesbians and gay men disproportionate to their numbers. Insemination was the innovation many credited with motivating the lesbian baby boom, facilitating biological parenting without requiring marriage, subterfuge, or heterosexual intercourse. I focus on this method of "choosing children" not only in deference to its centrality within discussions of lesbian parenting during the 1980s, but also because of its implications for the larger discourse on gay kinship. As the practice of alternative insemination spread among lesbians, relations conceived as blood ties surfaced where one might least expect them: in the midst of gay families that had been defined in *opposition* to the biological relations gays and lesbians ascribed to straight family.

In large part it is the prospect of physical procreation, the body of the child emerging from the body of the mother at a moment when she claims her lesbian identity, that renders "the lesbian mother" at once icon and conundrum. Babies conceived after a woman has come out demand a reconciliation of a nonprocreative lesbian identity with procreative practice. Any such reconciliation will be complicated by the notions of gender and personhood embedded in particular ideologies of kinship.

Alternative insemination, in particular, is a technique for acquiring children that challenges conventional understandings of biological offspring as the visible outcome of a gendered difference grounded in the symbolics of anatomy. In the United States, new reproductive technologies have collided with ideologies that picture a child as the "natural" product of the union of a woman and a man in an act of sexual intercourse that gives expression to contrasting gender identities. Significantly, biological offspring conceived through alternative insemination need not necessarily be "conceived" as the product of two persons in this sense.[3]

Most lesbians in the Bay Area used the gender-neutral term "donor" to describe a man who supplies semen for insemination. Because all parties to insemination theoretically construed the male contribution to procreation as a donation, freely given, a donor's continued involvement in a child's future was never assumed. Whether an individual donor would identify as a parent or participate in childrearing had to be determined on a case-by-case basis. Some of the lesbians I met who were planning to have children specifically sought men who were prepared to coparent. For their part, not all donors were eager to assume the responsibilities of changing diapers or contributing money to a child's support. Ray Glaser, a gay man who intended to donate sperm to a lesbian friend, had no intention of becoming a father. Although he was willing for the child to know his identity, he had opted to become what he called an uncle or godfather, a more distant relationship defined by agreement with the child's lesbian parents.

With a view to possible legal complications or a desire to legitimate a nonbiological mother's claim to parental status, some lesbian mothers preferred not to know a donor's identity. A few went so far as to use sperm from several donors to make it difficult to trace a child's genitor. There was always the danger that a donor would have a change of heart, redefining his contribution from gift of sperm to possession of the shared biological substance that would give him grounds for a custody case. Though widely practiced, anonymous donor insemination remained highly controversial in the Bay Area. Lesbians who had been adopted as children and lesbian birth mothers who had once given children up for adoption took the lead in formulating a critique that portrayed anonymous insemination as detrimental to a child's well-being in a society that privileges biological inheritance (Liljesfraund 1988).

Because insemination eliminates body-to-body contact, participants could minimize the male contribution to procreation with relative ease. Rather than focusing on donors, some lesbian parents-to-be referred only to "semen," making the procreative pair (if any) woman plus sperm, gendered person plus gender signifier. More is involved here than some strategic separation of genitor from (social) parent. To lesbian parents who had chosen an anonymous donor, their child might appear as the physical offspring of a single person, the child's biological mother. In this context, even so conventional a question as, "Does he take after his father?" directed by a stranger toward the baby in the stroller forces the issue of coming out.

This separation of personhood and parenthood from the male's physiological contribution to procreation is in no way intrinsic to insemination as a technique. In her study of married heterosexual couples enrolled in an in vitro fertilization program, Judith Modell (1989) found that women in the program considered adoption a preferable alternative to insemination in the event that the in vitro procedure failed. These women associated insemination with adultery and extramarital sex, believing that the method would introduce an unwanted third party into the relationship with a husband. For most Bay Area lesbians, in contrast, semen did not substitute for a contribution that would otherwise have come from their sexual partners. They defined the link to a donor as nonsexual, and insemination as an approach to procreation that circumvented any need for heterosexual intercourse or an ongoing heterosexual alliance.

Alternative insemination was initially associated with developments in biotechnology, although the syringe method favored by lesbians certainly represents a "low-tech," economical application. As insemination grew in popularity among lesbians, there was a corresponding move to change its linguistic modifier from "artificial" to "alternative," presumably in order to avoid invoking "natural" as a contrasting category. Labeling new reproductive technologies "artificial" resonated uncomfortably with the stigmatization of lesbian and gay sexualities as somehow unnatural. Were procreative sex reducible to methods of getting sperm to egg, this rhetorical shift might have proved adequate to avoid such associations. But the combination of two differently gendered persons destined to achieve substantive form in the new person about to be born, is as naturalized, as taken-for-granted, a part of procreation in the United States as the act of heterosexual intercourse symbolizing that union.

Viewed through the prism of a gendered difference predicated on the symbolic union of male and female in heterosexual relationships, the image of the lesbian mother can appear as much ironic as iconic. The butch stereotype of lesbians seems diametrically opposed to the nurturance and caretaking so closely associated with motherhood in the United States (Hanscombe and Forster 1982). If childbearing stands as a sign of gender fulfilled, the mark of maturity and becoming a "real woman," how can it coexist with a category like "butch," popularly understood as a woman who desires to be a man? This perceived contradiction rests upon a contested ideology of womanhood, along with a very one-dimensional and inaccurate portrait of what it means to be butch. Although the majority of lesbians in the 1980s did not identify as either butch or fem, most had grappled with stereotypes about what it means to be gay, and developed a high degree of consciousness about issues of gender identity in the process of coming out.

Lesbian parents in the Bay Area were very well aware of heterosexual concerns about the effect of "same-gender" parents on a child's own gender and sexual identities. Joking about butch/fem contrasts accompanied lively debates over the importance of incorporating male "role models" into their children's lives. One woman might tease another about the inexpert styling of her young daughter's hair ("I never wore barrettes, and I *still* can't figure out where to put them!" protested the target of these friendly jibes). On another occasion, a woman who identified as a fem delighted in trading tips on makeup with the teenage daughter of a woman who had recently joined her household. A "mid-life butch crisis" was how Diane Kunin, in her late thirties, sarcastically referred to her recent, unprecedented thoughts of having a child. Humor aside, in cases where lesbian parents in a couple did identify as butch and fem, there seemed to be no preordained correspondence between biological motherhood and their respective gendered identifications. The fem-identified woman might or might not have physically given birth to their child(ren), contrary to what one would expect from a simplistic mapping of butch/fem categories onto the culturally constructed masculine/feminine contrast.

From radio and television talk shows to private conversations, one of the most frequently raised objections to lesbian and gay parenting invoked kinship terminology: What would the child call the (biological) mother's lover? The question assumes, of course, an idealized mother-and-father form of parenting in which the persons rearing a child coincide neatly with genetrix and genitor. In actuality large numbers of children in the United States have been raised by single or adopted parents, grandparents, aunts and uncles, older siblings, or multiple coparents. When heterosexual parents divorce and remarry, children often acquire more than two parents. Although they classify these relations as stepparents, "stepdad" and "stepmother" are not terms of address. Some children resolve the issue by calling their stepparents by first name alone; others apply the same kinship term to more than one individual; still others use different variants of a term for different parents (e.g., "Father" and "Dad").

Similarly, children in the United States have two sets of grandparents, yet they manage to avoid confusing one with the other. Terms of address vary regionally, but a common method of distinguishing between maternal and paternal grandparents employs some combination of kinship term plus first or last name. This strategy was the same employed by some lesbian mothers, whose children knew them as "Mama X" and "Mama Z." In other instances, lesbian parents marked a blood tie as primary by teaching the child to address the biological parent simply as "Mama" and the nonbiological parent(s) as "Mama (or Papa, or Mommy, or Daddy) So-and-So." Claire Riley (1988) reported lesbian couples in New York City who used "Mommy" for one parent and a word for "mother" in a second language for her partner. Of course, the entire debate about kinship terminology ignores single lesbian parents, as well as lesbians who share childcare with men who may or may not identify as fathers.

This widespread heterosexual preoccupation with nomenclature, coupled with an inability to imagine solutions to the terminological "problem," seems curious—curious, that is, unless one takes into account the belief that lesbian and gay relationships must resolve themselves into "roles" patterned on heterosexually gendered relations. Consider these all-too-typical remarks by Mark Grover, a columnist for the *Boston Ledger:* "It may be my ignorance, but I can't help but wonder what a child would do whose parents are two males; are they both referred to as 'Daddy?' Or does the child learn to refer to one of the men as 'Mom?' " (Westheimer 1987). In his discomfort with gay parenting, Grover feared what seemed to him the inevitable outcome of a system of mutually exclusive gender categories-one man would have to be "the father," leaving "the mother" as the only identity available to the remaining partner.

Lest heterosexuals bear sole blame for perpetuating this line of cultural reasoning, listen for a moment to Paul Jaramillo, an interview participant whose opinions, while exceptional among gay men and lesbians, are not unknown:

> It seems like it's the latest thing now, to be a lesbian mother. And to me, that is *so* strange to me, two people of the same sex raising children. . . . It's gonna sound bad, but it seems to me there's no balance there. Maybe there is; I don't know. Again, focusing mostly in biology. I'm just so used to seeing a man and a woman. Sorts of masculine traits, sorts of female traits. Combining and raising this [child] together. And when it comes to lesbians, I'm totally ignorant. I admit that fact. I see them as being very good mothers, but I'm just curious as to how these kids are gonna be when they grow up. Is this gonna be a challenge, or a hardship, or is it gonna be something that's wonderful for them?

Rather than wondering who would take which (presumably fixed and given) "role," Paul worried that a child could find it confusing to have two mothers. His account invokes cultural associations that link parenting and procreation to gendered difference, and not just any sort of gendered difference, but one constituted through a heterosexual relationship.

Paul's version of the terminological objection refracts relationships between lovers through the looking-glass imagery critiqued in the earlier discussion of lesbian and gay couples. There I argued that the abstract likeness which appears to characterize "same-same" (woman-woman or man-man) ties cannot be assumed for lesbian and gay relationships, but must be meaningfully specified and interpreted in context. To my knowledge most lesbian mothers who shared responsibility for raising a child made no special effort to minimize their differences, but with respect to parenting, they often formulated those differences in terms of a new and gender-neutral contrast. For lesbian parents who had practiced alternative insemination, the salient category shifted from "*the* mother" (a "role" that only a single individual can fill) to "*the one* having the baby." This reclassification still defined parental identities through difference, but it became a difference organized in terms of biological versus nonbiological parenthood rather than mother versus father. One effect of this shift was to underscore the congruence between procreative potential and lesbian identity, positioning lesbian mothers as mediators of these ostensibly contradictory categories. At the same time, it allowed for the possibility of coparents in excess of two, consistent with the fluid boundaries of gay families.

More relevant in this context than the construction of any sort of gendered contrast between parents is the notion, shared by some lesbians and gay men in the United States with their heterosexual counterparts, that children complete or legitimate a family. "What would make your relationship with Gloria a family?" I asked one woman. "If there were at least three people, like a child, involved," she replied. "I always felt that Nancy and I could be a family by ourselves," another woman with young children told me. "But she felt very strongly no, that being a family *meant* having kids. And [after having kids] I think I see what she means." In a play on the old adage, "and baby makes three," and a poke at the proliferation of "alternative" families, a gay theater company in San Francisco recently produced a comedy entitled, "And Baby Makes Seven" (Vogel n.d.), which featured a pregnant lesbian, her lover, their gay male housemate and coparent-to-be, and several fantasy children. The lack of any prescribed number or gender for lesbian and gay parents, combined with the possibility (but *not* necessity) of a biological connection among those parents as contributors of egg or sperm, opened the way for some novel alliances between lesbian mothers and the gay men they had imaged as brothers previous to the lesbian baby boom.

MALE-FEMALE REVISITED: INSEMINATION AND AIDS

Generally speaking, gay men have been every bit as excited as lesbians about the baby boom and the prospect of becoming parents. If they had not personally donated sperm or assumed childrearing responsibilities, many gay men in the Bay Area knew of others who had. Dick Maynes, for example, had a friend he described as "ga ga" over the child he was coparenting: "All you have to do is mention the child, and he goes wild. Pulls out pictures and all the rest of it!" Craig Galloway had maintained a limited commitment to care for the son of a lesbian friend one weekend each month since the child was born five years earlier. Art Desautels got involved as a "bumblebee," the go-between who transfers semen from a donor to a lesbian trying to get pregnant when the two wish their identities to remain confidential.

Meanwhile, Arturo Pelayo was searching for a lesbian of color who would want a gay man both to donate sperm and to play an active part in raising a child:

> I've been really, really envious of lesbians for being able . . . for the options that they have. Just two weeks ago I went to see [the film] *Choosing Children*. I was just in my mood again! But I did talk to someone who said that she had been thinking about that. She's a black woman, and she said she was thinking about at some point in her life, she'd like to consider having children with another Third World gay man. Of course I got excited! You know, whoa!

Arturo's enthusiasm reflected the prospect of suddenly being able to envision something that had never before seemed possible, a parenthood categorically denied to lesbians and gay men in the past. His dream of one day having children encompassed the irony and the ecstasy of two persons culturally defined as nonprocreative beings uniting for the specific purpose of procreation. At one time, cooperation between lesbians and gay men as partners in alternative insemination and adoption seemed to offer the promise of healing some of the rifts in a "gay community" deeply divided by gender, race, and class.

As the vicissitudes of history would have it, it was AIDS (Acquired Immune Deficiency Syndrome), rather than AID (Alternative [Artificial] Insemination by Donor), that drew lesbians and gay men together after the 1970s.[4] Lesbians adopted a variety of positions with respect to AIDS, as with any issue. There were those who stereotyped gay men by condemning them for "promiscuity," ignoring findings that linked the disease to unsafe sexual practices rather than number of sexual partners. Others, however, responded to the crisis by working together with gay men in hospice programs, political action groups, and AIDS organizations that offer support services to people with the disease. "It's changing," said Charlyne Harris, "to be on an empathetic level now with the men and know what they're going through. [There's] a closeness. . . . [Before] there was a barrier: gay men, they have their own lives—I'm a lesbian, I have my own. And it's not like that anymore. They experience the same things we do."

As they encountered the lack of government support for AIDS

research, programs, and drug trials, many newly politicized gay men learned firsthand the meaning of the feminist slogan, "the personal is political." They began to build bridges, however imperfectly constructed, to the feminist sector of the lesbian population. Although some lesbians criticized the racism and sexism within community-based AIDS organizations, renewed concern for the situation of gay men seemed to prevail. Even lesbians not directly involved in AIDS organizing work mentioned making gay male friends when previously they had had few or none.

The onset of AIDS had a dramatic effect on the donor pool available to lesbians for alternative insemination. Before AIDS surfaced, the preferred means of facilitating lesbian motherhood had been to ask gay men to contribute sperm. The general feeling among lesbians was —and continues to be—that gay men represent that category of males most likely to recognize the lover of the biological mother as a full-fledged parent, and to abide by any parenting and custody agreements reached in advance of a child's birth.[5] For many, economics was also a factor in locating a donor, since informal arrangements are far less expensive than paying the high fees charged by sperm banks. But in light of the devastating losses AIDS has inflicted upon gay men in the Bay Area, and the risks for child and mother-to-be of contracting the HIV virus through insemination, by the mid-1980s most lesbians and gay men had become hesitant to pursue this strategy (Pies and Hornstein 1988).

In the absence of effective treatments for AIDS, many men were reluctant to take the antibody test and skeptical about claims that test results would remain confidential. "I don't feel like I would want to be the biological father of anybody," Craig Galloway told me, with the grim wit that has threaded its way through this epidemic, "simply because I don't know whether or not my sperm is radioactive." Louise Romero had originally anticipated asking a close gay male friend to donate semen. "I wanted to have his child, and I won't do it now because I'm afraid of AIDS," she said. "Actually, that's kind of wrecking my plans." Not everyone completely ruled out the combination of gay male genitor and lesbian genetrix, but almost everyone regarded it as an option fraught with deadly hazard. Misha Ben Nun described the changes in her approach to becoming a biological parent:

> I had definitely been looking at different gay men that were possibilities to me, or just feeling very secure that I would be able to find a gay man in the community who was into it. And then I gave that up completely. And then just recently, last week, my housemate was saying that you can feel safe enough, as long as he takes the [HIV antibody] test the day that you inseminate, each time you inseminate. And that's pretty intense to ask someone to do. But I'm also really interested in having whoever is the donor be also the father. So if someone's gonna make that kind of commitment, I expect them to be able to do something like take the test each time.

Notice the usage of "father" in the exclusively social sense of a male who assumes active responsibility for parenting, a person quite discrete from a genitor or donor. Influenced perhaps by her strong desire to find a gay donor, Misha offered a somewhat inaccurate assessment of the risks involved in insemination. If HIV (Human Immunodeficiency Virus) does indeed cause or contribute to AIDS, that virus has an incubation period during which exposure may not be detectable because the body has not yet manufactured the relevant antibodies. This picture is complicated by the unreliability of the HIV antibody test, along with ethical and emotional consequences of submitting to a diagnostic device with the potential to introduce severe stress and discrimination into a person's life if he or she tests positive or if test results become known.

The devastating impact of AIDS on gay men in San Francisco led many lesbians to look elsewhere for sperm donors. Toni Williams and her lover, Marta Rosales, had been seriously considering alternative insemination when they found themselves casting about for new possibilities.

> We wanted it to be a gay father. But with AIDS coming around and stuff like that, I'm very afraid. . . . [Q: Why did you originally want a gay father?] Because it would be very difficult to have a straight person involved in a gay relationship, in a lesbian relationship. It would take a very special person to be that understanding and accepting of how Marta and I are together. You're just this extra person here. You're part of us, but—it's more tension than needs to be. And plus, there's so many gay men that want to have children. And they can't because their lovers cannot

have babies. So we assumed that it would be nice for a gay man, and that he would really want that child. . . . And then, the whole fact that they are gay, and that they accept that in themselves, would make it easier. In the relationship that we have, all three of us or all four of us. God, I don't know how it would work out! (laughs) But now we just decided that we would try to get one of Marta's brothers to donate sperm. God, I don't know how that would work out legally.

In legal terms relationships between gay and lesbian lovers lack recognition in the United States, leaving lesbian and gay parents dependent on the good will of authorities who oversee nonbiological parenting arrangements like foster care or adoption and of sperm donors with a biological claim to parenthood. There is little judicial precedent for granting custody or visitation rights to nonbiological parents, whether lesbian, gay, or heterosexual, unless they have formalized their relationship to a child through adoption. By 1990 most courts still would not allow another person of the same sex as a biological parent to adopt a child without causing the biological parent to forfeit all legal relationship to that child. In only a very few cases had courts allowed lesbian or gay couples to adopt children jointly ("Rare . . . " 1989). Although lawyers urged lesbians and gay men to draw up contracts specifying the rights and obligations entailed in relationships with donors and coparents, such documents did not always hold up in court. This precarious legal situation greatly accentuated the importance of finding sperm donors who would not challenge the status of gay people as parents.

During the 1980s the stigmatization of homosexuality and protective attitudes toward children continued to impact the courts' evaluation of what makes someone a "fit" or "unfit" parent. Judges handed down mixed rulings in custody cases, although more lesbian mothers seemed to be winning custody than in previous years, and in one instance custody of the adolescent son of a gay man with AIDS was awarded to his lover after his death (Bull 1987a; Hunter and Polikoff 1976). Such decisions came in the context of a broad range of legal challenges, from palimony suits to visitation rights for surrogate mothers, that sought recognition for relationships which seemed to fall between the cracks of laws framed with a genealogical grid and legally sanctioned marriage in mind.

When alternative insemination first became common, most lesbians chose gay male partners for their foray into procreation, regardless of whether they elected to minimize the donor's identity as a person or invited him to participate in childrearing. By the 1980s lesbians were still likely to turn to gay men for prospective coparents. But the response of embattled gay and lesbian communities to AIDS has channeled gay fatherhood in the direction of a social rather than physical contribution. While the epidemic may have narrowed the options available for gay men wishing to become parents, it has not dampened their enthusiasm for raising children. Neither has AIDS changed the way alliances of lesbians and gay men as parents in one or another sense of the word embody a male-female symmetry between allegedly nonprocreative beings. Gay and lesbian parents invoke, only to disrupt, the unity of gendered opposites symbolically incarnated in the act of heterosexual coitus that represents a culturally standardized means to reproduction.

OF DEATH AND BIRTH

In conversations about the changes in their midst, gay men and lesbians in the Bay Area sometimes linked the lesbian baby boom to AIDS by juxtaposing the two as moments in a continuous cycle of life's passing and regeneration. New lives replaced lives lost, implicitly reasserting "community" as a unit which, like the disease itself, spanned divisions of gender, race, age, and class. Children (whether biological, foster, or adopted) brought generational depth to this community, along with the promise of a future in what some saw as genocidal times. To understand how deeply this sense of moving between the cultural poles of birth and death resonated in individual experience, one needs to understand something of the encompassing effects of AIDS in the Bay Area.[6]

San Francisco differs from other urban locales around the United States in that the vast majority of its persons with AIDS are gay or bisexual. Because doctors diagnosed the first AIDS cases in the West in gay men, the disease was initially labeled GRID (Gay-Related Immune Deficiency). Although AIDS has disproportionately affected people at the bottom of class and race hierarchies in the United States, physiologically speaking the disease is no respecter of social classifications. Despite efforts to reshape public opinion, however, many people still associate AIDS with sexual identity rather than with unsafe sexual acts practiced across a range of sexualities. The very categorization of AIDS as a sexually transmitted disease (versus an affliction of the blood or immune system that may be transmitted in many ways) constructs particular images of the AIDS patient and divides the disease's so-called "victims" into innocent and guilty, morally responsible or irresponsible (Gilman 1988; Watney 1987). While I was in San Francisco, "here comes walking AIDS" was an epithet of choice hurled by young heterosexuals at any man perceived to be gay. Gay organizations have shouldered the principal burden of AIDS education, with the unintentional effect of strengthening this association (Epstein 1988a). Lesbians occupy the paradoxical position of facing discrimination at the hands of those who link AIDS with gay identity, while lesbians with AIDS and lesbians who test HIV-positive remain relatively invisible to service providers. Although lesbians as a whole fall into a low-risk category based on incidence of the disease, and no fully documented cases link sex between women to AIDS transmission, there are lesbians who have acquired the HIV virus through intravenous drug use (sharing needles), blood transfusions, or sex with men.[7]

The rising incidence of anti-gay violence in the Bay Area, coupled with renewed discrimination in insurance, jobs, and housing, indicated a widespread tendency to view every gay man (and sometimes every lesbian) as a potential person with AIDS. Deeply resented, too, were the subtler indignities of being treated as a pariah in the course of everyday life. "People are less likely to offer a hug than they were a few years ago," said one man, the sadness in his voice almost palpable. Ronnie Walker, who cleaned houses for a living, had lost business in recent years. "Straight people are gonna be freaked out about some guy coming in and coughing on their toilet paper and then they're gonna die," he explained. "There's so much AIDS phobia going around." In his opinion, the phobia had proved far more contagious than the disease.

Like the baby boom among lesbians, AIDS has had an impact and significance reaching far beyond the numbers who have contracted the disease. Add the "worried well" to those who have tested HIV-positive and those diagnosed with AIDS or ARC (AIDS-Related Complex), and you have a group virtually synonymous with the population of self-defined gay men in San Francisco. Almost every gay man I met, as well as many lesbians, had friends or acquaintances who had died from AIDS. Some had the disease themselves. One of the few men who told me that he hardly ever thought about AIDS found himself face-to-face with it just six months later, when his closest friend developed ARC. A glance at the number of obituaries and articles on AIDS in gay periodicals, the constant round of funerals and memorial services, and the tremendous size of the AIDS contingent in the annual Gay Pride Parade offered other gauges of the epidemic's powerful presence in gay and lesbian lives.

At times of celebration like Halloween, the Castro Street Fair, and even Saturday nights, the mood in gay neighborhoods was subdued. No bubble machines sent their offerings up into the evening sky, and few men stood out on the balconies joking or flirting.[8] While there were some men who practiced "safer sex" long before there was need for the term, others found it quite an adjustment. Confusion prevailed regarding whether monogamy effectively prevents individuals from contracting the HIV virus (it does not), while heated polemics examined the politics of "settling down" with a single partner.[9] Initially some men were concerned that people would "go straight" for fear of AIDS or that gay communities would disappear, but no such trends developed (R. Marks 1988). Central gay institutions such as the baths shut their doors, however, in response to loss of patronage and governmental decree.

While Simon Watney (1987:85–86) has justly criticized media coverage of AIDS for its "slippage from 'gay' to 'Aids' to 'death,' " the epidemic has elicited an awareness among gay men of death as an ever-present possibility. Before AIDS, who would have mentioned dying as an experience comparable to claiming a gay identity, or portrayed encountering mortality as a second coming out? Some men tried to put AIDS out of their minds, feeling that beyond practicing safer sex they had little control over whether or not they would develop symptoms. Marty Rollins, who had had several close friends die from AIDS-related illnesses, adopted the philosophy of trying to "keep a good head on my shoulders and live each day one at a time." Others, like Brian Rogers, found themselves thinking about AIDS "every day. Almost every hour. Almost every minute. . . . Thoughts of mortality. Am I ready to die now? Have I done everything I want to do?" Drawing on his small income, Brian found a way to bring each of his brothers and sisters to spend time with him in San Francisco. He spoke about his plans for the future with the urgency and deliberateness of a man making a final settlement of his affairs. Experientially, AIDS had subjected gay men in the Bay Area to a kind of random terror. For them it was not homosexuality but death which appeared perverse, a formidable and elusive opponent that hunts down its targets and strikes without warning (cf. Ariès 1981).

At the risk of succumbing to what Dennis Altman (1986) has called a peculiarly "American" propensity to search for the silver lining in every cloud, I should emphasize that the epidemic has not left an unmitigatedly bleak landscape in its wake. Through self-help and educational activities, fundraising, and provision of crucial services to PWAs, volunteers developed organizational skills and social ties. Persons with AIDS began to organize in an effort to formulate their own needs, rather than accept the role of clients passively shuttled through the byways of social service programs. They introduced the acronym PLWA—Persons Living With AIDS—to stress that they were not victims submitting to an automatic sentence of death, but people coping with the impact of serious illness on their daily lives.[10] While Allan Bérubé (1988) has rightly cautioned against the tendency to read positive meaning and intent into an epidemic devoid of reason or sense, credit must be given to those who have struggled to create something worthwhile from disaster.

Situated historically in a period of discourse on lesbian and gay kinship, AIDS has served as an impetus to establish and expand gay families. In certain cases blood relations joined with gay friends and relatives to assist the chronically ill or dying. Sometimes a family of friends was transformed into a group of caregivers with ties to one another as well as the person with AIDS. Community organizations began to offer counseling to persons with AIDS "and their loved ones," while progressive hospitals and hospices modified residence and visitation policies to embrace "family as the client defines family." Implicit in a phrase like "loved ones" is an open-ended notion of kinship that respects the principles of choice and self-determination in defining kin, with love spanning the ideologically contrasting domains of biological family and families we create.

When gay men and lesbians greeted the baby boom, then, it was in a lived context that presented contrasts between life and death as something much more than a cognitive opposition of transcendent categories. In practice, lesbian and gay parenting countered longstanding associations of sex with death in Western cultures, including the nineteenth-century link between homosexuality and morbidity that seems to have found a twentieth-century counterpart in judgments that blame persons with AIDS for their own affliction. According to the hygienic ideologies that have blossomed periodically in the United States since 1800, illness is not part of a "natural" order, but an evil arising from individual violations of physiological laws, from living contrary to one's "nature" (Ariès 1981; Whorton 1982).[11] Drawing on the characterization of homosexual sex as "unnatural acts," heterosexist commentators have portrayed AIDS as the deserved product of some mythically unitary "gay lifestyle." Lesbian and gay parenting counters representations of homosexuality as sterile and narcissistic by courting life, establishing new family ties where critics expect to find only tragedy, isolation, and death.

Parenting constructs a particular type of kinship tie, an age-differentiated relationship that has added a generational dimension to gay "community." Before the baby boom, lesbians and gay men were accustomed to speaking of generations in a strictly nonprocreative sense that excluded biological referents. In this context, age cohorts represented generations of a sort, defined by symbolic events that incorporated new periodizations of history: the Stonewall generation, the lesbian-feminist generation, the AIDS generation. Generation and descent also surfaced in transmission models that posited a unified "lesbian culture" or "gay lore." Judy Grahn (1984:3), for instance, used the language of inheritance to describe peer relations through time when she set out to record "oral history we heard in a line passed on from our first lover's first lover's first lover." A notion of gay generations also informed political struggles intended to improve conditions for "kids coming out now." Their activist elders depicted themselves working for a society in which younger gays and lesbians "won't have to go through what we went through." This is a rhetoric familiar from discussions of class mobility, the hope voiced by parents seeking a better life for their children. In many Western societies, at least before the disillusionment of a postmodern era, the succession of generations had come to represent visions of unilinear progress fulfilled (Mannheim 1952). This movement toward a world without heterosexism, which enlists the idealism of gays and lesbians to benefit generations yet to come out, looks with expectancy to the children raised within gay families for empathy and acceptance in the future.

Rather than grouping biological and adopted children together with blood family, lesbian and gay parents in the Bay Area considered both part of their gay families. For a child, belonging to a gay family did not depend upon claiming a gay identity, any more than a straight adult would be expected to modify his or her sexual identity to be integrated into families we create. What qualified children for inclusion was being chosen by a self-identified lesbian or gay man. Contrary to the fears of some heterosexuals that gay men and lesbians will raise gay children, lesbian and gay parents tended to see themselves substituting the freedom to choose a sexual identity for the generalized social pressure to be heterosexual. Craig Galloway, coparent to a young boy, emphasized that he took great care "to remind him that the door out is always open. Instead of saying, 'Yeah, you *better* be gay when you grow up.' You know, just like everyone told me when I was a kid: 'You *better* be straight when you grow up.' "

The spatial imagery of children growing up within lesbian and gay communities may offer a clue to the symbolic weight given to children who have been chosen after a parent has come out, children situated squarely within gay families in a manner uncomplicated by ties to former spouses or heterosexual partners.[12] A fruitful parallel can be drawn between the straight children raised in gay families and the hearing children of deaf adults:

> The only hearing people who are ever considered full members of the deaf community are the hearing children of deaf parents for whom Sign is a native language. This is the case with Dr. Henry Klopping, the much-loved superintendent of the California School for the Deaf. One of his former students, talking to me at Gallaudet, signed, "He is deaf, even though he is hearing" (Sacks 1988).

In similar fashion, children raised by lesbian and gay parents carry gay families forward into what for many will be a heterosexual future, moving through ideological space from families we choose to blood family rather than vice versa, but accompanied by a firsthand knowledge of at least some sectors of the diverse range of lesbian and gay experience.

BLOOD RELATIVES RESPOND

Like holidays and coming out, parenthood and AIDS have opened opportunities to renegotiate relationships with blood relatives. In these contexts, however, straight and gay families tended to meet on the terrain of body and biology (adoption, again, retaining a biological referent). When David Lowry's mother, a staunch Catholic, wrote him one Christmas promising to care for him if he ever developed AIDS, it was the first time I had seen this friend of ten years cry. In many instances the epidemic forced the issue of coming out to biological or adoptive relatives, which in turn meant facing the possibility of being disowned at a time of acute need. "Living a lie is one thing," Joseph Beam (1986:241) has written, "but it is quite another to die within its confines." For Ronald Sandler, whose brother had already died from an AIDS-related illness, what strengthened his relationship with his mother "almost overnight" was confiding to her that he, too, had been diagnosed with AIDS. Not all stories had such happy endings. The number of PWAs without homes, family, or resources has grown year by year. When people told relatives and friends they had AIDS, kin ties were reevaluated, constituted, or alienated in the act, defined by who (if anyone) stepped forward to offer love, care, and financial assistance for the protracted and expensive battles with opportunistic infections that accompany this disease.

Kevin Jones took the threat of AIDS extremely seriously, having lived through the death of a good friend. Though he had already come out to his parents, when he contemplated the possibility of contracting the disease himself he felt pulled between two types of family:

> I don't want my parents to go through me dying of AIDS. I'm almost more worried about *them* having to bury me dying of AIDS, than *me* catching AIDS. . . . I've thought about, would I tell my parents? Would I tell my mom and dad I have AIDS, or would I just wait and just die out here? It's scary to me.

Contesting definitions of family can become all too evident in conflicts over a course of medical treatment or hospital visitation rights. Some people had drawn up powers of attorney authorizing persons they considered gay family to take charge of their affairs in the event of incapacitation or death, but these documents sometimes do not hold up under legal challenge by blood relations. When a gay man or lesbian dies, disputes over whether families we choose constitute "real" or legitimate kin can affect wills, distribution of possessions (including property held in common with lovers, friends, or housemates), listings of survivors in obituaries, and disposition of the body.

Tensions surrounding the legitimacy and kinship character of the social ties elaborated through families we choose also manifest themselves in struggles to define what relationship children raised in gay families will have to a lesbian or gay parent's blood relatives. Before the lesbian baby boom received widespread media coverage, the most common parental reaction when someone came out was to assume that having a gay son or daughter meant giving up any hope of grandchildren. Paulette Ducharme's father gave her sister with five children a piece of furniture he had originally promised to Paulette because he concluded that a lesbian would not be having children to whom she could "pass it down." Months after Amy Feldman came out, she felt it necessary to challenge her father's presumption that childbearing and childrearing would be out of the question for her as a lesbian:

> One thing my father did say to me about this thing, he said, one, he was sorry that I wasn't gonna be a mother, and I wasn't gonna have children. And I told him he was wrong. Even if I was straight, I wouldn't be having children right now. That's not the issue. . . . And he *will* get the chance to be a grandfather. And I told him that. He was jazzed about that!

Others described parents urging them to "go straight" or arrange a marriage of convenience in order to have children. Those with a strong racial or ethnic identity sometimes associated pressure to have children with ethnicity, contending that not having children was considered anathema in categories ranging from "a traditional Italian family" to "Cuban culture."

In Rona Bren's case, both she and her brother had come out as gay from a sibling set of two. She felt sorry for her parents, who lived in what she portrayed as a very kinship-conscious Jewish community:

> They can't go anywhere without people flashing baby pictures, grandchildren, wedding pictures. Everywhere they go it's children and children and children and children in their whole community. And everybody looks at them with sorrow. Everybody feels sorry for them—not that everybody knows their kids are gay, just the fact that we're not married and we haven't given them any grandchildren.

Ironically, Rona was the proud nonbiological mother of a child her parents refused to acknowledge as kin:

> They don't want anything to do with us. And I've been talking to them for years about having my own child. My mother says she's got enough trouble, she doesn't need a bastard to top it off . . . in the family. . . . When I first told them that Sarah was pregnant, they just said, "Well, she's not doing that kid any favors," and then they stopped calling after she was born because they didn't want to hear the baby crying, because it bothered them. Because they want grandchildren so desperately and to them it was just like another reminder that they didn't have them.

Parents are surely no less complex in their reactions than their lesbian daughters and gay sons. After their adult children presented motherhood or fatherhood as a possibility, some parents had offered encouragement and support to see them through the stresses of adoption applications or alternative insemination. What these mixed responses by blood relatives indicate is that the birthing and the raising, no less than the coming out and the dying, have become arenas of contention in which discourse on gay kinship is formulated even as transformations of kinship ideologies are hammered out.

PARENTS AND PERSONS

Why should alternative insemination have dominated the discussions of lesbian and gay parenting that have arisen within a wider discourse on gay families? The experience of coming out to relatives convinced many that elements of choice shape even the ostensibly fixed substance of biological ties. Selectivity manifested itself in the discretionary power to judge the closeness of relationships and to alienate kinship ties in response to revelations of a gay or lesbian identity. It should not be surprising, then, to find families we choose capable of integrating biological relations. Because insemination highlights physical procreation, it subsumes notions of biology under the organizing metaphors of choice and creation that have defined gay kinship in opposition to blood family. Such incorporations represent not contradictions, but rather the interplay between any two terms that define an ideological contrast through difference.

When the gay men and lesbians I met spoke of blood ties, they did so in ways that generally did not challenge cultural notions of biology as a static, material "fact." However, they considered a nonbiological mother, father, or coparent no less a parent in the absence of legal or physiological connection to a child. Of those who responded with a simple "yes" when asked whether they wanted to have children some-day, many envisioned a lover or close friend as the biological mother. Most did not consider a sperm donor to be intrinsically a parent, much less a partner, in relationship to a child conceived through alternative insemination; unless the donor shared parenting responsi-bilities, his semen tended to be spoken of simply as a catalyst that facilitates conception. Biological relatedness appeared to be a subsidi-ary option ranged alongside adoption, coparenting, and so on, *within* the dominant framework of choice that constituted families we create. At the same time, the distinction many gay people made between biological and nonbiological parents perpetuated the salience of biol-ogy as a (though not *the*) categorical referent for kinship relations.

There were those who felt that ethnicity was irrelevant, and those who dreamed of adopting "a child from every race" if money were no object. But had some method existed to fuse egg with egg, many lesbian couples planning to parent a child would have preferred that both partners contribute to the child's makeup biologically. The topic of parthenogenesis—procreation utilizing gametes of a single sex, which would completely obviate the need for sperm—came up in conversation from time to time. In the absence of such a method, many desired that children of alternative insemination bear a physical resemblance to the lover who would not physically be having the baby.

When searching for a donor, prospective parents frequently speci-fied race or ethnicity: "[My lover] said, 'I really want an Hispanic to give me sperm so that the baby looks like you.' " Some, especially after AIDS complicated the task of finding a gay male donor, mixed metaphors in attempting to "create" a more direct "biological" link by asking brothers or cousins of a nonbiological parent to contribute sperm. At a workshop for lesbians considering parenthood, one par-ticipant recalled thinking about asking her adult son for sperm when her lover wanted to get pregnant. The arrangement would have cre-ated a legally recognized blood tie to the child that could have sup-ported a custody claim if her lover were to die. After she realized that a genealogical mode of reckoning kinship would make her the child's

190 | PARENTING IN THE AGE OF AIDS

grandmother, she rejected the plan as "too intense." Her fear was that perceived differences in generation would complicate her relationship to lover and child alike.

Appearance tended to carry as much symbolism as genetic connection. Resemblance between parent and child might signify an intention toward creating ethnic or cultural continuity (popularly understood as passing along "traditions"), as well as the union of the child's parents. Heterosexual couples, too, often sought their union and reflection in their children, with comments about which parent a child "takes after" in looks, likes, or behavior. Yet the situation of lesbian mothers choosing a donor for insemination differed in that they could very deliberately select for certain physical characteristics, sometimes in a conscious attempt to reinforce the legally vulnerable tie to a lover. By drawing on the social significance that infuses notions of biology, a lesbian couple can effectively make a statement about who constitutes the child's "real" parents. This subtle emphasis comes in the face of court decisions requiring the biological mother to alienate all legal right to a child in order for her partner to become its adoptive parent, and forbidding a newborn conceived through alternative insemination from assuming the biological mother's lover's surname. In the latter case, the New York State Supreme Court argued that assuming the mother's lesbian lover's name would not be in the child's best interests. For her part, "The child's mother called the use of her lover's last name important as a 'symbolism of family' " (Gillis 1985).

An ideological stress on planning and choosing children pervades the titles for organizations, conferences, and films on lesbian and gay parents. Of course, heterosexuals can plan their children as well, but lesbians and gay men argued with conviction that they must choose in every case, effectively eliminating any contrast between "wanted" and "unwanted" children. In this context, biological ties no longer appeared as a given but as something consciously created, with choice representing a necessary and structural condition of parenting for anyone otherwise exclusively engaged in nonprocreative sex.[13] By situating relationships between parent and child within the metaphor of choice that defines gay families, this argument underlined the implicit contrast between gay and straight parenting.

I think we think more than heterosexual people. I see some very thinking people [among lesbians and gays]. I see my sisters as, they didn't think about having kids. They just did it. And lesbians and gays, they think about *how* they want to raise that child. If they can afford it. They don't just go out [and do it].

Prospective parents applied the notion of choice to the entire context of making a decision to have children, including the division of childcare responsibilities. Very often individuals engaged in extensive discussions and interviews before selecting coparents or sperm donors. Their own finances and job security typically came under scrutiny, especially when state agencies were involved. Many saw themselves enlisting "creativity" to work out the details of coparenting agreements.

The phrase "choosing children" also resonates with the variety of methods available for bringing children into one's life. Some gay men and lesbians would not consider parenting without a lover; others had elected to become single parents. Then there were those who assumed more restricted obligations, like Mara Hanson, who taught karate to children that her lover cared for once each week. L. J. Ewing was not, as she put it, a "formal coparent," but she had helped care for a girl now age 14 since the child was four years old. "She's my little buddy," boasted L. J., confident that this experience had given her a sense of what parenting her "own" child would be like.

Over dinner one evening, Brook Luzio surprised me by talking about a new desire to "help somebody who has kids already." When I saw her again several months later, the picture of a seven-year-old adorned her refrigerator door. After ending a long-term relationship with the biological mother of her daughter, Leslie Aronson continued to care for the child on a regular basis. On the other side of the city, Dave Vorlicek helped two lesbian friends through what he called a "family emergency" by letting their child live with him for the greater part of a year. Older gays and lesbians even had the option to become a grandfather or grandmother, as in this classified advertisement carried by *Gay Community News* : "Have Love Will Travel—Does your baby need a grandma? Middle-aged lesbian couple need grandchild to dote on." The very variety of these arrangements reinforced the belief that no models or code for conduct applied to gay families (aside from love), leaving lesbians and gay men freer than heterosexuals to experiment with alternative childrearing methods and novel parenting agreements.

The long history of state interventions into relationships between lesbians, gay men, and their children has supplied ample reasons for them to approach parenting with a healthy regard for tactical considerations. Custody battles remain a major concern. Former spouses, parents, and grandparents are the most frequent plaintiffs in custody cases that involve lesbians and gay men; such suits typically cite the parent's "lifestyle" as detrimental to the child or contest a lover's status as parent if the child's biological mother or father dies. Judges have mandated HIV antibody tests in some child custody cases, in one instance for heterosexual grandparents who had cared for a son with AIDS (Kenschaft 1987). Scattered custody disputes between lesbian coparents have arisen in conjunction with the baby boom, exacerbated by the uncertain legal status that positions gay relationships to one side of the "nature"/"law" divide. During the 1980s the Presidential Task Force on Adoption recommended against allowing lesbians and gay men to become adoptive parents, while foster care policy in several states became more restrictive, assigning lesbians and gay men to the status of parents of last resort (Bull 1987b). In the Bay Area the consensus seemed to be that planning and deliberation increase the chances that children will not be forcibly wrested from their parents at a later date.

Many lesbian and gay parents portrayed their children not only as the products of considered reflection, but as beings who *introduced* commitment and planning into everyday life. Rona Bren, the nonbiological mother of a two-year-old, spent much of her time and discretionary income on the child, caring for her three days each week in an apartment carpeted with toys:

> She's totally a part of my life, totally, every single way. You know, I consider myself her parent. . . . I don't make decisions without thinking about her. I mean, I don't think, "She's with her mother," and I go through life and do what I want. She's very much a part of every decision, of every thought, everything that I do in my life. Every plan that I make.

For all that Western societies have rooted kinship in a biological relatedness that invokes the act of heterosexual intercourse, becoming a genetrix or genitor has long carried cultural undertones of creation and responsibility for another human being (Schneider 1984). Among the lesbians and gay men in the Bay Area who had incorporated children into their lives, however, the persons who were parents rarely corresponded to genitor and genetrix. Although gay families have proved capable of subsuming childbirth along with adoption, erotic ties, and friendship, families we choose do not rest directly upon a genealogical referent. By the time the lesbian baby boom entered the discourse on gay families, kinship in the United States could no longer be reduced to procreation, or procreation to the image of differently gendered persons locked in heterosexual embrace.

EIGHT

THE POLITICS OF GAY FAMILIES

> Whomever one seeks to persuade, one acknowledges as
> master of the situation.   —KARL MARX

"Ever since they were small," remarked Jeanne
Riley, "my kids have been playing same-same-different games." We
sat on the couch watching her two-year-old daughter arrange small
toys in rows of three, laughing to herself with delight as she pulled
one away from each row and set about working on new combinations.
After a few moments, a look of concern replaced the wistful pride in
Jeanne's face. "The thing is, as they get older and go out into the
world, they're going to realize that their family's different. *Substan-
tially* different. How will this handle that? How will we help them
handle that?"

Lesbian and gay parents are part of the "we" in families we choose,
but from a child's perspective, as Jeanne put it, the "context is going
to be defined by having different parents. And she didn't *choose* it.
She just *has* it." How can you knowingly saddle a child with the
stigma of gay or lesbian parents, ask heterosexual critics, invoking
cultural notions of childhood innocence. This is an argument that
would deny children to the poor, the racially oppressed, and members
of all other groups not assigned to the mythical mainstream of society,
respond the defenders of gay families.

Earlier that afternoon, Jeanne had recounted her battle to include
the children on her health insurance policy. The Internal Revenue
Service considered them her dependents, but the insurance company
had pronounced them ineligible for benefits because they were "related by blood" only to her lover and not to Jeanne herself. Jeanne
pursued the issue with a tenacity that grew out of her fierce loyalty to
her children. Though she was ultimately successful in adding them to

her policy, the experience impressed her with a deep sense of just how different and lacking in legitimacy gay families remain.

The emergence of gay families represents a major historical shift, particularly when viewed against the prevalent assumption that claiming a lesbian or gay identity must mean leaving blood relatives behind and foregoing any possibility of establishing a family of one's own, unless a person is willing to make the compromise of hiding out in a marriage of convenience. Given that homosexuality became firmly allied with identity only at the end of the nineteenth century, and that the major period of urban gay population growth and institutional consolidation in the United States did not occur until after World War II, this entire shift has happened within a relatively brief period of time.

As constituted in the 1980s, gay families exhibited some distinct advantages over both nuclear families and the unattainable ideal of a unified, harmonious gay community. Face-to-face relations gave families we choose a fighting chance to encompass conflict and dissent without denying the difference that crosscutting identities (of race, class, etc.) can make or the divisions that can come between people. Significantly, many lesbians and gay men in the Bay Area cited a relationship's ability to weather conflict as itself a sign of kinship. Flexible boundaries released chosen families from the genealogical logic of scarcity and uniqueness that, for example, would limit a child to one mother and one father. Unlike nuclear families, gay families were not intrinsically stratified by age or gender. Their capacity to continue to embrace former lovers represents another strength. Consider how chosen families shed a different light on the issue of the alleged instability or *inconstancia* of gay couples. Opinion among both gays and heterosexuals remains divided as to whether lesbian and gay couples stay together as long as heterosexual partners. If, however, the question is reformulated to take account of contemporary discourse on gay families, which allows a former partner to make the transition from (erotic) lover to (nonerotic) friend without alienating the kinship tie, one could make a good case that gay relationships endure longer on average than ties established through heterosexual marriage. If two people cease being lovers after six years but remain friends and family for another 40, they have indeed achieved a relationship of long standing.

For every way in which families we choose seem to depart from hegemonic understandings of kinship, however, there is another way in which the two appear to be cut from the same cloth. Certainly discourse on gay families reworks meanings and symbols that already enjoy wide currency wherever people in the United States think about, argue about, and practice kinship. Even within the relation that opposes straight to gay families, the "same" elements of blood and choice surface on both sides of the contrast between these "different" categories of kin. Chosen families incorporate the physiological contributions to procreation of gay men who donate sperm and lesbians who bear children, while biological family encompasses the elements of selectivity implicit in counting someone as a close relative or severing kinship ties. At best, gay families and other family forms can be classified as simultaneously like and unlike. Just as the looking-glass language of sameness and difference obscures the complexities of relationships between lovers, so it provides a reductionist view of the relationship between gay families and more conventional interpretations of kinship.

ASSIMILATION OR TRANSFORMATION?

In the absence of close attention to history and context, there is the constant temptation for a person to view phenomena new to her experience as a reflection, extension, or imitation of something she thinks she already knows. Imagine you come across two women dressed as bride and groom, tossing rice over the heads of a crowd of onlookers. Would you consider them essentially the same as a heterosexual couple who had just been married? Different from a straight couple because both are women? Within the relationship, are they "like" based upon a common gender identity? Are they different from each other, and from the majority of lesbians, in their practice of butch/fem? What significance would you attribute to the inversion of throwing rice at the crowd, when the custom at weddings in the United States is for onlookers to throw rice toward the newlyweds? Perhaps you would revise your earlier conclusions if you learned that these women, dressed as bride and groom, were not stepping out of a chapel but rather riding a motorcycle down Market Street in San Francisco's annual Gay Pride Parade. After discovering more about its context, the scene immediately lends itself to reinterpretation. You might well find yourself searching for evidence of parodic intention and noticing the appreciative laughter of bystanders as the couple drives by.

Consider, then, the way most discussions of gay families have evaluated the political significance of laying claim to kinship as either inherently assimilationist or inherently progressive, without respect to social or historical context. Though less hotly contested than in former years, debate continues as to whether or not the struggle to relocate lesbians and gay men within the domain of kinship will, in the long run, move gay people in a conservative direction. Some gay commentators have argued that chosen families represent an impossible bid for respectability, a misguided attempt to become just like the happily, heterosexually married Joneses who live down the street. Was this the goal of gay liberation, they ask: to deflect charges of deviancy by becoming the proud possessors of the very institution no upstanding citizen can do without? On the other side of the issue, advocates praise chosen families for leading to a decisive break with genealogically calculated relations. Those who fear assimilation into a predominantly heterosexual society tend to identify "the family" solely with procreation and heterosexuality, while those who believe that gay kinship offers an authentic alternative often accept at face value ideologies that depict chosen families as independent of all social constraint.

Since the gay movement of the 1970s, certain activists have contended that having no family should constitute a point of pride for gay people, or at least remain a distinguishing feature of being lesbian or gay. To quote Dennis Altman (1979:47), a gay proponent of the "straight is to gay as family is to no family" thesis: "The homosexual represents the most clear-cut rejection of the nuclear family that exists, and hence is persecuted because of the need to maintain the hegemony of that concept." In 1978, Michael Lynch (1982) reported some gay men looking down upon gay fathers for having failed to escape "the family." E. M. Ettore (1980:20) has argued that lesbian and gay identity, in and of itself, denies the primacy of family. In place of family ties, Guy Hocquenghem (1978) encouraged gay people to elaborate friendship networks, which he portrayed as a more democratic form than kinship and a welcome alternative to Freud's derivation of significant relationships from filiation. In this view, kinship itself becomes a symbol of assimilation and marks the boundary between heterosexual and gay identity.[1] Why speak of lovers, friends, or even children as kin? "We" (gay men and lesbians) should develop "our" own terminology to describe "our" (presumably distinct) experiences, rather than adopting "their" (heterosexual) language and institutions. In a twist whose irony has yet to be fully appreciated, activists organizing against the same New Right that accuses homosexuals of being anti-family ended up condemning gay people for trafficking in kinship.

"We know how myths work: "through the impoverishment of history," Hortense Spillers (1984:185) has written. In the Bay Area many who argued against gay families interpreted kinship in a strictly procreative sense, taking it as a biogenetic given. By treating family as always and everywhere the same entity, they generally overlooked the context-dependent meanings that have given life to the concept and allowed it to become an object of contention. Gay families emerged in the context of historical developments that made coming out to relatives a possibility contemplated by most self-identified lesbians and gay men. Also related to the timing and content of this discourse was a legacy of building nonerotic solidarities among gay people, followed by a period of community-building and the subsequent deliberation of differences that brought the concept of a unified gay community into disrepute. The very complexity of this history demonstrates that the appearance of families we choose during the 1980s represented something more than a knee-jerk reaction to the "pro-family" politics of the New Right during the same decade. To formulate a critique of gay families in the abstract is to ignore the very circumstances that brought lesbians and gay men to the place of claiming and constructing kinship ties.

More useful than rhetorical attacks on a monolith called "the family" are ethnographically and historically grounded accounts that ask what families mean to people who say they have or want them. A basic insight to emerge from feminist examinations of kinship has been that the meanings carried by "family" can and will differ according to individual circumstances, identities, and intention to persuade (Thorne with Yalom 1982). In the words of Kenneth Burke (1945:105), "When you have a 'Rome' term to which all roads lead, you thereby have as many different variants of the motive as there are roads." Because family is not some static institution, but a cultural category that can represent assimilation *or* challenge (again, in context), there can be no definitive answer to the debate on assimilationism. Rather than representing a crystallized variation of some mythically main-stream form of kinship, gay families simply present one element in a broader discourse on family whose meanings are continuously elaborated in everyday situations of conflict and risk, from holidays and custody disputes to disclosures of lesbian or gay identity.

Significantly, lesbians and gay men have not abandoned the distinction between heterosexual and gay identity in the course of refusing to accept continued exile from kinship. Relocating the straight/gay boundary *within* the mediating domain of kinship made it possible for the establishment of a gay family to signify not assimilation, but (like coming out) a "point of exit" from heterosexuality (K. Jay 1978:28). Yet it is also entirely possible for some people to talk about gay families with the expectation that this new category will allow them to fit more comfortably into a predominantly heterosexual society. Others, with an interest in developing new forms of families, may portray their chosen families strictly as social experiment. A lesbian can choose to bear a child in the hope of gaining acceptance from "society" and straight relatives, or she can embark on the same course with a sense of daring and radical innovation, knowing that children tend to be "protected" from lesbians and gay men in the United States. For someone who associates kinship very closely with racial or cultural identity, the threat of assimilation might lie not in embracing the notion of gay families but in claiming membership in a lesbian or gay "community" where whites maintain hegemony. Politics do not inhere in the term "family" per se, but in its deployment in particular contexts.

All this is not to say that discourse on gay families lacks a radical *potential*. The notion of choice, for example, is very much an individualistic formulation, elevated in discourse on gay kinship to the level of a principle organizing a certain type of family. In the United States people often tend to image social organization as the additive end-product of a series of voluntary choices: individuals create groups (like families) which in turn create society (Varenne 1977). Yet gay families can also structure lived experiences which mitigate the utopianism that is always a danger in adopting any concept so closely tied to individualism. Many lesbian mothers, for example, spoke about their peers without children as though the latter had been deluded by the ideologies of freedom and creativity that inform chosen families. Jeanne Riley contrasted her own experience as the mother of two young children with the idealism of friends who had heard about "choosing children" but lacked personal experience as parents.

> Last night, [my best friend] calls me and she says, "Let's talk." I said, "I can't. I have my two kids, and I have a little boy over here visiting. So I have three kids, I really can't. I have to feed them dinner." So she says, "Well, I'm just home alone." So I said, "Well, I'm here. Why don't you come over?" She said, "With three kids?" It's real clear that no matter how much your friends love you, if they don't want to be around kids, they're no longer your friends. They resent and chafe at the fact that they have to incorporate the family into their social environment. There's not that spontaneity. "Let's go watch whales." (laughter) You kidding?

It is ironic that parenting, one of the phenomena within gay families most frequently taken as a sign of accommodation to "the traditional," should also become a place where people can come to realize that social conditions impose limits on ostensibly unrestricted choice.

There is also a radical potential associated with the one sense in which gay men and lesbians consistently concern themselves with "reproduction" in forming their own families. If "society" wants to define us as nonreproductive beings in the physical sense, some asked, why should we "reproduce" social arrangements that further the status quo? This double-edged usage of reproduction lends itself to a social critique that extends beyond gender and sexual identity to issues such as class which lie beyond the arena of concerns customarily attributed to gay people.

Having always assumed that he would marry, Stephen Richter said he had had to reevaluate everything after coming out made him realize that his life would not be "like" his parents'. People whose parents had pursued managerial or professional careers sometimes formulated a class critique by invoking images of a suburban home with its picket fence, signifiers of the complacent bourgeois life they attributed to their straight families. If he had not come out, Andy Wentworth insisted,

> I would have just followed the same path that I was expected to, that everybody else did, that society says you should. And it's very easy to just continue the same traditions over and over again,

get the same white picket fence that your grandparents have and your children will have after you. Where as soon as I realized I was gay, I said, hey, I've got a totally different situation going on here. My parents' expectations are now meaningless. Society's expectations are now meaningless. I have to build my own life. So that gave me more inner strength and durability and ability to be creative and in control of my environment.

Individuals from working-class backgrounds tended to experience coming out somewhat differently from Stephen and Andy. If they had determined to live openly as lesbians or gay men, they often perceived this not so much as declining to copy their parents' lives, but as departing from their parents' dream of upward mobility. Believing that heterosexism and anti-gay discrimination might render that dream unattainable, they saw themselves failing to reproduce not their parents' situation but rather their parents' ambitions. In the process, they sometimes began to question the value of those ambitions.

Viewed through the timeless sort of chronology that reproduction represents, a family can be pictured as an endless chain in which each individual replicates, exceeds, or fails to attain what "your grandparents have and your children will have after you." Gay families, in contrast, have not incorporated the chronological succession implicit in the Anglo-European notion of genealogical descent. Although chosen families can incorporate biological symbolism through childbearing and adoption, the children raised in gay families are not expected to go on to become gay or to form gay families of their own. Following the principle of choice, the kind of families these children establish should depend on their own sexual identities, and whether they establish families at all should be left to their discretion. By substituting images of creation and selection for the logic of reproduction and succession, discourse on gay families can—and does—remind people of their power to alter the circumstances into which they were born.

COMMON GROUND

Gay families not only dispute exclusively procreative interpretations of kinship, but introduce a new basis for rendering heterosexuality and lesbian or gay identity commensurable. Put simply, two things that are commensurable are capable of being compared. In the context of the symbolic contrast between straight and gay families, kinship effectively bridges the opposition of straight versus gay by providing a third term capable of relating each to the other. Because commensurability reserves the distinctive identities of its contrasting terms in the course of establishing this common ground, it is not to be confused with the notion of likeness that informs an identity politics. In the case of gay families, the opposition between biological and chosen families reaffirms the straight/gay boundary even as the vocabulary of kinship links categories of beings hitherto isolated by the species difference often attributed to homosexuality.

To view gay identity as a species difference is to regard gay people as beings so separate, so different in kind, that many heterosexuals believe they do not know and have never met a lesbian or gay man (cf. Hollibaugh 1979). To make such an assertion with certitude implies a belief that the difference gay identity makes is so significant it should be immediately detectable. Stereotyping that reduces gay men and lesbians to sexual beings only reinforces this perception of utter otherness. But "in real life, and usually in good novels and films, individuals are not defined only by their sexuality. Each has a history, and his or her eroticism is involved in a certain situation" (Beauvoir 1972:26). Being a lesbian "is more than somebody I sleep with," protested Charlyne Harris. "I mean, that's just like saying to a straight woman that a man, is that a big part of your life?" By countering any tendency to view gay people as what one lesbian dubbed "a walking sex act," a discourse on gay families that encompasses nonerotic as well as erotic ties invites heterosexuals to abandon the standpoint of the voyeur in favor of searching for areas of shared experience that join the straight self to the lesbian or gay other.

Despite their overt allegiance to values of autonomy and individualism, people in the United States tend to conceive commonality through a notion of humanity, and species membership through kinship more than other sorts of social bonds. Former soldiers interviewed by Studs Terkel (1984) described how, during World War II, they found it relatively simple to shoot at a nameless, faceless enemy. In their narratives it is not the name of a captured soldier on identification papers, or even a glimpse of the eyes, mouths, and faces of fallen enemy troops, that shocks combatants into recognition of a shared humanity. Instead, recognition and regret come with the discovery of a letter in a dead soldier's pocket written by sister or sweetheart, or from stumbling across kin gathered around the picture of a boy in soldier's uniform at a residence in the war zone. The enduring image that organizes these stories of wartime, recounted nearly half a century later, is a transformation of "the enemy" into a person—someone "just like me"—at the very moment of learning about relatives he cared for and who cared for him in return.

The concept of humanity as a unified species is deeply rooted in the procreative bias of a culture that dissociates gay men and lesbians from family by defining them as nonprocreative beings. Thus the notion of a species difference that divides gay from straight resonates with the strategic location of gay people outside the domain of kinship. Viewed against the backdrop of species difference, a seemingly matter-of-fact situation such as walking into the building that two gay lovers call home can evoke a startled recognition reminiscent of the emotion felt by Terkel's veterans when enemy soldiers assumed human form in the context of familial relations. In his coming-out narrative, Stephen Richter described one of his initial encounters with another gay person:

> The first time I was in a home where two men were living . . . I went off to the baths and I met a man there who had a lover and he introduced me, had me to dinner with he and his friend. And it was a very normal-looking house. I looked around and there was a sofa, and tables, and lamps. And I thought, "Isn't it amazing that two gay men can have a house that looks just like anybody else's house!" That was a fascination for me.

Situated in relation to symbols like home that carry kinship (as well as gender, class, and ethnicity), gay men and lesbians suddenly appear as social creatures rather than as self-absorbed and sex-obsessed caricatures of what a person might be. That "gay people have furniture!" look says worlds about just how incommensurable essentialized notions of identity can become, and what it can take to bring them back into relation with one another.

By advancing a claim to kinship, discourse on gay families bears the potential to break apart what Michel Foucault (1978:48) has called the "frozen countenance of the perversions" without discarding lesbian or gay identity in the process. Alfred Kinsey (1948) long ago depicted homosexuality and heterosexuality as aspects along a single continuum of human sexuality. Evelyn Hooker's (1967) finding that psychiatrists could not sort homosexuals from heterosexuals on the basis of psychological tests was considered revolutionary in its time. Alan Bell and Martin Weinberg (1978) painstakingly documented the tremendous diversity among gay men and lesbians in order to argue that relatively little separates gays from straights. Yet such studies have had a negligible impact on the continued objectification of gay men and lesbians by those who write "Kill Queers" on alley walls, or those who place a lower value on gay lives by failing to approve adequate funding for AIDS programs.

I am not arguing here that gay people are "just like" heterosexuals, or even that because Alfred Kinsey once placed the two along a sexual continuum that a continuum offers the best way to imagine their relationship. As a cultural category now linked to gay identity, kinship opens up new possibilities for relating gay to straight that shift discussion away from the tired rhetoric of sameness and difference. In discourse on gay families, straight remains opposed to gay, the two identities distinct but rendered commensurable through the vocabulary of kinship that conveys a common humanity to most people in the United States. The product of this discourse need not be a humanism that, like metaphor, dissolves difference into a larger whole. When lesbians and gay men can present themselves as fully social persons capable of laying claim to families, their distinctive sexual identities need no longer sharply segregate them as members of a species unto itself.

THE BIG PICTURE

After exposing the often oppressive ways in which families construct age and gender and organize inequitable divisions of labor, feminists have often been highly critical of "the family." In their works on kinship, they have warned of the twin dangers of ignoring power relations within families, and examining familial relations in isolation from relations of power in society at large. The vignette of the monkey cage introduced in chapter 1 offers an example of how families can structure hierarchies and gendered divisions of labor. Surely it is no coincide that of all five creatures in the cage, the animal labeled the "mommy monkey" ended up being the one who "left to make lunch." Knowing the ways such all-too-common representations are inextricably linked to practice, Michèle Barrett and Mary McIntosh (1982:8) have called for "the total eradication of familial ideology," while Susan Harding (1981:73) has asked feminists to set about the task of "creating kinship without families."[2]

Without doubt many travesties have been perpetrated in the name of family, including attempts to bar gay people from homes and workplaces across the United States. Because gay families are not structured through hierarchically ordered categories of relationship, however, they do not systematically produce gendered divisions of labor or relations stratified by age and gender. Such stratification is not incompatible with chosen families and, in particular instances, hierarchies can emerge within them, especially when children are involved. But neither is hierarchy essential to the constitution of gay families, which are often comprised primarily of relationships with peers. Rather than being organized through marriage and childrearing, most chosen families are characterized by fluid boundaries, eclectic composition, and relatively little symbolic differentiation between erotic and nonerotic ties. Where kinship terminology has developed in association with gay families, it has not been particularly marked by gender ("lover" and "biological [or nonbiological] parent" offer two cases in point).

Families we choose interpose face-to-face relationships between what Bonnie Zimmerman (1985) has called the "isolating structure" of identity and a more holistic, but exclusive, vision of a unified community. Does embracing gay families then mean abandoning all hope of resurrecting a notion of gay and/or lesbian community? Lesbian and gay activists have traveled a long road since the time when community seemed to some "the place we feel at home—a radical kinship in the making" (Zita 1981:175). By the late 1980s even white activists situated in the most privileged of circumstances had realized that not all lesbians and gay men have participated in this "we," just as not everyone felt at home in what once passed for an encompassing community. To some activists who have spent hours negotiating their way through the politics of identity and difference, the unresolved problem seems to be how to create "a new sense of political community which gives up the desire for the kind of home where the suppression of positive differences underwrites familial identity" (Martin and Mohanty 1988:204–205).

I have suggested that discourse on gay families offers one response to the differences and divisions encountered in the search for the holy grail of community, though probably not the one sought by those feminists who have devoted a considerable amount of energy to analyzing the drawbacks of familialism. In the Bay Area, families we choose were not constructed solely by people willing to pay any price to create a zone of comfort or a retreat from the weariness attendant upon years of political activism. People tended to describe their chosen families in terms that were as much about sustenance as safety. Gay families have created a cultural space in which people can love but also fight, without expecting their chosen kin to walk away, much less go off to organize a faction. These families are not opposed to collectivism, nor are they inherently privatizing; on the contrary, they have proved capable of integrating relationships that cross household lines, exchanges of material and emotional assistance, coparenting arrangements, and support for persons with AIDS. Although families we choose do not offer a substitute for political organizing, neither do they pose an inherent threat to political action or collective initiatives.

This is an idealized portrait, of course. There are problems raised by identity politics that gay families may well never address. Following the individualized logic of choice, many people have a tendency to create ties primarily with people they perceive to be "like" them, using one criterion or another to gauge similarity. In that case, difference once again disappears below the personal and political horizon. At the same time, however, families we choose offer novel possibilities for healing some of the rifts and wounds left over from a painful decade of learning to deal in difference. By this point it should be evident that family can mean very different things from person to person and situation to situation. During the 1980s some women of color labeled the feminist critique of "the family" as a *white* feminist critique that took as its point of departure the nuclear family ideal of the white "middle class" (see Joseph and Lewis 1981). Speaking about black feminists, Barbara Smith (1983:li) explained, "Unlike some white feminists who have questioned, and at times rightfully rejected, the white patriarchal family, we want very much to retain our blood connections without sacrificing ourselves to rigid and demeaning sex roles." The same year, Cherríe Moraga (1983:54) had written: "Being Chicana and having family are synonymous for me." For some people of color who felt marginal to "gay community"—partly due to experiences of racism in gay contexts, but also because they associated claiming a lesbian or gay identity with exile from kinship—discourse on gay families offered an opportunity to bring ethnicity and gay identity into a relationship of integration rather than constant tension. Such a reconciliation of identities is by no means predetermined, however; witness the lesbians and gay men of color described in chapter 2 who found it difficult to accept the authenticity of gay families, and who linked their rejection of the concept of chosen kin to a particular racial or ethnic identification.

At this point it remains unclear how the emerging discourse on gay families will unfold, or in what directions lesbians and gay men will pursue the political implications of families organized by choice. Rayna Rapp (1987) has noted that in a period when kinship has become highly politicized, lesbians and gay men have been somewhat less successful than others in making their bid for recognition of so-called alternative family forms. In the landmark *Bowers v. Hardwick* (1986:2844) decision that upheld Georgia's sodomy law and convicted one man for having consensual sex with another in the privacy of his own home, Justice White, in formulating the opinion of the Court, justified its finding that most areas of family law were inapplicable to the case by concluding, "No connection between family, marriage, or procreation on the one hand and homosexual activity on the other has been demonstrated."

One measure of the challenge gay families pose to the status quo is to ask whether basic changes in the social, economic, and political order would be required to grant gay families legitimacy and legal recognition, or whether chosen families could be accommodated by simply extending certain "rights" to lesbians and gay men and treating them as members of another minority group. From insurance companies to the courts, major institutions in the United States will find it easier to validate domestic partnerships, custody rights for lesbian and gay parents, and the right to jointly adopt children, than to recognize gay families that span several households or families that include friends.

Because the relationship of lovers, like marriage, brings together two individuals united by the symbolism of sex and love, many in the United States have drawn analogies between this bond and more customary affinal arrangements. Relatives and judges alike perceive the option of treating gay or lesbian lovers as they would a childless heterosexual couple: as an exceptional relationship in a procreative world. Likewise, they have the option of treating lesbian or gay coparents as though only the gender of individual parents has changed, while everything else about the social conditions in which childrearing occurs remains unaffected. Due to this sort of reasoning by analogy from heterosexual relations, coming out seems to make a much clearer statement about kinship when a person has a partner or is the non-biological coparent to a child. Without either of these ties, many gay people have reported finding it difficult to demonstrate the importance of friendship as kinship or to convince heterosexuals that lesbian and gay identity involves anything other than sex.

Pressure is building even now to take the path of least resistance. In the years to come it will be important that gay men and lesbians not become so concerned about gaining recognition for their families that they settle for whatever sort of recognition it seems possible to get. For lesbian and gay organizations that take up the issues raised by discourse on gay families, the future will bring difficult questions about where to devote limited resources. Should they work toward the legalization of same-sex partnerships, following Sweden's example (see Ettelbrick 1989; Stoddard 1989)? Does marriage have political implications that families per se do not? If gay people begin to pursue marriage, joint adoptions, and custody rights to the exclusion of seeking kinship status for some categories of friendship, it seems likely that gay families will develop in ways largely congruent with socio-economic and power relations in the larger society. This accommodationist thrust is already apparent in the requirements for shared residence or cohabitation for a specified period of time that are built in to most domestic partner legislation (Green 1987). Following the logic of chosen families, an individual should be able to pick any one person as a partner—domestic or otherwise—and designate that person as the recipient of insurance or other employment benefits, even when that choice entails crossing household boundaries.

If legal recognition is achieved for some aspects of gay families at the expense of others, it could have the effect of privileging certain forms of family while delegitimating others by contrast. The most likely scenario would involve narrowing the definition of gay families to incorporate only couples and parents with children, abandoning attempts to achieve any corresponding recognition for families of friends. Legal recognition for friends, or at least measures that would eliminate any automatic elevation of blood ties over ties of friendship, must also assume its place on lesbian and gay political agendas. Relatives calculated by blood should not be able to break a properly executed will that leaves possessions to a relative calculated by choice —whether that chosen relative be friend or lover—simply because the former can lay claim to a genealogical connection to the deceased.[3] In the widest political and economic arenas, taking advantage of the transformative potential of discourse on gay families—for it is only a potential—will require great care and attention to cultural context in framing legislation, laying the basis for court cases, and selecting particular kinship-related practices to challenge as exclusionary.

REENGINEERING BIOGENETICS

Change and continuity are more closely related than many people tend to think. No search is more fruitless than the one that seeks revolutionary forms of social relations which remain "uncontaminated" by existing social conditions. Not surprisingly, then, discourse on gay families transfigures the exclusively procreative interpretations of kinship with which it takes issue in such a way that it remains of them but no longer completely contained within them.

By implicitly identifying family with procreation, the equation "straight is to gay as family is to no family" concedes the entire domain of kinship to heterosexuality. Only when displaced onto one side of the relation that opposes straight to gay families does procreatively organized kinship become marked as "biological family" and qualified as one subset of a larger kinship universe. Although this transformation does not challenge the interpretation of biology as a "natural fact," it represents a truly significant departure from more conventional constructions of kinship in that it displaces biology onto a particular type of family identified with heterosexuality. Some gay men and lesbians in the Bay Area had chosen to create families and some had not, some had become parents and some had not, but almost all associated their sexual identities with a release from any sort of procreative imperative. In this sense the radical potential of a discourse on gay families is not limited to contesting the species difference of homosexuality, the "reproduction" of class relations, or even the individualism implicit in notions of choice.

In the absence of a notion of genealogy, David Schneider (1984:112) has argued, kinship would cease to have meaning as a cultural domain: "Robbed of its grounding in biology, kinship is nothing." After examining discourse on gay families, however, it would seem more accurate to say that, robbed of its *relation* to biology, kinship is nothing. Families we choose are defined through contrast with biological or blood family, making biology a key feature of the opposing term that conditions the meanings of gay kinship. To put it another way, biological family and chosen families are mutually constituted categories related through a principle of determinism that opposes free will to biogenetic givens. Through this relationship biology remains implicated in the concept of a family that can be chosen. On the one hand, discourse on gay families refutes any claim by procreation to be the privileged, precultural foundation for all conceivable forms of kinship. On the other hand, by retaining biology on one side of the symbolic opposition between straight and gay families, this same discourse removes procreation from center stage without dissolving kinship into the whole of social relations.

Lesbians and gay men have defined their own families not so much by analogy as by contrast, however overdrawn the opposition between gay and straight families might sometimes become as individuals argue for the distinctiveness of "their" type of family. Defined through their difference, blood family and chosen families assume equivalent status as they move away from the dualism of real versus ideal and authentic versus derivative concealed within the concept of fictive kinship. Through the fear and sometimes the experience of being disowned or rejected after coming out to blood relatives, many lesbians and gay men come to question not so much the "naturalness" of a biological tie, but rather the assumption that shared biogenetic substance in itself confers kinship. This heightened awareness of the selectivity incorporated into genealogical modes of calculating relationship has shaped the constitution of gay families as families we choose, and allowed gay people to argue that their chosen families represent something more than a second-best imitation of blood ties.

Nevertheless, isn't there a danger that by subjecting kinship to choice, the concept of family will lose its significance? A similar sort of dilution has occurred with the concept of community: people now speak blithely of "the community of artists," "the sports community," and even "the straight community." With respect to family, some tendency in this direction also exists. Of late, any assemblage of persons within a household, from halfway houses for people recovering from addiction to retirement homes sheltering hundreds, may be billed as a site for the development of familial relationships. Where discourse on gay families differs from these cases is in its emergence from a specific history of categorical exclusion from participation in kinship relations, an exclusion associated with claiming a lesbian or gay identity. A second characteristic that sets this discourse apart is its application of the term "family" to face-to-face ties that already carry deep attachment and commitment in the absence of any corresponding recognition from society at large.

Descriptively speaking, the categories of gay kinship might better be labeled families we struggle to create, struggle to choose, struggle to legitimate, and—in the case of blood or adoptive family—struggle to keep. Among gay men and lesbians, there is the pervasive sense that, as Diane Kunin put it, "gay people really have to work to make family." In a sense, people of all sexual identities "work" to make kinship. The Victorian depiction of family as a domestic retreat from the working world disguises a variety of labors, from housework and childrearing to the more intangible emotional work believed necessary to sustain relationships (Thorne with Yalom 1982). Yet gay men and lesbians encounter added dimensions that complicate the practice of constructing kin ties: parenting children in a heterosexist society, maintaining erotic relationships without viewing them through the one-dimensional lens of a gendered sameness, risking kin ties in coming out to straight relatives, interweaving peer relationships in multiples of three or four or seven, consistently asserting the importance of relationships that lack social status or even a vocabulary to describe them. Always in the background are strictly procreative interpretations of kinship, relative to which the opposition between biological and chosen families has taken shape. Too often in the foreground are opponents, well-meaning or otherwise, who reduce gay families to a metaphorical rendition of more conventional kinship arrangements, treating them as pretended family relations that will never quite measure up to a heterosexual standard.

When cast in narrative form, the shift from the identification of gayness with the renunciation of kinship (no family) to a correspondence between gay identity and a particular type of family (families we choose) presents a kind of collective coming-out story: a tale of lesbians and gay men moving out of isolation and into kinship. By the 1980s, when gay people came out to relatives by blood or adoption, they often were hoping not only to maintain and strengthen those biologically calculated bonds, but also to gain recognition for ties to lovers and other chosen relatives who could not be located on any biogenetic grid. If disclosure led to the pain of rejection, they were able to remind themselves that blood ties no longer exhausted the options open to them within the domain of kinship.

Like most stories, however, this one adopts a particular point of view. Without careful attention to the context from which gay kinship has emerged, an observer could easily overlook the rich history of friendships, erotic connections, community-building, and other modalities of lesbian and gay solidarity that have preceded the contemporary discourse on families we choose. In a sense, gay people have come full circle. According to John D'Emilio (1983a), a key precondition for the historical appearance of a gay or lesbian identity was the possibility of establishing a life *outside* "the family" once the expansion of commodity production under capitalism offered wage work to individuals in return for their formally "free" labor.[4] By the end of the twentieth century, many lesbians and gay men were busy establishing families of their own.

Any attempt to evaluate the political implications of a particular discourse must take into account Michel Foucault's (1978) contention that power feeds upon resistance, and knowledge upon its apparent negation.[5] Inversions that protest a given dominance, like the opposition of liberation to repression or anti-family to pro-family, remain trapped within terms that frame the act of resistance as a protest *against* a given representation or paradigm. Significantly, chosen families do not directly oppose genealogical modes of reckoning kinship. Instead, they undercut procreation's status as a master term imagined to provide the template for all possible kinship relations. In displacing rather than disallowing biogenetic symbolism, discourse on gay families moves obliquely toward the future, responding to hegemonic forms of kinship not with a defensive countermove, but by deftly stepping aside to evade the paradigmatic blow.

APPENDIX

TABLE 1. RACIAL/CULTURAL IDENTITY

	Women	Men	Total
Asian(-American)	3	2	5
Chinese-American	1	0	
Japanese national	2	1	
Korean-American	0	1	
African-American/Black	4	5	9
Latina/Latino	5	6	11
Cuban-American	1	1	
Mexican-American/Chicana/Chicano	2	4	
Nicaraguan-American	0	1	
Peruvian national	1	0	
Puerto Rican	1	0	
Native American/American Indian	1	1	2
Cherokee	1	0	
Paiute	0	1	
Multiple Identities	2	0	2
African-American/Native American	1	0	
Japanese-American/Native American	1	0	
White	25	26	51
Jewish (Ashkenazi)	7	4	9
TOTAL:	40	40	80

NOTE: The two participants who claimed more than one racial identity are grouped in following tables according to their primary identifications (Japanese-American and African-American, respectively). In a few cases people were technically citizens of another country but had lived in the Bay Area for a period of time. They considered themselves (and were considered by others) part of the local lesbian and gay population.

TABLE 2. CLASS BACKGROUND BY GENDER IDENTITY

	Women	Men	Total
Working	23	18	41
Managerial/ Professional	17	22	39
TOTAL:	40	40	80

TABLE 3. CLASS BACKGROUND BY RACIAL AND GENDER IDENTITY

	Working		Managerial/ Professional	
People of Color	16	(8/8)	13	(7/6)
Asian(-American)	1	(1/0)	5	(3/2)
African-American	7	(3/4)	3	(2/1)
Latina/o	7	(4/3)	4	(1/3)
Native American	1	(0/1)	1	(1/0)
White	25	(15/10)	26	(10/16)
Jewish	5	(4/1)	6	(3/3)
TOTAL:	41		39	

(Figures in parentheses denote the ratio of women to men.)

TABLE 4. PRESENT CLASS BY GENDER IDENTITY

	Women	Men	Total
Working	26	20	46
Managerial/ Professional	14	20	34
TOTAL:	40	40	80

TABLE 5. PRESENT CLASS BY RACIAL & GENDER IDENTITY

	Working Class	Managerial/ Professional Class
People of Color	20 (12/8)	9 (3/6)
Asian(-American)	5 (3/2)	1 (1/0)
African-American	8 (4/4)	2 (1/1)
Latina/o	6 (4/2)	5 (1/4)
Native American	1 (1/0)	1 (0/1)
White	26 (14/12)	25 (11/14)
Jewish	5 (3/2)	6 (4/2)
TOTAL:	46	34

(Figures in parentheses denote the ratio of women to men.)

TABLE 6. CLASS MOBILITY BY RACIAL AND GENDER IDENTITY

	Working to Working	Managerial to Managerial	Working to Managerial	Managerial to Working
People of Color	13 (8/5)	6 (3/3)	3 (0/3)	7 (4/3)
Asian(-American)	1 (1/0)	1 (1/0)	0	4 (2/2)
African-American	6 (3/3)	1 (1/0)	1 (0/1)	2 (1/1)
Latina/o	6 (4/2)	4 (1/3)	1 (0/1)	0
Native American	0	0	1 (0/1)	1 (1/0)
White	16 (10/6)	16 (6/10)	9 (5/4)	10 (4/6)
Jewish	4 (3/1)	5 (3/2)	1 (1/0)	1 (0/1)
TOTAL:	29	22	12	17

(Figures in parentheses denote the ratio of women to men.)

TABLE 7. CLASS MOBILITY BY GENDER IDENTITY

	Women	Men	Total
Working to Working	18	11	29
Managerial to Managerial	9	13	22
Working to Managerial	5	7	12
Managerial to Working	8	9	17
TOTAL:	40	40	80

TABLE 8. ANNUAL INCOME BY RACIAL IDENTITY
(to nearest $1,000)

	0–6	6–10	10–15	15–20	20–25	25–30	30+
People of Color	7	7	7	4	2	0	2
Asian(-American)	2	2	2	0	0	0	0
African-American	0	3	3	2	1	0	1
Latina/o	3	2	2	2	1	0	1
Native American	2	0	0	0	0	0	0
White	6	6	13	4	13	4	5
Jewish	2	1	3	1	2	1	1
TOTAL:	13	13	20	8	15	4	7

TABLE 9. ANNUAL INCOME BY GENDER IDENTITY (in dollars)

	Women	*Men*	*Total*
0— 5,999	8	5	13
6,000— 9,999	4	9	13
10,000—14,999	10	10	20
15,000—19,999	5	3	8
20,000—24,999	8	7	15
25,000—29,999	2	2	4
30,000+	3	4	7
TOTAL:	40	40	80

TABLE 10. AGE

	Women	*Men*	*Total*
Under 20	1	0	1
20–29	13	13	26
30–39	18	20	38
40–49	8	3	11
50–59	0	1	1
60+	0	3	3
TOTAL:	40	40	80

TABLE 11. HIGHEST LEVEL OF EDUCATION

	Women	Men	Total
High School	12	4	16
Some College	5	13	18
College Graduate	12	17	29
Graduate School	11	6	17
TOTAL:	40	40	80

TABLE 12. REGIONAL ORIGIN

	Women	Men	Total
East	18	14	32
Midwest	3	6	9
South	2	7	9
West	14	9	23
(California)	(14)	(4)	(18)
Born Abroad	3	4	7
TOTAL:	40	40	80

TABLE 13. RURAL/URBAN ORIGIN

	Women	Men	Total
Rural	6	6	12
Urban	34	34	68
TOTAL:	40	40	80

TABLE 14. PRESENT RELIGION

	Women	Men	Total
Buddhist	2	2	4
Jewish	1	1	2
Protestant	5	9	14
Roman Catholic	2	1	3
Spiritual/New Age	12	10	22
None/Atheist	14	14	28
Undecided	3	2	5
Declined to answer	1	1	2
TOTAL:	40	40	80

TABLE 15: RELIGIOUS UPBRINGING

	Women	Men	Total
Buddhist	1	1	2
Jewish	4	3	7
Protestant	12	17	29
Roman Catholic	19	17	36
None/Atheist	4	2	6
TOTAL:	40	40	80

TABLE 16. PREVIOUS HETEROSEXUAL MARRIAGE?

	Women	Men	Total
Yes	6	2	8
No	34	38	72
TOTAL:	40	40	80

TABLE 17. PARENT ("Biological" or "Social")?

	Women	Men	Total
Yes	6	3	9
No	34	37	71
TOTAL:	40	40	80

TABLE 18. LONGEST RELATIONSHIP WITH SAME-SEX LOVER

	Women	Men	Total
Under 1 year	5	12	17
1–2 years	8	10	18
3–5 years	15	8	23
6–9 years	10	7	17
10+ years	2	3	5
TOTAL:	40	40	80

NOTES

ONE. THE MONKEY CAGE AND THE RED DESOTO

1. For more on the Thompson and Kowalski case, see Thompson and Andrzejewski (1988). On state actions and policies that maintain or intervene in sexualities, see G. Rubin (1984).

2. I employ the term "discourse" in an effort to circumvent arbitrary divisions that oppose real to ideal, structure to superstructure, and material determination to ideological expression. For critiques of these analytic oppositions, see Coward and Ellis (1977) and R. Williams (1978). Rather than isolating an ideological system or ideological shift for the purposes of analysis, this usage of discourse treats meaning and activity, sense and event, as bound up together in practice (Foucault 1972; Patton 1985:104; Ricoeur 1976).

3. On in vitro insemination, see Arditti et al. (1984) and Modell (1989). On surrogate motherhood, see Andrews (1989), Gostin (1990), and Pies and Hornstein (1988). On aging and cooperative living, see Streib et al. (1984). Harrison and Bluestone (1988) link public policy and socioeconomic conditions to kinship relations, income distribution, and poverty. For a journalistic treatment of some social and legal issues raised by competing definitions of family, see Gutis (1989).

4. In referring to heterosexism here and throughout, I follow Nungesser's (1983) rejection of "homophobia" as an inadequate term to describe the sum of lesbian and gay oppression, anti-gay practices, and anti-gay sentiment. With its allusion to psychiatric diagnostic categories, homophobia not only implies a pathological and exceptional condition, but lays all responsibility at the foot of the individual. Heterosexism, in contrast, acknowledges that gay and lesbian oppression is socially structured and multiply determined.

5. For an impressionistic account of gay men and lesbians living in small towns and medium-sized cities across the U.S., see Miller (1989).

6. See the discussion that follows on the methodological problems that preclude obtaining a representative sample for this population. DeLeon and Brown also sort their data by age, reporting that 13 percent of the women and

21 percent of the men in the 18–29 age group placed themselves in one of these categories, compared to 9 percent of the women and 37 percent of the men aged 30–49, and 7 percent of the women and 11 percent of the men aged 50 or over.

7. One woman and one man initially presented themselves as lesbian and gay, respectively, but during the interview defined themselves as bisexual.

8. For a sample of readings on homosexuality in societies that do not necessarily ground same-sex eroticism in a notion of sexual identity, see Blackwood (1986), Caplan (1987), Greenberg (1988), Herdt (1984, 1987), Newton (1988), and W. Williams (1986).

9. On the demographic skewing of most studies of gay men and lesbians, see Berger (1982b) and Krieger (1985).

10. On older lesbians and gay men, see Adelman (1986), Berger (1982a, 1982b), Dunker (1987), Gay (1978), Harry (1984), Kehoe (1989), Laner (1979), Lyon and Martin (1979), Macdonald (1983), Minnigerode and Adelman (1978), and Vacha (1985). On gay youth, see Fricke (1981), Herdt Hefner (1989), and Autin (1978), and Heron (1983). With respect to levels of educational attainment, remember that the age cohort in their twenties and thirties at the time of the study had reached adolescence during a period when financial aid was widely available, higher education was expanding, and unprecedented numbers of children from poor and working-class homes had enrolled in colleges or junior colleges in the U.S.

11. Cf. Perin (1988), who purposefully traveled abroad before beginning fieldwork in her own culture, in an effort to defamiliarize herself with her accustomed surroundings. On parallels between the conventions of arrival scenes in ethnographies and travel writing, see M. L. Pratt (1986).

12. Although, to be sure, every situation carries its exoticisms, insofar as the exotic is always defined in relation to a set of assumptions held by the observer. Ethnographic writing on the U.S. and Europe includes frequent expressions of surprise and even shock which can only be explained with reference to perceptions or experiences that contradicted a researcher's preconceived expectations.

13. In contrast to some kinds of folklore for which differential identity constitutes a performance requirement (Bauman 1972). Narratives tend to be relatively self-contained, and as such more immune to audience control than other speech acts (Fowler 1981, M. L. Pratt 1977). Knowing that performed narrative generally lessens self-conscious monitoring of speech, I also hoped to put participants at ease and minimize the observer effect in the artificial situation of an interview (cf. Labov 1972).

14. On the concept of hegemony, see Gramsci (1971).

TWO. EXILES FROM KINSHIP

1. See Godwin (1983) and Hollibaugh (1979).

2. For an analysis that carefully distinguishes among the various senses of

reproduction and their equivocal usage in feminist and anthropological theory, see Yanagisako and Collier (1987).

3. On the distinction between family and household, see Rapp (1982) and Yanagisako (1979).

4. On relational definition and the arbitrariness of signs, see Saussure (1959).

5. For Lévi-Strauss (1963b:88), most symbolic contrasts are structured by a mediating third term. Apparently conflicting elements incorporate a hidden axis of commonality that allows the two to be brought into relationship with one another. Here sexual identity is the hidden term that links "straight" to "gay," while kinship mediates the oppositions further down in the chart. This sort of triadic relation lends dynamism to opposition, facilitating ideological transformations while ensuring a regulated, or structured, relationship between the old and the new.

My overall analysis departs from a Lévi-Straussian structuralism by historically situating these relations, discarding any presumption that they form a closed system, and avoiding the arbitrary isolation of categories for which structuralism has justly been criticized in the past (see Culler 1975; Fowler 1981; Jenkins 1979). The symbolic oppositions examined in this chapter incorporate indigenous categories in all their specificity (e.g., straight versus gay), rather than abstracting to universals of increasing generality and arguably decreasing utility (e.g., nature versus culture). Chronicled here is an ideological transformation faithful to history, process, and the perceptions of the lesbians and gay men who themselves identified each opposition included in the chart. For the deployment of these categories in everyday contexts, read on.

6. Notice how the contrasts in the chart map a relationship of difference (straight/gay) first onto a logical negation (family/no family, or A/NA), and then onto another relation of difference (biological [blood] family/families we choose [create], or A:B). On the generative potential of dichotomies that are constituted as A/B rather than A/NA, see N. Jay (1981:44).

7. See Foucault (1978) on the practice of grouping homosexuality together with other nonprocreative sex acts, a historical shift that supplanted the earlier classification of homosexuality with adultery and offenses against marriage. According to Foucault, previous to the late eighteenth century acts "contrary to nature" tended to be understood as an extreme form of acts "against the law," rather than something different in kind. Only later was "the unnatural" set apart in the emerging domain of sexuality, becoming autonomous from adultery or rape. See also Freedman (1982:210): "Although the ideological support for the separation of [erotic] sexuality and reproduction did not appear until the twentieth century, the process itself began much earlier."

8. See di Leonardo (1984), who criticizes the transmission model for its lack of attention to the wider socioeconomic context that informs the ways people interpret the relation of kinship to ethnicity.

9. See also Joseph and Lewis (1981:76), Kennedy (1980), McAdoo (1988), and Stack (1974). For a refutation and historical contextualization of allega-

tions that African-Americans have developed "dysfunctional" families, or even no families at all, see Gresham (1989).

10. Abercrombie et al. (1980) lay out many of the objections to treating culture as a shared body of values and knowledge determinative of social relations. For theoretical formulations critical of the assumption that ideology mechanically reflects a more fundamental set of material conditions, see Jameson (1981), Lichtman (1975), and R. Williams (1977). For different approaches to examining the influence of context, embodiment, and power relations on the formulation and interpretation of cultural categories, see Rosaldo (1989), Vološinov (1973), and Yanagisako (1978, 1985).

THREE. COMING OUT TO "BLOOD" RELATIVES

1. There are many versions of what happened at Stonewall. Interview participants asked to relate their knowledge of these events sometimes incorporated details related to their own identities. Only people of color, for example, mentioned that gays of color were among those who resisted. Women were less likely than men to have heard of Stonewall. No one numbered women among the resisters, although contemporary newspaper accounts reported the arrest of a lesbian patron (see Stein 1979).

2. "Coming out" was (and is) also occasionally used to mean having sex with another man or woman for the first time.

3. For analytical treatments of coming out in the first sense of coming out to self, see Altman (1979), Coleman (1982), Cronin (1975), Dank (1971), R. Marks (1988), McDonald (1982), Ponse (1978), Rofes (1983), T. S. Weinberg (1978), and Wooden et al. (1983). For a sampling of narrative accounts, see Adair and Adair (1978), Adelman (1986), Bulkin (1980), Fricke (1981), Grahn (1984), Hamilton (1973), Hefner and Autin (1978), Heron (1983), Kantrowitz (1977), Larkin (1976), Moraga and Anzaldúa (1981),Vojir (1982), and Wolfe and Stanley (1980).

4. For further discussion of changing attitudes toward lesbians in the military during this period, see Bérubé and D'Emilio (1985) and D'Emilio (1989a).

5. But see the older gay men interviewed by Berger (1982:15), who reported experiencing less concern than formerly about whether others knew of their sexual identities.

6. In the early 1980s, lesbian and gay activists enshrined a "backlash" to the gay movement as a third term in this historical sequence. While the concept of a backlash mitigates the progressive, evolutionary character of the sequence by identifying the present as a less "open" era, it cannot explain continuities in institutional intervention through time, or persistence of the relatively recent concern with coming out to blood and adoptive kin.

7. On fears and pejorative beliefs about homosexuality and homosexuals, see Nungesser (1983).

8. A trend marked by the proliferation of advice manuals on how best to handle coming out. Representatives of this genre include G. G. Beck (1985), Berzon (1978, 1979), Borhek (1983), Clark (1977), Córdova (1975), Much-

more and Hanson (1982), Silverstein (1977), G. Weinberg (1972), and Zitter (1987).

9. In 1978, former city supervisor Dan White shot and killed Milk along with then mayor George Moscone. For more on coming out as a political strategy, see Adam (1987), D'Emilio (1983b), and Lee (1977).

10. But see Ehrenreich (1983), who questions whether "sexual liberation" ever happened.

11. One exception would be the extremely controversial practice of "outing," in which a gay person "exposes" someone—usually a celebrity or political figure—as gay or lesbian without the latter's consent.

12. This may partially explain why so many studies of homosexuality in the United States have found symbolic interactionism congenial as a theoretical approach (e.g., Plummer 1975). The theatrical metaphors adopted by Goffman (1959, 1963) resonate with descriptions that liken attempts to conceal sexual identity to "playing a part." Unlike Goffman, however, most lesbians and gay men in the Bay Area did not regard acting as an inevitable condition of social relations, but rather as a pose that could and ideally should be dropped.

13. Cf. the Freudian contrast between the conscious and the unconscious, which images the unconscious as a storehouse of hidden truths that can be excavated through psychoanalysis. Descriptions of a compartmentalized and conflicted self date at least to Augustine (1961:170): "My inner self was a house divided against itself. In the heat of the fierce conflict which I had stirred up against my soul in our common abode, my heart, I turned upon Alypius."

14. For more on the stresses and management of nondisclosure, see Brooks (1981), Derlega and Chaikin (1975), and Moses (1978). For those interested in continuities and contrasts with passing in the context of racial identity, see Cliff's (1980) observations and Larsen's (1969) fictional treatment of passing for white. Goodwin (1989) discusses humor and other communication strategies that signal gay identity to others "in the know."

15. For parental perspectives on learning of a child's lesbian or gay identity, see Griffin et al. (1986), Muller (1987), Myers (1982), and Rafkin (1987).

16. Cf. the Japanese-American respondent in Wooden et al. (1983:240) who characterized Issei and Nisei (first and second generations, respectively) as "more rigid and non-accepting" than third- and fourth-generation Japanese-Americans (Sansei and Yonsei).

17. For accounts that link contemporary gay identity to *berdache*, see Kenny (1988), Roscoe (1987, 1988a, 1988b), and W. Williams (1986). For arguments against drawing direct links between the two, see Gutiérrez (1989), Midnight Sun (1988), and Whitehead (1981). Compare also the comments of Lee Staples, member of a gay American Indian organization in Minnesota, on *berdache*: "The idea of two 'masculine' men having a socially sanctioned relationship didn't fit into the American Indian tradition any more than it did into white culture" (in Miller 1989:193).

18. On the cultural representations, material conditions, and power rela-

tions that have not only shaped household composition but also configured discourse on "the family" in the United States, see Rapp (1982, 1987) and Thorne with Yalom (1982).

19. Speakers generally applied this theory to race or ethnicity but not class background. Whites, in contrast, sometimes stereotyped people of color as more anti-gay than the white population. Most lesbians and gay men of color did not disagree that heterosexism exists among people of color, but believed that it is equally prevalent among whites.

20. In choosing interview participants I made a conscious effort not to allow advance billing of coming-out stories to influence my selection. Some interviewees, of course, were not out to any blood or adoptive relatives. Cf. Mendola (1980:107), who found that of the lesbians and gay men in couples she surveyed, 40 percent reported that their parents invited them to family gatherings, 36 percent were not out to their parents, 21 percent said their parents "treat their relationships as simply two friends living together with no commitment," while only 3 percent had parents who unilaterally refused to see their son or daughter and his or her partner.

21. That this re-situation does not represent a unidirectional process of "liberation" from medical authority is obvious from the remedicalization of homosexuality in responses to the AIDS epidemic (Altman 1986; Epstein 1988; Kyle 1989; Watney 1987).

22. This generalization seemed to hold whether individuals regarded sexuality as the single, almost trivial, difference separating gays from heterosexuals (cf. Bell and Weinberg 1978), or whether they believed that particular sex acts constitute one of the few things shared by differently structured gay and straight "worlds."

23. Cf. Elisabeth Craigin (1975:50), writing in the 1930s, who maintained a basically positive conception of her sexual relationship with another woman: "I concealed it passionately, in a kind of maternal anxiety to keep it from harm, from the defilement of false interpretation. I felt it would have killed me if my love had suffered mishandling in the minds of others."

24. But see Umans (1988) for excerpts from coming-out letters, some of them written to parents.

25. Cf. Herdt (1989), who argues that with the drop in the mean age of claiming a gay identity in urban areas, young lesbians and gay men are now more likely to experience problems associated with coming out and with adolescence simultaneously.

26. Reinforced, no doubt, by a long history in the United States of polarizing "free will" and determinism.

FOUR. KINSHIP AND COHERENCE

1. Cf. Zimmerman's (1983) discussion of similarities between the lesbian novel of development and the *Bildungsroman*. Each chronicles the protagonist's growth into adulthood and subsequent confrontation with a hostile world, the movement of the individual into the social.

2. On the creation of coherence in presentations of self, including auto-biography, see Martin 1988.

3. Compare this account from a Jewish woman who had enrolled in a drug treatment program as a teenager: "[The counselors] wanted me to get a box and paint it a color that symbolized myself. They wanted me to get another box and buy a doll and put the doll inside the box and get a ribbon. 'Cause in the Jewish religion, when you're mourning death, you wear a black ribbon. And they wanted me to say . . . a prayer that only men say in the Jewish religion, which is a prayer you only say when somebody in your immediate family dies. And they wanted me to bury the lesbian part of myself. They wanted it to be dead and buried and out."

4. For a discussion of parental reactions to interethnic marriage in the United States, see Sollors (1986:224–225): "The [ethnic] purists' own unwill-ingness to accept the mixed after-generations as theirs is seen as the 'loss' of the children."

5. This is one of several points in the narrative marked by a change from the conversational historical present ("and he says . . . ") to the past tense ("and I said . . . "), a shift that highlights the query-response sequence (Wolfson 1978).

6. Jane Tompkins' (1981:89) comment on *Uncle Tom's Cabin* might equally well be applied to Louise Romero's story: "The truths that Stowe's narrative conveys can only be reembodied, never discovered, because they are already revealed from the beginning."

FIVE. FAMILIES WE CHOOSE

1. Schneider (1968) represents the classic anthropological text on "Ameri-can kinship." For a critique of Schneider's account as overly coherent and systematized, as well as insensitive to contextual shifts in meaning, see Yana-gisako (1978, 1985). For a discussion of models in culture theory, see Geertz's (1973:93–94) distinction between "model of" and "model for."

2. Cf. Riley (1988), who found in a small study of 11 lesbians in New York City that those friends characterized as family were "intimate" rather than "social" friends.

3. For a discussion of the theme of uncharted lives in lesbian autobiogra-phy, see Cruikshank (1982).

4. In practice this generalization may hold more for lesbians than for gay men, although many gay men also shared the ideal of transforming the formerly erotic tie to an ex-lover into an enduring nonerotic bond.

5. Chapter 7 explores relations to children within gay families.

6. The notion of a substitute family can also be criticized as functionalist in that it assumes all people have a need for family. Social scientists have applied theories of surrogate family to many marginalized groups in the U.S. See, for example, Vigil (1988) on barrio gangs in southern California.

7. Cf. Hooker (1965) on the importance placed on friendship by gay men of an earlier era.

8. Foucault (in Gallagher and Wilson 1987:33–34) has speculated that the devaluation of male friendship in eighteenth-century Europe was historically linked to the problematization of sex between men.

9. To my knowledge less is documented concerning lesbian usage of kinship terminology during this period. Among gay men, this application of kinship terminology persists in the form of camp references. In the specialized context of drag balls and competitions, gay male novices enter all-gay "houses" in which "the 'mother' and 'father' supervise the training and activities of their 'children' " (Goldsby 1989:34–35).

10. For a comprehensive discussion of the development of urban gay communities in the postwar years, see D'Emilio (1983b). On the emergence of a social movement grounded in gay identity, see also Adam (1987).

11. Epstein (1987) explores in more depth the limitations of analogies between ethnicity and gay identity.

12. On the formation of "new types of collective subjectivity" in association with postwar movements that invoked racial identity, see Omi and Winant (1983:37).

13. See, for example, Hoffman (1968), Hooker (1967), Simon and Gagnon (1967b), and Warren (1974).

14. Written before the emergence of discourse on gay families, Murray's piece identified lack of kinship as the major difference distinguishing urban gay communities from urban ethnic communities.

15. On the relation of gentrification to public policy and wider economic trends during the Reagan years, see Harrison and Bluestone (1988).

16. For an application of Turner's concept of *communitas* to feminist and lesbian-feminist organizing before the politics of difference questioned the notion of sisterhood, see Cassell (1977).

17. Cf. Anderson (1983), who has elaborated the notion of imagined community with respect to nation-states.

18. Cf. Lockard (1986:85), writing about lesbians in Portland: "The Community may be seen as a partial alternative form of family unit for Community members."

19. On the limitations of sisterhood as an all-embracing concept intended to bring women together across lines of race, age, ethnicity, sexual identity, and class, see E. T. Beck (1982), Chrystos (1988), Dill (1983), Fox-Genovese (1979–80), Gibbs and Bennett (1980), Hooks (1981), Hull et al. (1982), Joseph and Lewis (1981), Macdonald (1983), Moraga and Anzaldúa (1981), and Smith (1983).

20. The term "speaking sameness" comes from Bonnie Zimmerman's (1985) discussion of identity politics among lesbians during the early 1980s.

21. Cf. M.B. Pratt (1984), who very eloquently refutes the notion of home as a space of safety and comfort. For a perceptive commentary on issues raised by Pratt's portrayal of home as a locus of exclusions and oppressions, see Martin and Mohanty (1988).

SIX. LOVERS THROUGH THE LOOKING GLASS

1. Many of the gay men and lesbians I met voiced dissatisfaction with the expressions available to describe gay couples. They generally felt that "lovers" understates commitment to a relationship and "partners" sounds too much like a business arrangement, while "boyfriends" or "girlfriends" minimizes the seriousness, maturity, and kinship status of committed relationships. I have elected to use "lovers" and "partners" interchangeably.

2. See Nungesser (1986) for stories of gay men with AIDS who describe learning about intimacy and affection through coping with the disease.

3. Cf. Harry and Lovely (1979:179), who found that only 14 percent of the gay men in their sample said they did not want a long-term lover.

4. On the arrival of the "new masculinity" among gay men in urban areas during the late 1960s, see Humphreys (1972).

5. Depiction and execution are, of course, two separate matters. What these characterizations demonstrated was the widespread application of egalitarian ideals to relationships.

6. For a sample of writings that apply psychological theories of merging and fusion to lesbian relationships, see Clunis and Green (1988), Hall (1978), Krestan and Bepko (1980), and Lindenbaum (1985).

7. Cf. Blumstein and Schwartz (1983), whose study of couples in the United States concludes that too many separate vacations and separate activities may be correlated with relationships that fail to last, for couples of all sexual identities.

8. Ryan (1975:59), in her account of women during the "American" colonial period, raises an apt historical critique of this psychoanalytic argument: "A woman of Puritan upbringing could not vainly presume that a child was her private creation and personal possession. Neither was any colonial woman likely to merge her identity with a child torn from her by the pain of parturition and in great danger of infant mortality."

9. But see Krestan and Bepko (1980), who consider merging the product of oppression as well as socialization. They argue that members of a couple may "turn in on themselves" and "rigidify" their boundaries when faced with a hostile environment.

10. On the American Psychiatric Association's decision to remove homosexuality from its list of psychiatric disorders, see Bayer (1981). On the classifications of deviance that have affected relations between gay people and social service providers, see also Pearson (1975).

11. See also Epstein (1988a) and Patton (1985), who link portrayals of AIDS as the "deserved" product of gay male decadence and irresponsibility to similar representations of other diseases historically associated with groups at the bottom of race and class hierarchies.

12. But see Varenne (1977), who argues that cooperation and an egalitarian reciprocity can facilitate rather than destroy individualism, making it possible to be both an individualist and a conformist simultaneously.

13. Cf. the condemnation of "particular friendships" among Roman Cath-

olic nuns as relationships inimical to the task of building religious community (see Curb and Manahan 1985).

14. Cf. Kitzinger (1987), who also argues for greater attention to the rhetorical conventions that frame accounts of research on lesbians, including the visual metaphor of bringing the previously hidden to light.

SEVEN. PARENTING IN THE AGE OF AIDS

1. Representative collections include Alpert (1988), Bozett (1987), Hanscombe and Forster (1982), and Pollack and Vaughn (1987).

2. Cf. Gantz (1983), who confines his analysis to children of divorced or separated parents. Despite disclaimers, a negative tone pervades his descriptions, in part because he makes little effort to distinguish between the children's feelings about their parents' sexual identities and their feelings about their parents' separation.

3. On the inseparability of the analysis of gender and kinship, see Yanagisako and Collier (1987). For discussion of "the person" as a cultural construct, see Carrithers et al. (1985) and Schneider (1968).

4. AID is also abbreviated "AI," for alternative (artificial) insemination.

5. Assuming, of course, that the biological mother has a lover and that the lover wishes to take on parental responsibilities.

6. Shilts (1987), for all its flaws, offers a chronicle of the progress of the epidemic and a critique of public policy responses. For approaches that address government inaction by integrating theory and activism, see Crimp (1987), Epstein (1988b), and Watney (1987).

7. On women and AIDS, see Richardson (1987) and Rieder and Ruppelt (1989). On some of the consequences of the initial labeling of AIDS as a gay disease, see Altman (1986). Reanalysis of statistics on AIDS cases issued by the Centers for Disease Control (CDC) has alleged bias in CDC classificatory procedures. CDC statistics have subsumed persons who both used intravenous drugs and engaged in homosexual sex within the risk group "homosexual and bisexual men" (Bisticas-Cocoves 1986). The same tabulations have also defined risk groups in terms of identities rather than activities.

8. But see Miller (1989), who speculates that this calmer atmosphere might have emerged by the 1980s even in the absence of AIDS.

9. For reflections on the effects of AIDS on gay men's sexuality and sexual identity, see Epstein (1988a), Kyle (1989), and Patton (1985).

10. Compare the gay men with AIDS interviewed by Nungesser (1986), many of whom experienced the disease as an opportunity to fight for life.

11. But see Sontag (1989), who argues that AIDS, unlike cancer, extends earlier metaphors of disease that greeted plagues as retribution for communal rather than strictly personal transgressions.

12. The disproportionate attention garnered by children recently born or adopted has not gone unnoticed by gay and lesbian parents already raising children from previous heterosexual relationships, who wryly suggested that

some of the romanticism that characterizes discussions about "choosing children" will fade once these infants reach adolescence.

13. Lesbian or gay identification, of course, does not guarantee that a woman will have sex exclusively with other women or a man solely with other men (see Clausen 1990). I am speaking here of categorical assertions.

EIGHT. THE POLITICS OF GAY FAMILIES

1. In contrast to most structural-functionalist studies of immigrant populations, which tend to take renunciation of "traditional" kinship structures as a sign of acculturation.

2. On feminist critiques of "the family," see Coward (1983), Dalley (1988), Flax (1982), Nicholson (1986), Rapp (1987), G. Rubin (1975), Thorne with Yalom (1982), and Vance (1983). Even feminist apologists for "the family," who range along the political spectrum from Jean Elshtain (1982) to Betty Friedan, largely limit their discussions of familial relations to the familiar terrain ordered by heterosexual and procreative relations.

3. On the implications of failing to clarify friendship and kinship, see Fineman (n.d.). In a study that compared parents' treatment of the partners of their lesbian daughters and gay sons with their treatment of the partners of their heterosexual children, Fineman discovered that some parents felt relatively comfortable incorporating gay partners into selected family activities in the status of friend, but that the same status allowed them to treat the gay partnerships as nonerotic and exclude gay partners from certain "family occasions" such as Mother's Day. Fineman also found other sorts of differential treatment related to the denial of kinship status to the partners of adult gay children, such as signing greeting cards to the gay partner with a first name but signing cards to the spouses of heterosexual siblings "Mom." In all cases, parents knew of the sexual character of their gay son's or lesbian daughter's relationship.

4. Cf. Murray (1984:27), who argues that "the welfare state's takeover of insurance against disaster (the 'safety net' function of the family)" contributed to the emergence of homophile organizations and, ultimately, the gay movement.

5. Cf. de Lauretis (1988), who argues that taking a position counter to something imputes the existence of a unified subject whose coherence is not achievable in practice. De Lauretis' point would also apply to the allegedly solidary collectivity known as "lesbians and gay men."

REFERENCES

Abercrombie, Nicholas, Stephen Hill, and Bryan S. Turner. 1980. *The Dominant Ideology Thesis.* Boston: Allen & Unwin.

Achilles, Nancy. 1967. "The Development of the Homosexual Bar as an Institution." In John H. Gagnon and William Simon, eds., *Sexual Deviance, pp. 228–244.* New York: Harper & Row.

Adair, Nancy and Casey Adair. 1978. *Word Is Out: Stories of Some of Our Lives.* New York: Dell & New Glide.

Adam, Barry D. 1986. "Age, Structure, and Sexuality: Reflections on the Anthropological Evidence on Homosexual Relations." In Evelyn Blackwood, ed., *Anthropology and Homosexual Behavior*, pp. 19–33. New York: Haworth Press.

—— 1987. *The Rise of a Gay and Lesbian Movement.* Boston: Twayne Publishers.

Adelman, Marcy. 1986. *Long Time Passing: Lives of Older Lesbians.* Boston: Alyson.

Allen, Ronnie. 1987. "Times Have Changed at the *Herald.*" *Gay Community News* (June 28–July 4).

Alpert, Harriet, ed. 1988. *We Are Everywhere: Writings by and about Lesbian Parents.* Freedom, Calif.: Crossing Press.

Altman, Dennis. 1979. *Coming Out in the Seventies.* Sydney: Wild & Woolley.

—— 1986. *AIDS in the Mind of America.* Garden City, N.Y.: Doubleday.

Anderson, Benedict. 1983. *Imagined Communities: Reflections on the Origin and Spread of Nationalism.* London: Verso.

Andrews, Lori B. 1989. *Between Strangers: Surrogate Mothers, Expectant Fathers, and Brave New Babies.* New York: Harper & Row.

Arditti, Rita, Renate Duelli Klein, and Shelly Minden, eds. 1984. *Test Tube Women: What Future for Motherhood?* Boston: Pandora Press.

Arensberg, Conrad M. 1954. "The Community-Study Method." *American Journal of Sociology* 60:109–124.

Ariès, Philippe. 1962. *Centuries of Childhood: A Social History of Family Life*. New York: Vintage Books.

—— 1981. *The Hour of Our Death*. New York: Alfred A. Knopf.

Augustine. 1961. *Confessions*. New York: Penguin Books.

Balzar, John. 1985. "American Views of Gays: Disapproval, Sympathy." *Los Angeles Times* (Dec. 20).

Bambara, Toni Cade. 1980. *The Salt Eaters*. New York: Random House.

Barnhart, Elizabeth. 1975. "Friends and Lovers in a Lesbian Counterculture Community." In Nona Glazer-Malbin, ed., *Old Family/New Family*, pp. 90–115. New York: Van Nostrand.

Barrett, Michèle and Mary McIntosh. 1982. *The Anti-Social Family*. London: Verso/NLB.

Bauman, Richard. 1972. "Differential Identity and the Social Base of Folklore." In Américo Paredes and Richard Bauman, eds., *Toward New Perspectives in Folklore*, pp. 31–41. Austin: University of Texas Press.

Bayer, Ronald. 1981. *Homosexuality and American Psychiatry*. New York: Basic Books.

Beam, Joseph. 1986. "Brother to Brother: Words from the Heart." In Joseph Beam, ed., *In the Life: A Black Gay Anthology*, pp. 230–242. Boston: Alyson.

Beauvoir, Simone de. 1972. *Brigitte Bardot and the Lolita Syndrome*. New York: Arno Press.

Beck, Evelyn Torton, ed. 1982. *Nice Jewish Girls: A Lesbian Anthology*. Watertown, Mass.: Persephone Press.

Beck, Gloria Guss. 1985. *Are You Still My Mother? Are You Still My Family?* New York: Warner Books.

Becker, Carol S. 1988. *Unbroken Ties: Lesbian Ex-Lovers*. Boston: Alyson.

Beer, Gillian. 1983. *Darwin's Plots: Evolutionary Narrative in Darwin, George Eliot and Nineteenth-Century Fiction*. London: Routledge & Kegan Paul.

Bell, Alan P. and Martin S. Weinberg. 1978. *Homosexualities: A Study of Diversity Among Men and Women*. New York: Simon & Schuster.

Bercovitch, Sacvan. 1978. *The American Jeremiad*. Madison: University of Wisconsin Press.

Berger, Raymond M. 1982a. "The Unseen Minority: Older Gays and Lesbians." *Social Work* 27(3):236–242.

—— 1982b. *Gay and Gray: The Older Homosexual Man*. Urbana: University of Illinois Press.

Bérubé, Allan. 1988. "Caught in the Storm: AIDS and the Meaning of Natural Disaster." *OUT/LOOK* 1(3):8–19.

—— 1989. "Marching to a Different Drummer: Lesbian and Gay GIs in World War II." In Martin Bauml Duberman, Martha Vicinus, and George Chauncey, Jr., eds., *Hidden From History: Reclaiming the Gay and Lesbian Past*, pp. 383–394. New York: New American Library.

Bérubé, Allan and John D'Emilio. 1985. "The Military and Lesbians During the McCarthy Years." In Estelle B. Freedman, Barbara C. Gelpi, Susan

L. Johnson, and Kathleen M. Weston, eds., *The Lesbian Issue: Essays from SIGNS*, pp. 279–295. Chicago: University of Chicago Press.

Berzon, Betty. 1978. "Sharing Your Lesbian Identity with Your Children." In Ginny Vida, ed., *Our Right to Love: A Lesbian Resource Book*, pp. 69–74. Englewood Cliffs, N.J.: Prentice-Hall.

—— 1979. "Telling the Family You're Gay." In Betty Berzon and Robert Leighton, eds., *Positively Gay*, pp. 88–100. Los Angeles: Mediamix Associates.

Bisticas-Cocoves, M. 1986. "U.S. AIDS Cases Pass the 20,000 Mark." *Gay Community News* (May 24).

Blackwood, Evelyn, ed. 1986. *Anthropology and Homosexual Behavior*. New York: Haworth Press.

Bloch, Maurice and Jean H. Bloch. 1980. "Women and the Dialectics of Nature in Eighteenth-Century French Thought." In Carol MacCormack and Marilyn Strathern, eds., *Nature, Culture and Gender*, pp. 25–41. New York: Cambridge University Press.

Blumstein, Philip and Pepper Schwartz. 1983. *American Couples: Money, Work, Sex*. New York: William Morrow.

Borhek, Mary V. 1983. *Coming Out to Parents: A Two-Way Survival Guide for Lesbians and Gay Men and Their Parents*. New York: Pilgrim Press.

Bourdieu, Pierre. 1977. *Outline of a Theory of Practice*. New York: Cambridge University Press.

Bowers v. Hardwick. 1986. 106 Supreme Court 2841.

Bozett, Frederick W., ed. 1987. *Gay and Lesbian Parents*. New York: Praeger.

Bronski, Michael. 1984. *Culture Clash: The Making of a Gay Sensibility*. Boston: South End Press.

Brooks, Virginia R. 1981. *Minority Stress and Lesbian Women*. Lexington, Mass.: D. C. Heath.

Brown, Laura S. 1988. "Lesbians and Family." *NWSA Journal* 1(1):103–108.

Bulkin, Elly. 1980. "An Old Dyke's Tale: An Interview with Doris Lunden." *Conditions* 2(3):26–44.

Bull, Chris. 1987a. "Gay Man Wins Custody of Lover's Son." *Gay Community News* (Nov. 15–21).

—— 1987b. "Presidential Group Slams Les/Gay Adoption." *Gay Community News* (Dec. 20–26).

—— 1988. "Fight Against Hate Crimes Heats Up." *Gay Community News* (Jan. 31–Feb. 6).

Burke, Kenneth. 1941. *The Philosophy of Literary Form*. Baton Rouge: Louisiana State University Press.

—— 1945. *A Grammar of Motives*. New York: Prentice-Hall.

Camus, Albert. 1955. *The Myth of Sisyphus*. New York: Vintage.

Caplan, Pat, ed. 1987. *The Cultural Construction of Sexuality*. London: Tavistock.

Carrithers, Michael, Steven Collins, and Steven Lukes. 1985. *The Category of the Person: Anthropology, Philosophy, History.* Cambridge: Cambridge University Press.

Casal, Mary. 1975. *The Stone Wall.* New York: Arno Press.

Cassell, Joan. 1977. *A Group Called Women: Sisterhood and Symbolism in the Feminist Movement.* New York: David McKay.

Castells, Manuel. 1983. *The City and the Grassroots: A Cross-Cultural Theory of Urban Social Movements.* Berkeley: University of California Press.

Castells, Manuel and Karen Murphy. 1982. "Cultural Identity and Urban Structure: The Spatial Organization of San Francisco's Gay Community." In Norman I. Fainstein and Susan S. Fainstein, eds., *Urban Policy Under Capitalism,* pp. 237–259. Beverly Hills, Calif.: Sage.

Cavan, Sherri. 1966. *Liquor License: An Ethnography of Bar Behavior.* Chicago: Aldine.

Chodorow, Nancy. 1978. *The Reproduction of Mothering: Psychoanalysis and the Sociology of Gender.* Berkeley: University of California Press.

Chrystos. 1988. *Not Vanishing.* Vancouver: Press Gang Publishers.

Clark, Don. 1977. *Loving Someone Gay.* Millbrae, Calif.: Celestial Arts.

Clausen, Jan. 1990. "My Interesting Condition." *OUT/LOOK* 2(3): 10–21.

Cliff, Michelle. 1980. *Claiming an Identity They Taught Me to Despise.* Watertown, Mass.: Persephone Press.

Clifford, James. 1988. *The Predicament of Culture: Twentieth-Century Ethnography, Literature, and Art.* Cambridge: Harvard University Press.

Clifford, James and George E. Marcus. 1986. *Writing Culture: The Poetics and Politics of Ethnography.* Berkeley: University of California Press.

Clunis, D. Merilee and G. Dorsey Green. 1988. *Lesbian Couples.* Seattle: Seal Press.

Coleman, Eli. 1982. "Developmental Stages of the Coming Out Process." *Journal of Homosexuality* 7(2/3):31–43.

Cook, Blanche Wiesen. 1977. "Female Support Networks and Political Activism: Lillian Wald, Crystal Eastman, Emma Goldman." *Chrysalis* 3:44–61.

Córdova, Jeanne. 1975. "How to Come Out Without Being Thrown Out." In Karla Jay and Allen Young, eds., *After You're Out: Personal Experiences of Gay Men and Lesbian Women,* pp. 89–95. New York: Links Press.

Cott, Nancy F. 1977. *The Bonds of Womanhood: "Woman's Sphere" in New England, 1780–1835.* New Haven: Yale University Press.

Couser, G. Thomas. 1979. *American Autobiography: The Prophetic Mode.* Amherst, Mass.: University of Massachusetts Press.

Coward, Rosalind. 1983. *Patriarchal Precedents: Sexuality and Social Relations.* Boston: Routledge & Kegan Paul.

Coward, Rosalind and John Ellis. 1977. *Language and Materialism: Developments in Semiology and the Theory of the Subject.* Boston: Routledge & Kegan Paul.

Craigin, Elisabeth. 1975. *Either Is Love.* New York: Arno Press.

Crimp, Douglas, ed. 1987. *AIDS: Cultural Analysis, Cultural Activism.* Cambridge: MIT Press.

Crisp, Quentin. 1968. *The Naked Civil Servant.* New York: Holt, Rinehart & Winston.

Cronin, Denise M. 1975. "Coming Out Among Lesbians." In Erich Goode and Richard T. Troiden, eds., *Sexual Deviance and Sexual Deviants*, pp. 268–277. New York: William Morrow.

Cruikshank, Margaret. 1982. "Notes on Recent Lesbian Autobiographical Writing." *Journal of Homosexuality* 8(1):19–26.

Culler, Jonathan. 1975. *Structuralist Poetics: Structuralism, Linguistics and the Study of Literature.* Ithaca, N.Y.: Cornell University Press.

Curb, Rosemary and Nancy Manahan, eds. 1985. *Lesbian Nuns: Breaking Silence.* Tallahassee, Fla.: Naiad Press.

Dalley, Gillian. 1988. *Ideologies of Caring: Rethinking Community and Collectivism.* London: Macmillan.

Dank, Barry M. 1971. "Coming Out in the Gay World." *Psychiatry* 34:180–195.

DeLeon, Richard and Courtney Brown. 1980. "Preliminary Estimates of Size of Gay/Bisexual Population in San Francisco Based on Combined Data from January and June S.F. Charter Commission Surveys." Mimeograph.

D'Emilio, John. 1983a. "Capitalism and Gay Identity." In Ann Snitow, Christine Stansell, and Sharon Thompson, eds., *Powers of Desire: The Politics of Sexuality*, pp. 100–113. New York: Monthly Review Press.

—— 1983b. *Sexual Politics, Sexual Communities: The Making of a Homosexual Minority in the United States, 1940–1970.* Chicago: University of Chicago Press.

—— 1989a. "The Homosexual Menace: The Politics of Sexuality in Cold War America." In Kathy Peiss and Christina Simmons with Robert A. Padgug, eds., *Passion and Power: Sexuality in History*, pp. 226–240. Philadelphia: Temple University Press.

—— 1989b. "Gay Politics, Gay Community: San Francisco's Experience." In Martin Bauml Duberman, Martha Vicinus, and George Chauncey Jr., eds., *Hidden From History: Reclaiming the Gay and Lesbian Past*, pp. 456–473. New York: New American Library.

Derlega, Valerian J. and Alan L. Chaikin. 1975. *Sharing Intimacy: What We Reveal to Others and Why.* Englewood Cliffs, N.J.: Prentice-Hall.

di Leonardo, Micaela. 1984. *The Varieties of Ethnic Experience: Kinship, Class, and Gender Among California Italian-Americans.* Ithaca: Cornell University Press.

Dill, Bonnie Thornton. 1983. "Race, Class, and Gender: Prospects for an All-Inclusive Sisterhood." *Feminist Studies* 9(1):131–150.

Dollard, John. 1935. *Criteria for the Life History: With Analyses of Six Notable Documents.* New Haven: Yale University Press.

Dreyfus, Hubert L. and Paul Rabinow. 1982. *Michel Foucault: Beyond Structuralism and Hermeneutics.* Chicago: University of Chicago Press.

Dunker, Buffy. 1987. "Aging Lesbians: Observations and Speculations." In Boston Lesbian Psychologies Collective, ed., *Lesbian Psychologies*, pp. 72–82. Urbana: University of Illinois Press.

Ehrenreich, Barbara. 1983. *The Hearts of Men: American Dreams and the Flight from Commitment.* Garden City, N.Y.: Anchor/ Doubleday.

Elshtain, Jean Bethke. 1982. "Feminism, Family, and Community." *Dissent* 29(4):442–449.

Epstein, Steven. 1987. "Gay Politics, Ethnic Identity: The Limits of Social Constructionism." *Socialist Review* 93/94:9–54.

Epstein, Steven. 1988a. "Moral Contagion and the Medicalizing of Gay Identity." *Research in Law, Deviance, and Social Control* 9:3–36.

—— 1988b. "Nature vs. Nurture and the Politics of AIDS Organizing." *OUT/LOOK* 1(3):46–53.

Ettelbrick, Paula L. 1989. "Since When Is Marriage a Path to Liberation?" *OUT/LOOK* 2(2):9, 14–17.

Ettore, E. M. 1980. *Lesbians, Women and Society.* Boston: Routledge & Kegan Paul.

Evans, Sara. 1979. *Personal Politics: The Roots of Women's Liberation in the Civil Rights Movement and the New Left.* New York: Vintage.

Fernandez, James. 1986. *Persuasions and Performances: The Play of Tropes in Culture.* Bloomington: Indiana University Press.

Fineman, Norman. n.d. "Kinship Relations Between Lesbians and Gay Men in Long-term Relationships and the Parents of Their Partners." Unpublished paper.

FitzGerald, Frances. 1986. *Cities on a Hill: A Journey Through Contemporary American Cultures.* New York: Simon & Schuster.

Flax, Jane. 1982. "The Family in Contemporary Feminist Thought: A Critical Review." In Jean Bethke Elshtain, ed., *The Family in Political Thought*, pp. 223–253. Amherst: University of Massachusetts Press.

Foucault, Michel. 1972. *The Archaeology of Knowledge.* New York: Harper & Row.

—— 1973. *The Birth of the Clinic: An Archaeology of Medical Perception.* New York: Pantheon.

—— 1977. *Discipline and Punish: The Birth of the Prison.* New York: Vintage Books.

—— 1978. *The History of Sexuality.* Vol. 1. New York: Vintage.

Fowler, Roger. 1981. *Literature as Social Discourse: The Practice of Linguistic Criticism.* Bloomington: University of Indiana Press.

Fox-Genovese, Elizabeth. 1979–1980. "The Personal is Not Political Enough." *Marxist Perspectives* 2(4):94–113.

Freedman, Estelle B. 1982. "Sexuality in Nineteenth-Century America: Behavior, Ideology, and Politics." *Reviews in American History* 10:196–215.

Fricke, Aaron. 1981. *Reflections of a Rock Lobster.* Boston: Alyson.

Frye, Marilyn. 1980. "Review of *The Coming Out Stories*." *Sinister Wisdom* 14:97–98.

Gallagher, Bob and Alexander Wilson. 1987. "Sex and the Politics of Identity: An Interview with Michel Foucault." In Mark Thompson, ed., *Gay Spirit: Myth and Meaning*, pp. 25–35. New York: St. Martin's Press.

Gantz, Joe. 1983. *Whose Child Cries: Children of Gay Parents Talk About Their Lives*. Rolling Hills Estates, Calif.: Jalmar Press.

Garfinkel, Harold. 1967. *Studies in Ethnomethodology*. Englewood Cliffs, N.J.: Prentice-Hall.

Gay, A. Nolder. 1978. *The View From the Closet: Essays on Gay Life and Liberation, 1973–1977*. Boston: Union Park Press.

Geertz, Clifford. 1973. *The Interpretation of Cultures*. New York: Basic Books.

Gibbs, Joan and Sara Bennett. 1980. *Top Ranking: A Collection of Articles on Racism and Classism in the Lesbian Community*. New York: Come! Unity Press.

Gilligan, Carol. 1982. *In a Different Voice: Psychological Theory and Women's Development*. Cambridge: Harvard University Press.

Gillis, Regina. 1985. *"You Call My Name* (But I'm Not There)." *Gay Community News* (Oct. 26).

Gilman, Sander L. 1988. *Disease and Representation: Images of Illness from Madness to AIDS*. Ithaca: Cornell University Press.

Godwin, Ronald S. 1983. "AIDS: A Moral and Political Time Bomb." *Moral Majority Report* (July).

Goffman, Erving. 1959. *The Presentation of Self in Everyday Life*. New York: Doubleday/Anchor.

—— 1963. *Stigma: Notes on the Management of Spoiled Identity*. Englewood Cliffs, N.J.: Prentice-Hall.

Goldsby, Jackie. 1989. "All About Yves." *OUT/LOOK* (2)1:34–35.

Goldstein, Richard. 1986. "The Gay Family." *Village Voice* (July 1).

Goodman, Gerre, George Lakey, Judy Lashof, and Erika Thorne. 1983. *No Turning Back: Lesbian and Gay Liberation for the '80s*. Philadelphia: New Society Publishers.

Goodwin, Joseph. 1989. *More Man Than You'll Ever Be: Gay Folklore and Acculturation in Middle America*. Bloomington: Indiana University Press.

Gostin, Larry, ed. 1990. *Surrogate Motherhood: Politics and Privacy*. Bloomington: Indiana University Press.

Gottlieb, Amy. 1986. "Amy Gottlieb Talks to Joan Nestle." *Rites* (April).

Grahn, Judy. 1984. *Another Mother Tongue: Gay Words, Gay Worlds*. Boston: Beacon Press.

Gramsci, Antonio. 1971. *Selections from the Prison Notebooks*. New York: International Publishers.

Green, Richard. 1987. "Domestic Partner Benefits: A Status Report to the ACLU." Washington, D.C.: Lesbian and Gay Rights Project, American Civil Liberties Union.

Greenberg, David F. 1988. *The Construction of Homosexuality*. Chicago: University of Chicago Press.

Gresham, Jewell Handy. 1989. "The Politics of Family in America." *The Nation* (July 24–31):116–122.

Griffin, Carolyn Welch, Marian J. Wirth, and Arthur G. Wirth. 1986. *Beyond Acceptance: Parents of Lesbians and Gays Talk About Their Experiences.* Englewood Cliffs, N.J.: Prentice-Hall.

Guilfoy, Chris. 1980. "Coming Out in the '40s and '50s." *Gay Community News* (Nov.).

Gutiérrez, Ramón A. 1989. "Must We Deracinate Indians to Find Gay Roots?" *OUT/LOOK* 1(4):61–67.

Gutis, Philip S. 1989. "How to Define a Family: Gay Tenant Fights Eviction." *New York Times* (April 27).

Hall, Marny. 1978. "Lesbian Families: Cultural and Clinical Issues." *Social Work* 23(4):380–385.

Hamilton, Wallace. 1973. *Christopher and Gay: A Partisan's View of the Greenwich Village Homosexual Scene.* New York: Saturday Review Press.

Hanscombe, Gillian E. and Jackie Forster. 1982. *Rocking the Cradle: Lesbian Mothers: A Challenge in Family Living.* Boston: Alyson.

Harding, Susan. 1981. "Family Reform Movements: Recent Feminism and Its Opposition." *Feminist Studies* 7(1):57–75.

Harrison, Bennett and Barry Bluestone. 1988. *The Great U-Turn: Corporate Restructuring and the Polarizing of America.* New York: Basic Books.

Harry, Joseph. 1984. *Gay Couples.* New York: Praeger.

Harry, Joseph and Robert Lovely. 1979. "Gay Marriages and Communities of Sexual Orientation." *Alternative Lifestyles* 2(2):177–200.

Hefner, Keith and Al Autin, eds. 1978. *Growing Up Gay.* Ann Arbor: Youth Liberation Press.

Height, Dorothy. 1989. "Self-Help-A Black Tradition." *The Nation* (July 24–31):136–138.

Helquist, M. 1985. "New Behavior Survey Released by SF AIDS Fdn." *Coming Up!* (Aug.).

Herdt, Gilbert. 1984. *Ritualized Homosexuality in Melanesia.* Berkeley: University of California Press.

—— 1987. *Guardians of the Flutes: Idioms of Masculinity.* New York: Columbia University Press.

Herdt, Gilbert, ed. 1989. Gay and Lesbian Youth. New York: Haworth Press.

Heron, Ann, ed. 1983. *One Teenager in Ten: Writings by Gay and Lesbian Youth.* Boston: Alyson.

Hidalgo, Hilda A. and Elia Hidalgo Christensen. 1976–1977. "The Puerto Rican Lesbian and the Puerto Rican Community." *Journal of Homosexuality* 2(2):109–121.

Hillery, George A. 1955. "Definitions of Community: Areas of Agreement." *Rural Sociology* 20:111–123.

Hocquenghem, Guy. 1978. *Homosexual Desire.* London: Alison & Busby.

Hoffman, Martin. 1968. *The Gay World: Male Homosexuality and the Social Creation of Evil.* New York: Basic Books.

Hollibaugh, Amber. 1979. "Sexuality and the State: The Defeat of the Briggs Initiative and Beyond." *Socialist Review* 9(3):55-72.

Hooker, Evelyn. 1965. "Male Homosexuals and Their 'Worlds.' " In Judd Marmor, ed., *Sexual Inversion*, pp. 83-107. New York: Basic Books.

—— 1967. "The Homosexual Community." In John H. Gagnon and William Simon, eds., *Sexual Deviance*, pp. 167-184. New York: Harper & Row.

Hooks, Bell. 1981. *Ain't I a Woman: Black Women and Feminism*. Boston: South End Press.

Hull, Gloria T., Patricia Bell Scott, and Barbara Smith, eds. 1982. *All the Women Are White, All the Blacks Are Men, But Some of Us Are Brave: Black Women's Studies*. Old Westbury, N.Y.: Feminist Press.

Humphreys, Laud. 1972. "New Styles in Homosexual Manliness." In Joseph A. McCaffrey, ed., *The Homosexual Dialectic*, pp. 65-83. Englewood Cliffs, N.J.: Prentice-Hall.

Hunter, Nan D. and Nancy D. Polikoff. 1976. "Custody Rights of Lesbian Mothers: Legal Theory and Litigation Strategy." *Buffalo Law Review* 25:691-733.

Jackman, Mary R. and Robert W. Jackman. 1983. *Class Awareness in the United States*. Berkeley: University of California Press.

Jakobson, Roman. 1962. *Selected Writings*. The Hague: Mouton.

Jameson, Frederic. 1981. *The Political Unconscious: Narrative as a Socially Symbolic Act*. Ithaca: Cornell University Press.

Jay, Karla. 1978. "Coming Out as Process." In Ginny Vida, ed., *Our Right to Love: A Lesbian Resource Book*, pp. 28-30. Englewood Cliffs, N.J.: Prentice-Hall.

Jay, Nancy. 1981. "Gender and Dichotomy." *Feminist Studies* 7(1):38-56.

Jenkins, Alan. 1979. *The Social Theory of Claude Lévi-Strauss*. New York: St. Martin's Press.

Johnston, Norman. 1973. *The Human Cage*. New York: Walker & Co.

Jones, Clinton R. 1978. *Understanding Gay Relatives and Friends*. New York: Seabury Press.

Joseph, Gloria I. and Jill Lewis. 1981. *Common Differences: Conflicts in Black and White Feminist Perspectives*. Garden City, N.Y.: Anchor/Doubleday.

Kantrowitz, Arnie. 1977. *Under the Rainbow: Growing Up Gay*. New York: William Morrow.

Katz, Jonathan. 1976. *Gay American History: Lesbians and Gay Men in the U.S.A.* New York: Thomas Y. Crowell.

Kazin, Alfred. 1979. "The Self as History: Reflections on Autobiography." In Marc Pachter, ed., *Telling Lives: The Biographer's Art*, pp. 74-89. Washington, D.C.: New Republic Books.

Kehoe, Monika. 1989. *Lesbians Over 60 Speak for Themselves*. New York: Harrington Park Press.

Kennedy, Theodore R. 1980. *You Gotta Deal With It: Black Family Relations in a Southern Community*. New York: Oxford University Press.

Kenny, Maurice. 1988. "Tinselled Bucks: A Historical Study in Indian Homosexuality." In Gay American Indians and Will Roscoe, eds., *Living the Spirit: A Gay American Indian Anthology,* pp. 15–31. New York: St. Martin's Press.

Kenschaft, Lori. 1987. "Parents of PWA Denied Visits to Grandchildren. Gay Community News" (Nov. 29–Dec. 5).

Kerr, Barbara T. and Mirtha N. Quintanales. 1982. "The Complexity of Desire: Conversations on Sexuality and Difference." *Conditions* 3(2):52–71.

Kingsdale, Jon M. 1980. "The 'Poor Man's Club': Social Functions of the Urban Working-Class Saloon." In Elizabeth H. Pleck and Joseph H. Pleck, eds., *The American Man,* pp. 255–283. Englewood Cliffs, N.J.: Prentice-Hall.

Kinsey, Alfred C., Wardell B. Pomeroy and Clyde E. Martin. 1948. *Sexual Behavior in the Human Male.* Philadelphia: W. B. Saunders.

—— 1953. *Sexual Behavior in the Human Female.* Philadelphia: W. B. Saunders.

Kitzinger, Celia. 1987. *The Social Construction of Lesbianism.* London: Sage.

Kleinberg, Seymour. 1980. *Alienated Affections: Being Gay in America.* New York: St. Martin's Press.

Krestan, Jo-Ann and Claudia S. Bepko. 1980. "The Politics of Fusion in the Lesbian Relationship." *Family Process* 19(3):277–289.

Krieger, Susan. 1983. *The Mirror Dance: Identity in a Women's Community.* Philadelphia: Temple University Press.

—— 1985. "Lesbian Identity and Community: Recent Social Science Literature." In Estelle B. Freedman, Barbara C. Gelpi, Susan L. Johnson, and Kathleen M. Weston, eds., *The Lesbian Issue: Essays from SIGNS,* pp. 223–240. Chicago: University of Chicago Press.

Kyle, Garland Richard. 1989. "AIDS and the New Sexual Order." *Journal of Sex Research* 26(2):276–278.

Labov, William. 1972. *Language in the Inner City: Studies in the Black English Vernacular.* Philadelphia: University of Pennsylvania Press.

Lacan, Jacques. 1977. *Écrits.* New York: W. W. Norton.

Laner, Mary Riege. 1979. "Growing Older Female: Heterosexual and Homosexual." *Journal of Homosexuality* 4(3):267–275.

Larkin, Joan. 1976. "Coming Out." *Ms.* 4(9):72–74, 84–86.

Larsen, Nella. 1969. *Passing.* New York: Arno Press.

Lasch, Christopher. 1978. *The Culture of Narcissism: American Life in an Age of Diminishing Expectations.* New York: Norton.

Lauretis, Teresa de. 1988. "Displacing Hegemonic Discourses: Reflections on Feminist Theory in the 1980's." *Inscriptions* 3/4:127–141.

Lazere, Arthur. 1986. "On the Job." *Coming Up!* (June).

Lee, John Allen. 1977. "Going Public: A Study in the Sociology of Homosexual Liberation." *Journal of Homosexuality* 3(1):49–78.

Lempke, Debbie. 1977. *Gay and Proud.* Performed by the Berkeley Women's Music Collective. Olivia Records, LF915A Stereo.

Lévi-Strauss, Claude. 1963a. *Structural Anthropology*. New York: Basic Books.
—— 1963b. *Totemism*. Boston: Beacon Press.
—— 1969. *The Raw and the Cooked*. New York: Harper & Row.
Lewin, Ellen. 1981. "Lesbianism and Motherhood." *Human Organization* 40(1):6–14.
Lewin, Ellen and Terri A. Lyons. 1982. "Everything in Its Place: The Coexistence of Lesbianism and Motherhood." In William Paul, James D. Weinrich, John C. Gonsiorek, and Mary E. Hotvedt, eds., *Homosexuality: Social, Psychological, and Biological Issues*, pp. 249–273. Beverly Hills: Sage.
Leznoff, Maurice and William A. Westley. 1967. "The Homosexual Community." In John H. Gagnon and William Simon, eds., *Sexual Deviance*, pp. 184–196. New York: Harper & Row.
Lichtman, Richard. 1975. "Marx's Theory of Ideology." *Socialist Revolution* 5(1):45–76.
Liebow, Elliott. 1967. *Tally's Corner: A Study of Negro Streetcorner Men*. Boston: Little, Brown & Co.
Liljesfraund, Petra. 1988. "Children Without Fathers: Handling the Anonymous Donor Question." *OUT/LOOK* 1(3):24–29.
Lindenbaum, Joyce P. 1985. "The Shattering of an Illusion: The Problem of Competition in Lesbian Relationships." *Feminist Studies* 11(1):85–103.
Lockard, Denyse. 1986. "The Lesbian Community: An Anthropological Approach." In Evelyn Blackwood, ed., *Anthropology and Homosexual Behavior*, pp. 83–95. New York: Haworth Press.
Long, Elizabeth. 1985. *The American Dream and the Popular Novel*. Boston: Routledge & Kegan Paul.
Louÿs, Pierre. 1932. *Aphrodite*. New York: Illustrated Editions.
Lynch, Michael. 1982. "Forgotten Fathers." In Ed Jackson and Stan Persky, eds., *Flaunting It!: A Decade of Gay Journalism from The Body Politic*, pp. 55–63. Vancouver: New Star Books.
Lynd, Robert S. and Helen M. Lynd. 1937. *Middletown in Transition*. New York: Harcourt, Brace.
Lyon, Phyllis and Del Martin. 1979. "The Older Lesbian." In Betty Berzon and Robert Leighton, eds., *Positively Gay*, pp. 133–145. Los Angeles: Mediamix Associates.
Macdonald, Barbara with Cynthia Rich. 1983. *Look Me in the Eye*. San Francisco: Spinsters/Aunt Lute.
Mannheim, Karl. 1952. *Essays on the Sociology of Knowledge*. New York: Oxford University Press.
Marcus, George E. and Michael M. J. Fischer. 1986. *Anthropology as Cultural Critique: An Experimental Moment in the Human Sciences*. Chicago: University of Chicago Press.
Marcuse, Herbert. 1969. "Repressive Tolerance." In Barrington Moore, Jr., Robert Paul Wolff, and Herbert Marcuse, *A Critique of Pure Tolerance*, pp. 81–117. Boston: Beacon Press.

Marks, Elaine. 1979. "Lesbian Intertextuality." In George Stambolian and Elaine Marks, eds., *Homosexualities and French Literature*, pp. 353–377. Ithaca, N.Y.: Cornell University Press.

Marks, Robert. 1988. "Coming Out in the Age of AIDS: The Next Generation." *OUT/LOOK* 1(1):66–74.

Martí, José. 1975. *Inside the Monster: Writings on the United States and American Imperialism*. New York: Monthly Review Press.

Martin, Biddy. 1988. "Lesbian Identity and Autobiographical Difference[s]." In Bella Brodzki and Celeste Schenck, eds., *Life/Lines: Theorizing Women's Autobiography*, pp. 77–103. Ithaca: Cornell University Press.

Martin, Biddy and Chandra Talpade Mohanty. 1986. "Feminist Politics: What's Home Got to Do with It?" In Teresa de Lauretis, ed., *Feminist Studies/Critical Studies*, pp. 191–212. Bloomington: Indiana University Press.

Martin, Emily. 1987. *The Woman in the Body: A Cultural Analysis of Reproduction*. Boston: Beacon Press.

Marx, Karl. 1963. *The 18th Brumaire of Louis Bonaparte*. New York: International Publishers.

McAdoo, Harriette P. 1988. *Black Families*. 2d ed. Newbury Park, Calif.: Sage.

McCoy, Sherry. and Maureen Hicks. 1979. "A Psychological Retrospective on Power in the Contemporary Lesbian-Feminist Community." *Frontiers* 4(3):65–69.

McDonald, Gary J. 1982. "Individual Differences in the Coming Out Process for Gay Men: Implications for Theoretical Models." *Journal of Homosexuality* 8(1):47–60.

McIntosh, Mary. 1981. "The Homosexual Role." In Kenneth Plummer, ed., *The Making of the Modern Homosexual*, pp. 30–44. Totowa, N.J.: Barnes & Noble.

McKinney, Kevin. 1987. "How to Become a Gay Father." *The Advocate* (Dec. 8):43–49, 52–55.

McKnight, Jennie. 1986. "Activists Testify in D.C. on Anti-gay Violence." *Gay Community News* (Oct. 19–25).

Mendenhall, George. 1985. "Mickey Mouse Lawsuit Remains Despite Disney Dancing Decree." *Bay Area Reporter* (Aug. 22).

Mendola, Mary. 1980. *The Mendola Report: A New Look at Gay Couples*. New York: Crown.

Midnight Sun. 1988. "Sex/Gender Systems in Native North America." In Gay American Indians and Will Roscoe, eds., *Living the Spirit: A Gay American Indian Anthology*, pp. 32–47. New York: St. Martin's Press.

Miller, Neil. 1989. *In Search of Gay America: Women and Men in a Time of Change*. New York: Atlantic Monthly Press.

Minnigerode, Fred and Marcy Adelman. 1978. "Elderly Homosexual Women and Men: Report on a Pilot Study." *Family Coordinator* 4(27):452–456.

Mintz, Sidney W. 1979. "The Anthropological Interview and the Life History." *Oral History Review* 17:18–26.

Modell, Judith. 1989. "Last Chance Babies: Interpretations of Parenthood in an In Vitro Fertilization Program." *Medical Anthropology Quarterly* 3(2):124–138.

Moraga, Cherríe. 1983. *Loving in the War Years*. Boston: South End Press.

Moraga, Cherríe and Gloria Anzaldúa. 1981. *This Bridge Called My Back: Writings by Radical Women of Color*. Watertown, Mass.: Persephone Press.

Morin, Stephen F. 1977. "Heterosexual Bias in Psychological Research on Lesbianism and Male Homosexuality." *American Psychologist* 32:629–637.

Moses, Alice E. 1978. *Identity Management in Lesbian Women*. New York: Praeger.

Muchmore, Wes and William Hanson. 1982. *Coming Out Right: A Handbook for the Gay Male*. Boston: Alyson.

Muller, Ann. 1987. *Parents Matter: Parents' Relationships with Lesbian Daughters and Gay Sons*. Tallahassee, Fla.: Naiad Press.

Murray, Stephen O. 1979. "The Institutional Elaboration of a Quasi-Ethnic Community." *International Review of Modern Sociology* 9:165–177.

—— 1984. *Social Theory, Homosexual Realities*. New York: Gai Saber.

Myers, Michael F. 1982. "Counseling the Parents of Young Homosexual Male Patients." *Journal of Homosexuality* 7(2/3):131–143.

National Organization of Gay & Lesbian Scientists & Technical Professionals (NOGLSTP). 1986. "Measuring the Gay and Lesbian Population." Pamphlet.

Nestle, Joan. 1987. *A Restricted Country*. Ithaca, N.Y.: Firebrand Books.

Newton, Esther. 1979. *Mother Camp: Female Impersonators in America*. Chicago: University of Chicago Press.

—— 1988. "Of Yams, Grinders and Gays: The Anthropology of Homosexuality." *OUT/LOOK* 1(1):28–37.

Nichols, Margaret. 1987. "Lesbian Sexuality: Issues and Developing Theory." In Boston Lesbian Psychologies Collective, ed., *Lesbian Psychologies*, pp. 97–125. Urbana: University of Illinois Press.

Nicholson, Linda J. 1986. *Gender and History: The Limits of Social Theory in the Age of the Family*. New York: Columbia University Press.

Nungesser, Lon G. 1983. *Homosexual Acts, Actors, and Identities*. New York: Praeger.

—— 1986. *Epidemic of Courage: Facing AIDS in America*. New York: St. Martin's Press.

Ollman, Bertell. 1976. *Alienation: Marx's Conception of Man in Capitalist Society*. 2d ed. New York: Cambridge University Press.

Olmstead-Rose, Lester. 1990. Personal communication.

Omi, Michael and Howard Winant. 1983. "By the Rivers of Babylon: Race in the United States, Part Two." *Socialist Review* 72:35–68.

Parsons, Elsie Clews. 1915. *Social Freedom: A Study of the Conflicts Between Social Classifications and Personality*. New York: Putnam.

Parsons, Talcott. 1942. "Age and Sex in the Social Structure of the United States." *American Sociological Review* 7(5):604–616.

Patton, Cindy. 1985. *Sex and Germs: the politics of AIDS*. Boston: South End Press.

Pearson, Geoffrey. 1975. *The Deviant Imagination: Psychiatry, Social Work and Social Change*. New York: Holmes & Meier.

Peplau, Letitia Anne. 1982. "Research on Gay Couples: An Overview." *Journal of Homosexuality* 8(2):4–8.

Peplau, Letitia Anne and Susan D. Cochran. 1981. "Value Orientations in the Intimate Relationships of Gay Men." *Journal of Homosexuality* 6(3):1–19.

Peplau, Letitia Anne, Susan Cochran, Karen Rook, and Christine Padesky. 1978. "Loving Women: Attachment and Autonomy in Lesbian Relationships." *Journal of Social Issues* 34(3):7–27.

Perin, Constance. 1988. *Belonging in America: Reading Between the Lines*. Madison: University of Wisconsin Press.

Pies, Cheri and Francine Hornstein. 1988. "Baby M and the Gay Family." *OUT/LOOK* 1(1):79–85.

Pleck, Joseph H. 1981. *The Myth of Masculinity*. Cambridge: MIT Press.

Pleck, Elizabeth H. and Joseph H. Pleck, eds. 1980. *The American Man*. Englewood Cliffs, N.J.: Prentice-Hall.

Plummer, Kenneth. 1975. *Sexual Stigma: An Interactionist Account*. Boston: Routledge & Kegan Paul.

Pollack, Sandra and Jeanne Vaughn. 1987. *Politics of the Heart: A Lesbian Parenting Anthology*. Ithaca, N.Y.: Firebrand Books.

Ponse, Barbara. 1976. "Secrecy in the Lesbian World." *Urban Life* 5:313–339.

—— 1978. *Identities in the Lesbian World: The Social Construction of Self*. Westport, Conn.: Greenwood Press.

Popert, Ken. 1982. "Neighbourly Sentiments." In Ed Jackson and Stan Persky, eds., *Flaunting It!: A Decade of Gay Journalism from The Body Politic*, pp. 73–90. Vancouver: New Star Books.

Pratt, Mary Louise. 1977. *Toward a Speech Act Theory of Literary Discourse*. Bloomington: Indiana University Press.

—— 1986. "Fieldwork in Common Places." In James Clifford and George E. Marcus, eds., *Writing Culture: The Poetics and Politics of Ethnography*, pp. 27–50. Berkeley: University of California Press.

Pratt, Minnie Bruce. 1984. "Identity: Skin Blood Heart." In Elly Bulkin, Minnie Bruce Pratt, and Barbara Smith, eds., *Yours in Struggle: Three Feminist Perspectives on Anti-Semitism and Racism*, pp. 11–63. New York: Long Haul Press.

Praunheim, Rosa von. 1979. *Army of Lovers*. London: Gay Men's Press.

Rabinow, Paul. 1977. *Reflections on Fieldwork in Morocco*. Berkeley: University of California Press.

Rafkin, Louise. 1987. *Different Daughters: A Book by Mothers of Lesbians*. Pittsburgh/San Francisco: Cleis Press.

Rapp, Rayna. 1982. "Family and Class in Contemporary America: Notes Toward an Understanding of Ideology." In Barrie Thorne with Marilyn Yalom, eds., *Rethinking the Family*, pp. 168–187. New York: Longman.

—— 1987. "Toward a Nuclear Freeze? The Gender Politics of Euro-American Kinship Analysis." In Jane Fishburne Collier and Sylvia Junko Yanagisako, eds., *Gender and Kinship: Essays Toward a Unified Analysis*, pp. 119–131. Stanford: Stanford University Press.

"Rare Joint Adoptions Won in Calif." 1989. *Equal Time* (Dec. 13).

Read, Kenneth E. 1980. *Other Voices: The Style of a Male Homosexual Tavern*. Novato, Calif.: Chandler & Sharp.

Reagon, Bernice Johnson. 1983. "Coalition Politics: Turning the Century." In Barbara Smith, ed., *Home Girls: A Black Feminist Anthology*, pp. 356–368. New York: Kitchen Table: Women of Color Press.

Rechy, John. 1963. *City of Night*. New York: Grove Press.

Rice, Louise. 1988. "The Nitty-Gritty Truth About Lesbian Parenting." *Gay Community News* (Jan. 31–Feb. 6).

Rich, Adrienne. 1980. "Compulsory Heterosexuality and Lesbian Existence." *Signs* 5:631–660.

Richardson, Diane. 1987. *Women and the AIDS Crisis*. Gainesville, Fla.: Pandora.

Ricoeur, Paul. 1976. *Interpretation Theory: Discourse and the Surplus of Meaning*. Fort Worth: Texas Christian University Press.

Rieder, Ines and Patricia Ruppelt, eds. 1988. *AIDS: The Women*. Pittsburgh: Cleis Press.

Riley, Claire. 1988. "American Kinship: A Lesbian Account." *Feminist Studies* 8(2):75–94.

Rodgers, Nile and Bernard Edwards. 1979. *We Are Family*. Performed by Sister Sledge. Cotillion Records, SD5209 Stereo.

Roe, K. 1985. "You Know How to Whistle, Don't You?" *Bay Area Reporter* (Nov. 11).

Rofes, Eric E. 1983. *"I Thought People Like That Killed Themselves": Lesbians, Gay Men and Suicide*. San Francisco: Grey Fox Press.

Rosaldo, Michelle Z. 1983. "The Shame of Headhunters and the Autonomy of Self." *Ethos* 11(3):135–151.

—— 1984. "Toward an Anthropology of Self and Feeling." In Richard Shweder and Robert Levine, eds., *Culture Theory: Essays on Mind, Self, and Emotion*, pp. 137–157. New York: Cambridge University Press.

Rosaldo, Renato. 1989. *Culture and Truth: The Remaking of Social Analysis*. Boston: Beacon Press.

Roscoe, Will. 1987. "Living the Tradition: Gay American Indians." In Mark Thompson, ed., *Gay Spirit: Myth and Meaning*, pp. 69–77. New York: St. Martin's Press.

—— 1988a. "Strange Country This: Images of Berdaches and Warrior Women." In Gay American Indians and Will Roscoe, eds., *Living the Spirit: A Gay American Indian Anthology*, pp. 48–76. New York: St. Martin's Press.

—— 1988b. "The Zuni Man-Woman." *OUT/LOOK* 1(2):56–67.

Rosenberg, Charles E. 1980. "Sexuality, Class and Role in Nineteenth-Century America." In Elizabeth H. Pleck and Joseph H. Pleck, eds., *The American Man*, pp. 219–254. Englewood Cliffs, N.J.: Prentice-Hall.

Rosenberg, Morris. 1979. *Conceiving the Self*. New York: Basic Books.

Rubin, Gayle. 1975. "The Traffic in Women: Notes on the 'Political Economy' of Sex." In Rayna R. Reiter, ed., *Toward an Anthropology of Women*, pp. 157–210. New York: Monthly Review Press.

—— 1984. "Thinking Sex: Notes for a Radical Theory of the Politics of Sexuality." In Carole S. Vance, ed., *Pleasure and Danger: Exploring Female Sexuality*, pp. 267–319. Boston: Routledge & Kegan Paul.

Rubin, Lillian. 1983. *Intimate Strangers: Men and Women Together*. New York: Harper & Row.

Ryan, Mary P. 1975. *Womanhood in America: From Colonial Times to the Present*. New York: New Viewpoints.

Sacks, Harvey. 1974. "An Analysis of the Course of a Joke's Telling in Conversation." In Richard Bauman and Joel Sherzer, eds., *Explorations in the Ethnography of Speaking*, pp. 337–353. New York: Cambridge University Press.

Sacks, Oliver. 1988. "The Revolution of the Deaf." *New York Review of Books* (June 2).

Saussure, Ferdinand de. 1959. *Course in General Linguistics*. New York: McGraw-Hill.

Schafer, Roy. 1976. *A New Language for Psychoanalysis*. New Haven: Yale University Press.

Schneider, David M. 1968. *American Kinship: A Cultural Account*. Englewood Cliffs, N.J.: Prentice-Hall.

—— 1972. "What is Kinship All About?" In Priscilla Reining, ed., *Kinship Studies in the Morgan Centennial Year*. Washington, D.C.: Anthropological Society of Washington.

—— 1977. "Kinship, Nationality, and Religion in American Culture: Toward a Definition of Kinship." In Janet L. Dolgin, David S. Kemnitzer, and David M. Schneider, eds., *Symbolic Anthropology*, pp. 63–71. New York: Columbia University Press.

—— 1984. *A Critique of the Study of Kinship*. Ann Arbor: University of Michigan Press.

Schneider, David M. and Raymond T. Smith. 1978. *Class Differences in American Kinship*. Ann Arbor: University of Michigan Press.

Scott, Joan W. 1988. "Deconstructing Equality-Versus-Difference: Or, the Uses of Poststructuralist Theory for Feminism." *Feminist Studies* 14(1):33–50.

Seifer, Nancy. 1976. *Nobody Speaks for Me!: Self-Portraits of American Working Class Women*. New York: Simon & Schuster.

Shi, David E. 1985. *The Simple Life: Plain Living and High Thinking in American Culture*. New York: Oxford University Press.

Shilts, Randy. 1987. *And the Band Played On: Politics, People, and the AIDS Epidemic*. New York: St. Martin's Press.

"Shotgun Wedding." 1989. *City Pages* (August 23).

Silverstein, Charles. 1977. *A Family Matter: A Parents' Guide to Homosexuality*. New York: McGraw-Hill.

—— 1981. *Man to Man: Gay Couples in America*. New York: Morrow.

Simon, William and John H. Gagnon. 1967a. "Homosexuality: The Formulation of a Sociological Perspective." *Journal of Health & Social Behavior* 8:177–185.

—— 1967b. "The Lesbians: A Preliminary Overview." In John H. Gagnon and William Simon, eds., *Sexual Deviance*, pp. 247–282. New York: Harper & Row.

Smith, Barbara, ed. 1983. *Home Girls: A Black Feminist Anthology*. New York: Kitchen Table: Women of Color Press.

—— 1987. "From the Stage." *Gay Community News* (Nov. 8–14).

Smith-Rosenberg, Carroll. 1975. "The Female World of Love and Ritual: Relations Between Women in Nineteenth-Century America." *Signs* 1(1):1–30.

Sollors, Werner. 1986. *Beyond Ethnicity: Consent and Descent in American Culture*. New York: Oxford University Press.

Sontag, Susan. 1989. *AIDS and Its Metaphors*. New York: Farrar, Straus, Giroux.

Spillers, Hortense J. 1984. "Interstices: A Small Drama of Words." In Carole S. Vance, ed., *Pleasure and Danger: Exploring Female Sexuality*, pp. 73–100. Boston: Routledge & Kegan Paul.

Stack, Carol B. 1974. *All Our Kin: Strategies for Survival in a Black Community*. New York: Harper & Row.

Stefan, Susan. 1989. "Whose Egg Is It Anyway?: Reproductive Rights of Incarcerated, Institutionalized, and Incompetent Women." *Nova Law Review* 13(2):405–456.

Stein, Cindy. 1979. "Stonewall Nation 69–79: What Happened, Anyhow?" *Gay Community News* (June 23).

Stoddard, Thomas B. 1989. "Why Gay People Should Seek the Right to Marry." *OUT/LOOK* 2(2):9–13.

Stone, Albert E. 1982. *Autobiographical Occasions and Original Acts: Versions of American Identity from Henry Adams to Nate Shaw*. Philadelphia: University of Pennsylvania Press.

Streib, Gordon F., W. Edward Folts, and Mary Anne Hilker. 1984. *Old Homes—New Families: Shared Living for the Elderly*. New York: Columbia University Press.

Swidler, Ann. 1980. "Love and Adulthood in American Culture." In Neil J. Smelser and Erik H. Erikson, eds., *Themes of Work and Love in Adulthood*, pp. 120–147. Cambridge, Mass.: Harvard University Press.

Terkel, Studs. 1984. *"The Good War": An Oral History of World War Two*. New York: Ballantine Books.

Thompson, Karen and Julie Andrzejewski. 1988. *Why Can't Sharon Kowalski Come Home?* San Francisco: Spinsters/Aunt Lute.

Thorne, Barrie with Marilyn Yalom, eds. 1982. *Rethinking the Family: Some Feminist Questions.* New York: Longman.

Tompkins, Jane P. 1981. "Sentimental Power: *Uncle Tom's Cabin* and the Politics of Literary History." In Walter Benn Michaels, ed., *Glyph* vol. 8, pp. 79–102. Baltimore: Johns Hopkins University Press.

Tremble, Bob, Margaret Schneider, and Carol Appathurai. 1989. "Growing Up Gay or Lesbian in a Multicultural Context." In Gilbert Herdt, ed., *Gay and Lesbian Youth*, pp. 253–264. New York: Haworth Press.

Turner, Victor. 1969. *The Ritual Process: Structure and Anti-Structure.* Ithaca: Cornell University Press.

Umans, Meg, ed. 1988. *Like Coming Home: Coming-Out Letters.* Austin, Texas: Banned Books.

Vacha, Keith. 1985. *Quiet Fire: Memoirs of Older Gay Men.* Trumansburg, N.Y.: Crossing Press.

Vance, Carole S. 1983. "Gender Systems, Ideology, and Sex Research." In Ann Snitow, Christine Stansell, and Sharon Thompson, eds., *Powers of Desire: The Politics of Sexuality*, pp. 371–384. New York: Monthly Review Press.

—— 1984. "Pleasure and Danger: Toward a Politics of Sexuality." In Carole S. Vance, ed., *Pleasure and Danger: Exploring Female Sexuality*, pp. 1–27. Boston: Routledge & Kegan Paul.

Varenne, Hervé. 1977. *Americans Together: Structured Diversity in a Midwestern Town.* New York: Teachers College Press.

Vetere, Victoria A. 1982. "The Role of Friendship in the Development and Maintenance of Lesbian Love Relationships." *Journal of Homosexuality* 8(2):51–65.

Vigil, James Diego. 1988. *Barrio Gangs: Street Life and Identity in Southern California.* Austin: University of Texas Press.

Vogel, Paula. n. d. *And Baby Makes Seven.* Unpublished play script.

Vojir, Dan. 1982. *The Sunny Side of Castro Street: A Diary of Sorts.* San Francisco: Strawberry Hill Press.

Vološinov, V. N. 1973. *Marxism and the Philosophy of Language.* New York: Seminar Press.

Warner, W. Lloyd et al. 1963. *Yankee City.* New Haven: Yale University Press.

Warren, Carol A. B. 1974. *Identity and Community in the Gay World.* New York: Wiley.

—— 1977. "Fieldwork in the Gay World: Issues in Phenomenological Research." *Journal of Social Issues* 33(4):93–107.

Watney, Simon. 1987. *Policing Desire: Pornography, AIDS, and the Media.* Minneapolis: University of Minnesota Press.

Weeks, Jeffrey. 1977. *Coming Out: Homosexual Politics in Britain from the Nineteenth Century to the Present.* London: Quartet Books.

—— 1985. *Sexuality and Its Discontents: Meanings, Myths and Modern Sexualities.* London: Routledge & Kegan Paul.

Weinberg, George. 1972. *Society and the Healthy Homosexual*. New York: St. Martin's Press.

Weinberg, Thomas S. 1978. "On 'Doing' and 'Being' Gay: Sexual Behavior and Homosexual Male Self-Identity. *Journal of Homosexuality* 4:143–68.

Westheimer, Kim. 1987. " 'Right Thinking' at the Ledger." *Gay Community News* (Jan. 4–10).

Weston, Kathleen M. and Lisa B. Rofel. 1985. "Sexuality, Class, and Conflict in a Lesbian Workplace." In Estelle B. Freedman, Barbara C. Gelpi, Susan L. Johnson, and Kathleen M. Weston, eds., *The Lesbian Issue: Essays from SIGNS*, pp. 199–222. Chicago: University of Chicago Press.

White, A. 1986. "Violence Rising, New Reports Show." *Bay Area Reporter* (April 17).

White, Edmund. 1980. *States of Desire: Travels in Gay America*. New York: Dutton.

Whitehead, Harriet. 1981. "The Bow and the Burden Strap: A New Look at Institutionalized Homosexuality in Native North America." In Sherry B. Ortner and Harriet Whitehead, eds., *Sexual Meanings: The Cultural Construction of Gender and Sexuality*, pp. 80–115. New York: Cambridge University Press.

Whorton, James C. 1982. *Crusaders for Fitness: The History of American Health Reformers*. Princeton: Princeton University Press.

Wilde, Oscar. 1982. *The Picture of Dorian Gray and Other Writings*. New York: Bantam Books.

Williams, Raymond. 1977. *Marxism and Literature*. New York: Oxford University Press.

Williams, Walter. 1986. *The Spirit and the Flesh: Sexual Diversity in American Indian Culture*. Boston: Beacon Press.

Winnicott, Donald Woods. 1971. *Playing and Reality*. London: Tavistock.

Wolf, Deborah Goleman. 1979. *The Lesbian Community*. Berkeley: University of California Press.

Wolfe, Susan J. and Julia Penelope Stanley, eds. 1980. *The Coming Out Stories*. Watertown, Mass.: Persephone Press.

Wolfson, Nessa. 1978. "A Feature of Performed Narrative: The Conversational Historical Present." *Language in Society* 7(2):215–237.

Wooden, Wayne S., Harvey Kawasaki, and Raymond Mayeda. 1983. "Lifestyles and Identity Maintenance Among Gay Japanese-American Males." *Alternative Lifestyles* 5(4):236–243.

Wyatt, Jean. 1986. " Avoiding Self-Definition: In Defense of Women's Right to Merge (Julia Kristeva and *Mrs. Dalloway*)." *Women's Studies* 13(1–2):115–126.

Yanagisako, Sylvia J. 1978. "Variance in American Kinship: Implications for Cultural Analysis." *American Ethnologist* 5(1):15–29.

—— 1979. "Family and Household: The Analysis of Domestic Groups." *Annual Review of Anthropology* 8:161–205.

—— 1985. *Transforming the Past: Tradition and Kinship among Japanese Americans*. Stanford: Stanford University Press.

Yanagisako, Sylvia Junko and Jane Fishburne Collier. 1987. "Toward a Unified Analysis of Gender and Kinship." In Jane Fishburne Collier and Sylvia Junko Yanagisako, eds., *Gender and Kinship: Essays Toward a Unified Analysis*, pp. 14–50. Stanford: Stanford University Press.

Zimmerman, Bonnie. 1983. "Exiting from Patriarchy: The Lesbian Novel of Development." In Elizabeth Abel, Marianne Hirsch, and Elizabeth Langland, eds., *The Voyage In: Fictions of Female Development*, pp. 244–257. Hanover: University Press of New England.

—— 1985. "The Politics of Transliteration: Lesbian Personal Narratives." In Estelle B. Freedman, Barbara C. Gelpi, Susan L. Johnson, and Kathleen M. Weston, eds., *The Lesbian Issue: Essays from SIGNS*, pp. 27–42. Chicago: University of Chicago Press.

Zita, Jacquelyn N. 1981. "Historical Amnesia and the Lesbian Continuum." *Signs* 7(1):172–187.

Zitter, Sherry. 1987. "Coming Out to Mom: Theoretical Aspects of the Mother-Daughter Process." In Boston Lesbian Psychologies Collective, ed., *Lesbian Psychologies*, pp. 177–194. Urbana: University of Illinois Press.

INDEX

Abercrombie, Nicholas, 226n10
Acceptance in coming out, 55-56, 95-97
Achilles, Nancy, 126
Adair, Casey, 226n3
Adair, Nancy, 226n3
Adam, Barry D., 227n9, 230n10
Adelman, Marcy, 224n10, 226n3
Adoption, 38
Adoptive relatives, see Blood relatives
Adulthood, coming out as validation of, 69-72
African-American families, 37, 58-60
Age discrimination, 132-33
Age of study participants, 12-13
AIDS: alternative insemination and, 175-80; blood relatives and, 185-88; death and, 182-83; gay couples and, 159-60, 182-83; in San Francisco Bay Area, 180-82; sex attitudes and, 141-42
Allen, Ronnie, 24, 157
Alpert, Harriet, 232n1
Alternative insemination, 169-71, 188-90; AIDS and, 175-80; donor link in, 170-71; gay men as donors, 175-80
Altman, Dennis, 127, 183, 198, 226n3, 228n21, 232n7
Anderson, Benedict, 230n17
Andrews, Lori B., 223n3
Androgyny, 145-46
Andrzejewski, Julie, 223n1
Anti-gay legislative initiative campaigns, 23-24
Anti-gay violence, 46
Anzaldúa, Gloria, 226n3, 230n19
Arditti, Rita, 223n3
Arensberg, Conrad, 124
Ariès, Philippe, 183, 184

Arrested development and homosexuality, 154-55
Assimilation debate, 197-202
Augustine, 227n13
Austin, Al, 133, 224n10, 226n3

Balzar, John, 47
Bambara, Toni Cade, 1
Barnhart, Elizabeth, 160
Barrett, Michèle, 205-6
Bars, 126, 130, 139
Bauman, Richard, 224n13
Bayer, Ronald, 47, 231n10
Beam, Joseph, 186
Beauvoir, Simone de, 203
Beck, Evelyn Torton, 230n19
Beck, Gloria Guss, 226n8
Becker, Carol S., 111
Bell, Alan P., 138, 205, 228n22
Bennett, Sara, 230n19
Bentham, Jeremy, 163
Bepko, Claudia S., 112, 231nn6, 9
Bercovitch, Sacvan, 126, 139
Berger, Raymond M., 13, 224nn9, 10, 226n5
Bérubé, Allan, 120, 183, 226n4
Berzon, Betty, 36, 226n8
Biological relatedness, parenting and, 188-89
Biology, kinship and, 34-35
Bisticas-Cocoves, M., 232n7
Blackwood, Evelyn, 224n8
Bloch, Jean H., 5
Bloch, Maurice, 5
Blood relatives, AIDS and, 185-88
Bluestone, Barry, 223n3, 230n15
Blumstein, Philip, 231n7

107; Jewish, 92-95; Korean-American, 58; Latino, 57, 58; love and, 107; Native American, 97-99; race and, 36-37, 56-61; rejection by, 61-64; *see also* Gay families.
Streib, Gordon F., 223n3
Study: age of participants, 12-13; interview participants, 9-12; researcher identity, 13-14; San Francisco Bay Area as fieldwork site, 7-8; terminology, 15-16
Suicide attempts, 82-83, 84

Terkel, Studs, 203, 204
Terminology, 15-16
Thompson, Karen, 1, 223n1
Thorne, Barrie, 107, 199, 212, 228n18, 233n2
Tompkins, Jane P., 229n6
Tremble, Bob, 37, 53
Turner, Victor, 126, 230n16

Umans, Meg, 228n24
Unconditional love, 64

Vacha, Keith, 224n10
Vance, Carole S., 233n2
Vaughn, Jeanne, 232n1
Varenne, Hervé, 124, 153, 200, 231n12
Vetere, Victoria A., 121
Vigil, James Diego, 229n6
Violence, *see* Anti-gay violence
Vogel, Paula, 175
Vojir, Dan, 226n3
Vološinov, V.N, 17, 226n10

Warner, W. Lloyd, 124
Warren, Carol A.B., 8, 230n13
Watney, Simon, 22, 181, 182, 228n21, 232n6
Weeks, Jeffrey, 65
Weinberg, George, 227n8
Weinberg, Martin S., 138, 205, 228n22
Weinberg, Thomas S., 68, 226n3
Westheimer, Kim, 173
Westley, William A., 121
Weston, Kathleen M., 132
White, Edmund, 46
White, Justice Byron, 208
Whitehead, Harriet, 227n17
Whorton, James C., 184
Wilde, Oscar, 137
Williams, Raymond, 223n2, 226n10
Williams, Walter L., 224n8, 227n17
Wilson, Alexander, 230n8
Winant, Howard, 130, 230n12
Winnicott, Donald Woods, 155
Wolf, Deborah, 123
Wolfe, Susan J., 226n3
Wolfson, Nessa, 229n5
Wooden, Wayne S., 226n3, 227n16
Wyatt, Jean, 152

Yalom, Marilyn, 107, 199, 212, 228n18, 233n2
Yanagisako, Sylvia J., 2, 35, 107, 137, 225nn2, 3, 226n10, 229n1, 232n3

Zimmerman, Bonnie, 206, 228n1, 230n20
Zita, Jacquelyn N., 206
Zitter, Sherry, 227n8